A Companion to the United States Constitution and Its Amendments

Fourth Edition

A COMPANION TO THE UNITED STATES CONSTITUTION AND ITS AMENDMENTS

Fourth Edition

John R. Vile

Westport, Connecticut
London

Library of Congress Cataloging-in-Publication Data

Vile, John R.
    A companion to the United States Constitution and its amendments / John R. Vile.—
4th ed.
      p. cm.
    Includes bibliographical references and index.
    ISBN 0–275–98932–1 ((cloth) : alk. paper)—ISBN 0–275–98957–7 ((pbk) : alk.
    paper) 1. Constitutional law—United States. I. Title.
    KF4550.V55 2006
    342.7302—dc22   2005032682

British Library Cataloguing in Publication Data is available.

Library of Congress Catalog Card Number: 2005032682
ISBN: 0–275–98932–1
     0–275–98957–7 (pbk.)

First published in 2006

Praeger Publishers, 88 Post Road West, Westport, CT 06881
An imprint of Greenwood Publishing Group, Inc.
www.praeger.com

Printed in the United States of America

The paper used in this book complies with the
Permanent Paper Standard issued by the National
Information Standards Organization (Z39.48–1984).

10 9 8 7 6 5 4 3 2 1

To my wife, Linda Christensen Vile

Contents

and the Structure of the Constitution • Bicameralism • The U.S. House of Representatives • Terms of Office and Qualifications • Representation and Taxation • The Three-Fifths Clause • Initial State Representation • House Vacancies, the Speaker, and Impeachment • The U.S. Senate • Representation, Voting, and Terms • Staggered Senate Terms and Vacancies • Qualifications • The Legislative Role of the Vice President • Other Senate Officers • Trials of Impeachment • Other Matters Involving Congressional Operations • Elections for Congress • Housekeeping Provisions • Congressional Compensation and Privilege • The Incompatibility Clause • Article I, Section 7—Procedures for Passing Laws • Revenue Bills • Procedures for Lawmaking and Presidential Vetoes • The Presentment Clause • Article I, Section 8—Powers Granted to Congress • Taxing, Spending, and Borrowing • Power to Regulate Commerce • A Note on Native Americans • Power Over Naturalization and Bankruptcies • Coining Money and Establishing Uniform Standards • Establishing a Post Office and Promoting Scientific Advances • Establishing Lower Courts • War Powers • Calling the Militia • Governing the District of Columbia • Implied Powers • Congressional Investigations • Article I, Section 9—Limits on Congressional Powers • Slave Importation • The Writ of Habeas Corpus • Bills of Attainder and Ex Post Facto Laws • Protections for the States • The Appropriation of Money • Titles of Nobility • Article I, Section 10—Limits on the States • Powers Reserved to the National Government • The Contract Clause • Other Limits on the States • References and Suggestions for Further Study

A Single Executive • The Presidential Term • Presidential Selection and the Electoral College • Presidential Qualifications • The Vice President and Presidential Disability • The Presidential Salary • The Presidential Oath • Presidential Duties • Commander in Chief • Getting Advice from the Cabinet • Power to Pardon and Reprieve • Negotiation and Ratification of Treaties • Presidential Appointment and Removal Powers • Interim Presidential Appointments • The State of the Union Address • Power to Convene and Adjourn Congress • The President as Chief Diplomat • Power to Execute the Laws and Executive Privilege • Commissioning of Military Officers • Presidential Impeachment • References and Suggestions for Further Study

Preface to Fourth Edition

In a classic tale, Goldilocks discovered during her visit to the house of three bears that porridge can be too hot or too cold, that chairs can be too big or too small, and that beds can be too hard or too soft. Alternatively, they can be "just right." So too, students and citizens seeking knowledge of the U.S. Constitution discover that books can be too long or too short, too ponderous or too breezy, too ideological or too lifeless. Contrariwise, they can be "just right." I have designed this book to fit into the "just right" category. To switch to an Aristotelian analogy, I have tried in this book to strike a "golden mean" between serious scholarship and reader accessibility in describing and explaining the U.S. Constitution, its amendments, and its interpretations.

I am especially interested in making materials that are currently found in erudite casebooks and commentaries on the U.S. Constitution accessible to citizens and to students in civics, American government, and constitutional law classes. Recognizing that scholars often validly disagree about such matters, I have emphasized both what those who wrote and ratified provisions of the Constitution meant and how others have subsequently interpreted them. Because the nation is now more than 200 years old, the U.S. Supreme Court has literally written hundreds of cases interpreting some provisions of the Constitution; as a result, in some books, case interpretations seem to swallow the document they are designed to explicate. I have attempted to describe and identify important judicial trees without therefore obscuring the view of the constitutional forest. I am grateful to the attentive students and professors alike who have responded positively to earlier editions of this book, in which I utilized this same approach.

I have designated this book as a "companion" to the Constitution in order to avoid the pretentiousness of designating it as a "guide" or the individualism of calling it an interpretation. I have included the texts of provisions from the Constitution directly in the text so that readers can compare what I say with the actual language of the document itself. Although I recognize that fallible individuals wrote and ratified the document, I believe it remains among the greatest examples of its kind.

I have extensively rewritten this book to make it more thorough and clearer. I have also updated it so that it covers all major legal developments through the 2004–2005 term of the U.S. Supreme Court, which turns out to have been the last term during which Chief Justice William Rehnquist presided. I hope that this edition, like its predecessors, will help readers both better understand and better appreciate the Constitution. I view this book as a way to repay part of the immense debt that I owe to my generous parents and teachers, to the brave and wise American forebears who committed themselves to establishing and preserving a system of liberty under law, and to men and women of good will who continue to cherish and defend constitutional government today.

Acknowledgments

In writing this book I am indebted to my students, especially those who have taken my classes in American government and in constitutional law, as well as to students and teachers who have utilized prior editions of this work and have encouraged me to continue to update it. Ever since I began full-time teaching in 1977, I have devoted at least a week or two in my introductory American government classes toward explicating the Declaration of Independence and the Constitution section by section and another similar period to dealing specifically with the Bill of Rights, the post-Civil War Amendments, and those of the Progressive Era. In my constitutional law classes, I have utilized a traditional casebook approach that has further emphasized constitutional interpretation and development. I enjoy reading cases and recognize that they are critical to understanding U.S. history, but the more cases I have read, the more convinced I have become that it remains important to return to the textual source of constitutional interpretations and that the text itself should be the beginning point for students of the subject.

In writing four editions of this book, I have been privileged to draw from research that I have written and edited or to which I have contributed. I believe that this edition will be especially enhanced by recent work I have done co-editing (with Hamline's David Schultz) and writing entries for *The Encyclopedia of Civil Liberties in America* (3 vols., M.E. Sharpe, 2005) and by my work authoring *The Constitutional Convention of 1787: A Comprehensive Encyclopedia of America's Founding* (2 vols., ABC-CLIO, 2005).

I want therefore to thank all those teachers, students, friends, colleagues, and administrators who have taught, encouraged, and challenged me and furthered my scholarly endeavors. I would also like to thank those at Middle Tennessee State University who have provided continuing research support, in part by providing a noninstructional assignment during the Spring 2005 semester. I would like to thank my student aide, Barbara Sidwell, for helping with proofreading and my secretary, Pam Davis, for her help with computer matters. I would also like to thank Hilary Claggett at Praeger, as well as Karyn Slutsky and Kate Lavallee at Westchester Book Services.

My friends know how indebted I am to my wife Linda. With God's help, she and I pledged our lives to one another in "a more perfect Union" of marriage just a week before the bicentennial celebration of the Declaration of Independence. Thankfully, our union has enabled us not only to pursue, but also to attain and enjoy considerable happiness. I deeply appreciate the affection, encouragement, and support that she has given to our daughters, Virginia and Rebekah, and their husbands, Keith Wesolowski and Kenny Johnston, and to me. She has done this while pursuing a successful career teaching elementary school. I am pleased to rededicate this volume, like its three predecessors and my dissertation, to Linda in deepest appreciation for her continuing affection and support.

Chapter 1

The Background of the Constitution

The U.S. Constitution established a system of self-government that distinguishes between liberty and license and between representative democracy and mob rule. The Constitution further embodies the rule of law, which is the foundation for freedom. In securing American rights, the Constitution has embodied universal principles. Both forebears and contemporaries have thought these values worth establishing and passing down to posterity, and some have sacrificed their very lives for them.

THE COLONIAL SETTING

Before the United States of America was born, settlers planted thirteen colonies in a newly discovered world an ocean away from Europe. Almost from the beginning, the distance largely forced colonists to govern themselves. Settlers at Virginia established a legislative branch, or House of Burgesses, in 1619, and settlers to the north at Plymouth in the next year signed a charter of government, or Mayflower Compact, even before they disembarked from their ship. Immigrants came to the New World to exercise freedoms that European rulers had denied them, and, although the colonists did not always grant others the freedom they sought for themselves, they continued to value liberty.

Over time, England came to rule all thirteen of the North American colonies (as well as Canada), but this rule was initially fairly mild, and the British policy of "salutary neglect" encouraged colonial self-governance. The distance between England and the colonies was simply too great, and

Britain had too many other obligations, for it to involve itself in the day-to-day affairs of the American colonies. Britain continued its relative inattention until the French and Indian War, which lasted from 1754 to 1763. The conflict in America, between French settlers (often allied with the Indians) and British colonists, was part of a larger worldwide conflict between French and British interests. At war's end, English leaders tried to collect taxes from the colonies for the troops that Britain had supplied. The colonists strongly resisted efforts by the English Parliament to tax them.

Most American colonists thought of themselves as British citizens who were fully entitled to all English rights. Beginning in 1215, the Magna Carta, which English noblemen wrested from a reluctant King John and which successors expanded, had established the principle of "no taxation without representation" as a critical right of British citizenship. English leaders claimed that, as citizens, the colonists were virtually represented in Parliament. Absent actual representation in Parliament, however, the colonists denied that this legislature had the authority, or sovereignty, to tax or legislate for them. They believed that such unaccountable power threatened not only their pocketbooks, but also their most basic liberties.

Although there were other points of controversy, this dispute over parliamentary authority was a primary cause of the American Revolution of 1776. The colonists openly questioned the constitutionality of laws like the Stamp Act, the Tea Tax, and the Townshend Duties through which the British unsuccessfully tried to tax them. During the initial controversy, most American colonists insisted that they were loyal English citizens who were simply asking for the rights to which English laws entitled them.

While denying parliamentary sovereignty, most colonists still acknowledged allegiance to the British king, whose predecessors had granted most colonial charters, which provided the antecedents to later state constitutions. Unfortunately, Britain's George III was no more sympathetic to colonial interests than the Parliament. As he rebuffed petitions from the continental congresses that the colonists convened, a permanent split seemed more and more likely. English-born Thomas Paine served as a catalyst to such action when he published *Common Sense* in January 1776. Pointing to all the disadvantages, including war and oppression, that he attributed to kingship and the practice of hereditary succession by which monarchs ascended the throne based on birth, Paine proposed that the colonists should declare their independence from Britain and proclaim that the law should be the only king in America.

Fighting between the colonists and the British had continued sporadically since the battles at Lexington and Concord in April 1775, and many colonists believed that a firm declaration of independence was the only remedy for their complaints. Thus, on June 7, 1776, Virginia delegate Richard

Henry Lee introduced three resolutions before the Second Continental Congress. The first resolution proclaimed:

> That these United Colonies are, and of right ought to be, free and independent States, that they are absolved from all allegiance to the British Crown, and that all political connection between them and the State of Great Britain is, and ought to be, totally dissolved (Solberg, *The Federal Convention and Formation of the Union of the American States*, p. 32).

Lee's other resolutions called for forming military alliances and for creating "a plan of confederation."

THE DECLARATION OF INDEPENDENCE

The Background of the Declaration

The Second Continental Congress appointed five men to a committee to write a Declaration of Independence. They were: John Adams, Benjamin Franklin, Roger Sherman, Robert Livingston, and Thomas Jefferson. Jefferson took the lead in authoring the document. Adams and Franklin made minor modifications before the Continental Congress enacted more substantial revisions. On his tombstone at Monticello, Virginia, Jefferson listed the Declaration of Independence as one of three accomplishments for which he wanted people to remember him—the other two omitted his presidency to highlight his authorship of the Virginia Statute for Religious Freedom and his establishment of the University of Virginia in nearby Charlottesville. Both Jefferson and Adams died on the fiftieth anniversary of the Declaration's adoption.

The Declaration of Independence remains one of the most important documents in American history. Jefferson did not intend for the document to be especially novel. Thus, writing to Richard Henry Lee in 1825, Jefferson said it was designed:

> Not to find out new principles, or new arguments, never before thought of, not merely to say things which had never been said before; but to place before mankind the common sense of the subject, in terms so plain and firm as to command their assent. Neither aiming at originality of principles or sentiments, nor yet copied from any particular or previous writing, it was intended to be an expression of the American mind (Becker, *The Declaration of Independence*, pp. 26–27).

The value of the Declaration of Independence rests not in its originality but in its expression of American sentiments. Those who later wrote the Constitution believed that they were furthering the objectives that the Declaration of Independence had articulated.

> When, in the Course of human events, it becomes necessary for one people to dissolve the political bands which have connected them with another, and to assume, among the powers of the earth, the separate and equal station to which the Laws of Nature and of Nature's God entitle them, a decent respect to the opinions of mankind requires that they should declare the causes which impel them to the separation.

The Purpose of the Document

However much the Second Continental Congress hoped the Declaration of Independence would mobilize opinion within the once separate colonies, its opening words indicate that its primary purpose was to explain to foreign nations why the colonies were declaring their independence. In so doing, Jefferson resorted to such common philosophic concepts of his day as "the laws of nature" and "nature's God." He further indicated that, whatever the former relations between Great Britain and America, the residents of the two areas were now distinct peoples.

> We hold these truths to be self-evident, that all men are created equal, that they are endowed by their Creator with certain unalienable Rights, that among these are Life, Liberty and the pursuit of Happiness.

The Idea of Equality of Human Rights

The most profound words of the Declaration are in the second paragraph. Although the document's reference to all *men* sounds underinclusive, in eighteenth-century times, as in today's, writers often used the male pronoun to include all members of the human race, including women. Moreover, although Jefferson was a slaveholder—albeit one who often expressed guilt over the nefarious institution—the Declaration did not explicitly limit its coverage to whites. Both blacks and whites, including Frederick Douglass, Abraham Lincoln, and Martin Luther King, Jr., have subsequently cited its words to condemn slavery, grant emancipation, and extend full rights to African Americans. Englishmen were most familiar with the kinds of rights that Jefferson cited, but because the onetime colonies were claiming their independence from Britain, Jefferson did not phrase his grievances in terms of the rights of Englishmen, but in broader terms of the rights of men.

The notion of human equality may not be as "self-evident" as Jefferson suggested. Individuals certainly vary immensely in their physical and intellectual endowments. These differences were so pronounced that the Greek philosopher Plato had declared in one mythical formulation in *The Republic* that individuals fell into three groups: those with souls of gold, those with souls of silver, and those with souls of bronze. Jefferson undoubtedly recognized and appreciated human differences; he often cited the need for an aristocracy of talent and virtue. More importantly, however, he recognized human likenesses. All humans are members of the same species, and, as God's creations, all are entitled to certain rights. Jefferson designated these rights as "Life, Liberty and the pursuit of Happiness." The last category is perhaps most fascinating for, if Jefferson had completely followed the lead of John Locke (1632–1704), a seventeenth-century English theorist whose views influenced the Declaration of Independence, he might have used the word "property" instead. The pursuit of happiness is more inclusive. Moreover, the term recognizes that although governments may provide the conditions for individuals to seek their own happiness, polities can rarely, if ever, guarantee its fulfillment.

That to secure these rights, Governments are instituted among Men, deriving their just powers from the consent of the governed,

---

The Purpose of Government

Different regimes have different purposes. Some seek chiefly to enforce their conception of the will of God. Other regimes aggrandize the self-interests of the person or persons in power. By contrast, Jefferson viewed the true end of government as serving all human beings by securing their rights. Agreeing with social contract theorists like Locke, Jefferson declared that governments derive their "just powers" not from the will of God—what James I and other English kings had designated as "the divine right of kings"—or the mandate of the leader, but from "the consent of the governed."

That whenever any Form of Government becomes destructive of these ends, it is the Right of the People to alter or to abolish it, and to institute new Government, laying its foundation on such principles and organizing its

continued on next page

> powers in such form, as to them shall seem most likely to effect their Safety
> and Happiness. Prudence, indeed, will dictate that Governments long esta-
> blished should not be changed for light and transient causes; and accordingly
> all experience hath shown that mankind are more disposed to suffer, while evils
> are sufferable, than to right themselves by abolishing the forms to which they
> are accustomed. But when a long train of abuses and usurpations, pursuing
> invariably the same Object evinces a design to reduce them under absolute
> Despotism, it is their right, it is their duty, to throw off such Government, and
> to provide new Guards for their future security.

The Right of Revolution

Jefferson tied his case for revolution to the purpose of government. Since
people create government to secure their happiness, they may rightfully
change or overthrow it when it fails to accomplish its objects. In pro-
claiming a right of revolution, Jefferson followed the lead of Locke and
other English theorists. Like them, he faced the problem of how to justify a
particular revolution without undermining future governments and creating
anarchy. Jefferson's solution was to argue that people should not revolt on a
whim, or for what he designated as "light and transient causes," but rather
only "when a long train of abuses and usurpations . . . evinces a design to
[create] . . . absolute Despotism."

> Such has been the patient sufferance of these Colonies; and such is now the
> necessity which constrains them to alter their former System of Government.
> The history of the present King of Great Britain is a history of repeated injuries
> and usurpations, all having in direct object the establishment of an absolute
> Tyranny over these States. To prove this, let Facts be submitted to a candid
> world. He has refused to Assent to Laws, the most wholesome and necessary
> for the public good.
>
>   He has forbidden his Governors to pass Laws of immediate and pressing
> importance, unless suspended in their operation till his Assent should be
> obtained; and, when so suspended, he has utterly neglected to attend to them.
>
>   He has refused to pass other Laws for the accommodation of large dis-
> tricts of people, unless those people would relinquish the right of represen-
> tation in the Legislature, a right inestimable to them, and formidable to tyrants
> only.
>
> *continued on next page*

He has called together legislative bodies at places unusual, uncomfortable, and distant from the depository of their Public Records, for the sole purpose of fatiguing them into compliance with his measures.

He has dissolved Representative Houses repeatedly, for opposing, with manly firmness, his invasions on the rights of the people.

He has refused for a long time, after such dissolutions, to cause others to be elected; whereby the Legislative Powers, incapable of Annihilation, have returned to the People at large for their exercise; the State remaining, in the mean time, exposed to all the dangers of invasions from without and convulsions from within.

He has endeavored to prevent the population of these states; for that purpose obstructing the Laws of Naturalization of Foreigners; refusing to pass others to encourage their migration hither, and raising the conditions of new Appropriations of Lands.

He has obstructed the Administration of Justice, by refusing his Assent to laws for establishing Judiciary Powers.

He has made Judges dependent on his Will alone, for the tenure of their offices, and the amount and payment of their salaries.

He has erected a multitude of New Offices, and sent hither swarms of Officers to harass our People and eat out their substance.

He has kept among us, in times of peace, Standing Armies, without the Consent of our legislatures.

He has affected to render the military independent of, and superior to, the civil power.

Charges Against the English King

Jefferson devoted the central portion of the Declaration to establishing that George III was a tyrant whom Americans should resist. Colonial spokesmen had already rejected the notion of parliamentary sovereignty. Jefferson therefore directed most of his accusations against the king.

Trained as a lawyer, Jefferson crafted his accusations against the king much like a legal brief to show a pattern of abuses that evidenced the king's hostile design toward the colonists. Many accusations related to abuses of the colonists' rights to self-government and thus pointed to the type of institutions that Americans would have preferred. Thus, for example, Jefferson accused the king of refusing to assent to laws, suspending laws, attempting to bargain with the people for their liberties, calling legislative bodies together "at places unusual and difficult," dissolving legislatures, delaying elections to the legislatures, and so forth.

A number of Jefferson's other indictments highlighted colonial concerns with the system of justice. Thus, he noted the British refusal to agree to a colonial justice system and British efforts to undercut judicial independence by keeping judges dependent upon the king for their tenure and salaries. So too, Jefferson accused the king of multiplying governmental officials, keeping standing armies in the colonies, and failing to maintain civilian control over the military.

He has combined with others to subject us to a jurisdiction foreign to our constitution, and unacknowledged by our laws, giving his Assent to their Acts of pretended legislation:

For quartering large bodies of armed troops among us:

For protecting them, by a mock Trial, from Punishment for any Murders which they should commit on the Inhabitants of these States:

For cutting off our Trade with all parts of the world:

For imposing taxes on us without our Consent:

For depriving us in many cases, of the benefits of Trial by Jury:

For transporting us beyond Seas, to be tried for pretended offenses:

For abolishing the free System of English Laws in a neighbouring Province, establishing therein an Arbitrary government, and enlarging its Boundaries so as to render it at once an example and fit instrument for introducing the same absolute rule into these Colonies:

For taking away our Charters, abolishing our most valuable Laws, and altering fundamentally the Forms of our Governments:

For suspending our own Legislatures, and declaring themselves invested with Power to legislate for us in all cases whatsoever.

Indictments Against the King and the Parliament

Jefferson extended blame to Parliament when he indicted the king for combining "with others" and for giving assent "to their Acts of pretended legislation." Jefferson listed grievances connected with troops, trade, taxes ("without our Consent"), trials on foreign soil without the protection of juries, alterations of charters, suspension of legislatures, and so forth.

He has abdicated Government here, by declaring us out of his Protection and waging War against us.

He has plundered our seas, ravaged our Coasts, burned our towns, and destroyed the lives of our people.

continued on next page

He is at this time transporting large armies of foreign mercenaries to complete the works of death, desolation, and tyranny already begun with circumstances of Cruelty & perfidy scarcely paralleled in the most barbarous ages, and totally unworthy the Head of a civilized nation.

He has constrained our fellow Citizens taken Captive on the high Seas to bear Arms against their Country, to become the executioners of their friends and Brethren, or to fall themselves by their Hands.

He has excited domestic insurrections among us, and has endeavoured to bring on the inhabitants of our frontiers the merciless Indian Savages, whose known rule of warfare, is an undistinguished destruction of all ages, sexes, and conditions.

War Atrocities and Slavery

Among the final charges Jefferson leveled against the British were those atrocities that they had perpetrated from the start of the armed conflict that had begun the previous April. Jefferson's original declaration included a powerful and extended condemnation of the British for introducing and perpetuating slavery:

> He has waged cruel war against human nature itself, violating its most sacred rights of life and liberty in the persons of a distinct people who never offended him, captivating & carrying them into slavery in another hemisphere or to incur miserable death in their transportation thither. This piratical warfare, the opprobrium of *infidel* powers, is the warfare of the *Christian* king of Great Britain. Determined to keep open a market where *Men* should be bought & sold, he has prostituted his negative for suppressing every legislative attempt to prohibit or to restrain this execrable commerce. And that this assemblage of horrors might want to fact of distinguished die, he is now exciting those very people to rise in arms among us, and to purchase that liberty of which he has deprived them, by murdering the people on whom he has obtruded them: thus paying off former crimes committed against the *Liberties* of one people, with crimes which he urges them to commit against the *lives* of another. (Wills, 1978, 377)

This indictment offended some southern representatives. Other delegates undoubtedly recognized that it was problematic both to proclaim that "all men are created equal" and simultaneously to indict the king for encouraging slaves to gain their freedom. The Continental Congress thus shortened Jefferson's indictment to "He has excited domestic insurrections among us."

In every stage of these Oppressions We have Petitioned for Redress in the most humble terms: Our repeated Petitions have been answered only by repeated injury. A Prince, whose character is thus marked by every act which may define a Tyrant, is unfit to be the ruler of a free People.

Nor have We been wanting in our attentions to our British brethren. We have warned them, from time to time, of attempts by their legislature to extend an unwarrantable jurisdiction over us. We have reminded them of the circumstances of our emigration and settlement here. We have appealed to their native justice and magnanimity, and we have conjured them by the ties of our common kindred, to disavow these usurpations, which, would inevitably interrupt our connections and correspondence. They too have been deaf to the voice of justice and of consanguinity. We must, therefore, acquiesce in the necessity, which denounces our Separation, and hold them, as we hold the rest of mankind, Enemies in War, in Peace Friends.

Recapitulation of Earlier Petitions

Jefferson recapitulated the history of colonial petitions to England to establish his earlier contention that the colonists had been patient and pursued peaceful means of change before resorting to revolution. Although he focused on the king, Jefferson also accused the people and the institutions of England of failing to heed colonial grievances. Jefferson believed that the colonists became free of parliamentary authority by their move to the New World. They, and not their English sponsors, had taken the initiative, and therefore the British Parliament had no continuing authority over them.

We, therefore, the Representatives of the United States of America, in General Congress, Assembled, appealing to the Supreme Judge of the world for the rectitude of our intentions, do, in the Name, and by the Authority of the good People of these Colonies, solemnly publish and declare, That these United Colonies are, and of Right ought to be FREE AND INDEPENDENT STATES; that they are Absolved from all Allegiance to the British Crown, and that all political connection between them and the state of Great Britain is and ought to

continued on next page

be totally dissolved; and that as Free and Independent States, they have full Power to levy War, conclude Peace, contract Alliances, establish Commerce, and do all other Acts and Things which independent States may of right do. And for the support of this Declaration, with a firm reliance on the protection of Divine Providence, we mutually pledge to each other our Lives, our Fortunes, and our sacred Honor.

Conclusion

Jefferson ended by appealing to God to establish the colonists' good motives and incorporating Richard Henry Lee's resolution for independence. Jefferson announced that the United Colonies would now take their independent places among the family of nations. In closing, the fifty-six members of the Second Continental Congress who signed the document mutually affirmed their lives, their fortunes, and their sacred honor.

The Second Continental Congress adopted the Declaration of Independence on July 4, 1776, just two days after voting to accept Richard Henry Lee's resolution for independence. The Congress subsequently prepared and the delegates signed the document not, as paintings of the event suggest, on a single day, but during a period of months. Once members of Congress adopted the document, they could not turn back. Benjamin Franklin reportedly observed that, from then on, the revolutionaries would hang together or find themselves hanging separately from the ends of British nooses!

THE ARTICLES OF CONFEDERATION

The Background

On the day that Richard Henry Lee introduced his resolution for independence, he also proposed that Congress should seek foreign allies and form a new confederation. Congress vested the initial job of writing such a confederation in John Dickinson of Pennsylvania, who submitted his work to the Continental Congress in August 1776. Faced with more urgent matters of war, Congress delayed consideration of this proposal. When the Second Continental Congress reviewed the plan in 1777, the delegates, influenced by North Carolina Governor Thomas Burke, weakened the central authority of the new government at the expense of the states, each of which had until this time been separate. The Articles of Confederation did not officially go into effect until Maryland ratified it in 1781. As a small state, Maryland had insisted that large states relinquish their western land claims before it would ratify the new confederacy.

The Principles and Structures

There are two primary facts to remember about the Articles of Confederation. First, it was as much a treaty, or league of friendship, as a central government. Second, the Articles vested chief power in the individual states. Thus, Article II of the Constitution of the Articles stated that:

> Each state retains its sovereignty, freedom and independence, and every Power, Jurisdiction and right, which is not by this confederation delegated to the United States, in Congress assembled.

The centrifugal forces of states' rights under the Articles were greater than the centripetal ones for central power.

Under the Articles of Confederation, Congress was essentially the only branch of government, and it had only one house or chamber. Although states could send from two to seven delegates, the Articles granted each state a single vote regardless of size. Moreover, state legislatures chose the representatives, who thus felt more accountable to them than to the people. Congress lacked power over interstate commerce. Moreover, in most matters, Congress depended on the states. If it needed taxes, it could petition, but not coerce, the states for such revenues. If it needed an army, Congress again had to depend upon the states, which often looked jealously at their neighbors before deciding how much to contribute. On most key matters, delegations from nine states had to agree before Congress could act. Because it was essentially a treaty, all the state legislatures had to approve amendments that Congress proposed.

The Problems

The Articles of Confederation served as a valuable trial government. Its achievements included winning the war with Great Britain. The Congress under the Articles also adopted the Northwest Ordinance of 1787 formulating government for the western territories.

Despite its accomplishments, the negative results of such a weak alliance were fairly predictable. The economy worsened as states enacted tariffs and other trade restrictions on one another's goods. Currency was not uniform from one state to another. Congress was too weak. On the foreign policy front, the new government had difficulty enforcing treaties, and foreigners treated American diplomats with disrespect. Politically, the new government lacked adequate power of taxation and defense, and when Congress proposed needed changes, the rigid requirements to adopt constitutional amendments stymied them.

States had their own problems. Although they had led the way to constitutional government, many had modeled their governments on that of the

Articles, with weak or practically nonexistent executive and judicial branches. Factional battles often created chaos in state legislatures.

PRELUDE TO THE CONSTITUTIONAL CONVENTION

These conditions prompted a series of events that led to the Constitutional Convention of 1787. Delegates from Virginia and Maryland met at George Washington's home at Mount Vernon to iron out problems concerning commerce on mutual waterways. After achieving some success, the delegates called a convention where all the states could deal with such problems. Initially, this Annapolis Convention appeared to fail because delegates from only five of the thirteen states attended. Nationalistic delegates like James Madison and Alexander Hamilton, however, used this convention to call for another meeting in Philadelphia to deal not only with problems of commerce, but also with the wider problems that had evidenced themselves.

Initially, it appeared that no more states would send delegates to this convention than to the last. In the winter of 1786–1787, however, a debtor's and taxpayer's rebellion in Massachusetts shocked many people, particularly those with wealth and influence. Designated Shay's Rebellion after its revolutionary leader, Daniel Shays, many elites saw this rebellion as the beginning of anarchy and as another demonstration of the impotency of the Articles. Congress subsequently approved the new convention by proposing that it be held in Philadelphia in May:

> for the sole and express purpose of revising the Articles of Confederation and reporting to Congress and the several legislatures such alterations and provisions therein as shall when agreed to in Congress and confirmed by the states render the federal constitution adequate to the exigencies of government and the preservation of the Union. (Text found in Jensen, 1976, 187)

Twelve of the thirteen states (all but Rhode Island) eventually sent delegates.

THE CONSTITUTIONAL CONVENTION

The Delegates

Consistent with the congressional resolution calling the convention, most delegates probably arrived in Philadelphia to revise rather than to scrap the Articles of Confederation. However, the delegates from Virginia, who introduced the first plan that the delegates discussed, came prepared to rethink the entire system of government. Once they advanced their plan, it set the agenda for a complete overhaul.

Altogether fifty-five of seventy-four appointed delegates attended the Constitutional Convention. These delegates represented the elite of the colonies, including state governors, men who had been active in writing state constitutions, and thirty-nine present or former members of Congress. Among the best known and most influential delegates were (from North to South): Nathaniel Gorham and Elbridge Gerry of Massachusetts; Roger Sherman and Oliver Ellsworth of Connecticut; William Paterson of New Jersey; Benjamin Franklin, James Wilson, and Gouverneur Morris of Pennsylvania; John Dickinson of Delaware; Luther Martin of Maryland; George Washington, James Madison, Jr., and George Mason of Virginia; Hugh Williamson of North Carolina; and cousins Charles Pinckney and Charles Cotesworth Pinckney of South Carolina. John Adams and Thomas Jefferson were serving respectively as diplomats to England and France, and a few other important leaders—most notably Patrick Henry, who, with his strong states' rights views, professed "to smell a rat"— refused to attend, but few assemblies have highlighted better educated or more serious men.

Sons of the Enlightenment, delegates hoped to apply the lessons of experience to the creation of a new government. At the same time, most were realists who recognized, as Madison argued in *Federalist* No. 51, that human beings were not angels and that governments must necessarily guard against destructive human impulses. Scholars have variously painted the framers as near demigods or condemned them as representatives of narrow social and economic interests. In his book, *Constitution Making*, Calvin Jillson has convincingly argued that the convention delegates attempted both to uphold cherished constitutional principles and to protect state and regional interests.

The Rules

The convention's first order of business was to choose a president. Two members of the convention, George Washington and Benjamin Franklin, had worldwide reputations. Although he was mentally alert, the eighty-one-year-old Franklin, the oldest member, was frail. With his blessing, fellow Pennsylvania delegate Robert Morris nominated Washington, whom the state delegations then in attendance unanimously selected. As the former commander of American forces during the Revolutionary War, the fifty-five-year-old Washington was quite mindful of his high place in the public mind, and he had ruminated for months about whether to attend the convention. His decision both to attend and to serve as the convention's president may ultimately have been decisive in the people's eventual acceptance of the Constitution. Although he rarely spoke during the convention, his very presence lent a special gravity to the proceedings.

The delegates adopted several rules that illumined their intentions and deliberations. As in the Articles of Confederation, delegates specified that each state delegation would have a single vote. The delegates did not record votes under individual names, and, when members of the convention desired to retake votes, they could do so. Delegates thus hoped to encourage reasonable argument and compromise. Finally, the convention voted to keep its proceedings secret. They feared that publicity might subordinate rational deliberation to power politics and perhaps even mob action in the streets of Philadelphia. Delegates could propose or discuss anything, knowing that the public would eventually approve or disapprove the final proposal.

The official secretary took only skeletal notes, but thirty-six-year-old James Madison recorded convention votes and debates. Madison had literally spent months reading books that his friend Thomas Jefferson had mailed to him from Europe and writing essays on needed changes in government. Positioning himself near the front of Washington's chair, Madison kept meticulous notes. Madison was the last delegate to the convention who died, and his notes of the proceedings were not published until after his demise. They remain the best record available of the proceedings.

The Virginia Plan

The Virginia delegates presented the first plan to the convention. The state's governor, Edmund Randolph, introduced the plan, which Madison appears largely to have authored. The Virginia Plan dominated the discussion for the first two weeks.

The plan called for significantly strengthening the national government, and its plan of representation favored populous states like Virginia. The Virginia Plan proposed establishing three branches of government. The Plan also proposed a bicameral legislature, rather than the unicameral congress under the Articles of Confederation. The Virginia Plan proposed apportioning both houses according to population. The people would elect members of the first chamber, who would choose members of the second from among members of state legislatures. Congress would choose the executive—probably a single individual—who the plan would limit to a single term. So too, congress would choose members of the judicial branch, who would serve during good behavior. The Virginia Plan also proposed a Council of Revision consisting of the executive and members of the national judiciary. Such a council would have had power to veto acts of state and national legislation, subject to an override by a congressional supermajority.

The Virginia Plan also proposed an amending process and contained provisions for admitting new states.

The New Jersey Plan

After about two weeks of discussion, New Jersey's William Paterson proposed an alternative to the Virginia Plan. Although it introduced an early variant of the supremacy clause, which courts have since used to establish the authority of the national government over the states, delegates who feared granting increased powers to the national government generally supported the New Jersey Plan over the Virginia Plan as more consistent with the Articles of Confederation and the call for the convention that Congress had issued. More obviously, the New Jersey Plan favored the interests of the small states.

Because Paterson introduced the New Jersey Plan after two weeks of discussion and agreement, it incorporated a number of features of the Virginia Plan. Thus, the New Jersey Plan accepted the idea that the new government would have three branches. Whereas the Virginia Plan proposed a bicameral legislature, however, the New Jersey Plan proposed keeping a unicameral congress, which would continue to represent the states equally. Moreover, the New Jersey Plan favored a plural executive, which Congress would appoint for a fixed term. The executive would appoint the judiciary. Although the New Jersey Plan did not mention an amending process or a Council of Revision, like the Virginia Plan, it wisely provided for the admission of new states.

Prominent Convention Issues

The convention soon decided to move ahead with the Virginia Plan, but delegates eventually incorporated many of the ideas of the New Jersey Plan into its final product. Most notably, in the most difficult issue the delegates faced, they reached a compromise utilizing the Virginia Plan's scheme for representation for one house of Congress and that of the New Jersey Plan for the second. This was called the Connecticut, or Great, Compromise.

The delegates had to work out many other compromises on issues that divided North and South, small states and large states, proponents of a strong nation and defenders of states' rights, and those who largely trusted and those who chiefly feared the people. Compromises resolved issues related to the taxation, representation, and importation of the slaves; selection of the president; state and national relations; and the powers of the Congress, the president, and the courts. The delegates often appointed committees to facilitate compromise, or, as in the case of the Committee of the Detail, to compile resolutions on similar topics into coherent articles and sections.

When the convention's work neared its end, it appointed a five-man Committee of Style to put the final touches on the document. The most influential member of the committee was Gouverneur Morris, the large Pennsylvania delegate with a peg leg. After he and the committee reported the document back to the convention, the delegates signed it on September 17, 1787. Most of the delegates agreed with the arguments that Benjamin Franklin advanced on the last day of the convention. He argued that, although it was not perfect, the document was the best distillation of collective wisdom that delegates could expect under the circumstances. Defenders of the Constitution also pointed out that the people could amend the document as problems developed. Thirty-nine of the remaining forty-two delegates (including Dickinson, who did so by proxy) signed the document. Virginia's Edmund Randolph and George Mason, as well as Elbridge Gerry of Massachusetts, did not.

A painter had embossed the image of the sun on the top slat of the stately Chippendale chair on which George Washington sat. As delegates were signing the Constitution, Benjamin Franklin observed that he now believed that the sun was rising rather than setting. Franklin and others hoped that the adoption of the Constitution would bring a new day of freedom, prosperity, and justice.

RATIFICATION OF THE CONSTITUTION

Bypassing requirements under the Articles of Confederation for unanimous state approval of any constitutional changes, the delegates specified that the new constitution would go into effect when a majority of delegates to nine or more state conventions ratified it. Almost as soon as the Constitutional Convention finished its work, the country divided into two groups. Calling themselves Federalists, proponents of the new constitution naturally pushed for its quick adoption. Pointing to the clear weaknesses of the Articles of Confederation and the need for change, they touted the new document as a way to maintain liberty while strengthening the national government so that it would be adequate to the crises it faced.

Antifederalist opponents of the Constitution in turn raised a variety of objections to the new Constitution. Some rested on unfounded fears of any change, but others were more substantial. Relying for primary support on the French philosopher Charles Louis the Second [the Baron] of Montesquieu (1689–1755), who had also advocated separation of powers, prominent Antifederalists argued that a national government over such a large land area would swallow the states and destroy civil liberties. They further thought that the absence of a bill of rights in the new Constitution confirmed either that its framers were unconcerned with civil liberties or that they had not adequately protected them. Antifederalists wanted to call for yet another convention to resolve such issues before the people ratified the new Constitution.

Many Federalists initially argued that a bill of rights was unnecessary and could even become counterproductive or dangerous if drafters inadvertently omitted some rights. Like Antifederalists, however, they favored rights, and they were quite concerned that another convention could destroy the work of the first, plunge the nation into renewed chaos, and further tarnish America's international image. These concerns led key Federalists to agree to work for a bill of rights once the states ratified the new Constitution.

Writing under the pen name Publius, Alexander Hamilton, James Madison, and John Jay launched a series of newspaper articles in New York, eventually published in book form as *The Federalist*, or *The Federalist Papers*. These essays argued for the new Constitution and sought to explain its meaning. Some essays attempted to refute Montesquieu's contention that democratic government was unsuited for governments over a large land area. In *Federalist* No. 10, James Madison argued that a government over such an extended area would better alleviate the perennial problem of faction, or injustice caused by self-interests, than would a small one. He pointed out that the new government the Constitution proposed was not a pure democracy, like classic examples of the past, but rather a republic, or indirect democracy. Such a republic would refine the public view through a system of representation and, by its very size and the varied interests that it therefore embraced, further reduce the possibility that private interest groups could successfully collude against the public interest.

In addition to such arguments, Federalists had a number of advantages in their contest with the Antifederalists. Federalists were proposing a positive solution to an obvious problem. Federalists were well-organized; many had been working for a new government not only during the long summer of 1787, but even earlier.

Although debates were intense and the votes were often close in the state ratifying conventions (especially in critical states like Massachusetts, Virginia, and New York), the required nine states soon ratified in 1788. Electors chose George Washington as president, and the Constitution went into effect in 1789. By the end of Washington's first term, all thirteen states had joined the new union.

REFERENCES AND SUGGESTIONS FOR FURTHER STUDY

Mortimer J. Adler, *We Hold These Truths: Understanding the Ideas and Ideals of the Constitution* (New York: Macmillan Publishing Company, 1987).

Akhil Reed Amar, *America's Constitution: A Biography* (New York: Random House, 2005).

George Anastaplo, *The Constitution of 1787: A Commentary* (Baltimore, MD: The Johns Hopkins University Press, 1989).

Thorton Anderson, *Creating the Constitution: The Convention of 1787 and the First Congress* (University Park: The Pennsylvania State University Press, 1993).

Bernard Bailyn, *The Ideological Origins of the American Revolution* (Cambridge, MA: Harvard University Press, 1967).

Lance Banning, *The Sacred Fire of Liberty: James Madison and the Founding of the Federal Republic* (Ithaca, NY: Cornell University Press, 1995).

Fred Barbash, *The Founding: A Dramatic Account of the Writing of the Constitution* (New York: Simon and Schuster, 1987).

Carl L. Becker, *The Declaration of Independence: A Study in the History of Political Ideas* (New York: Vintage Books, 1970).

Richard Beeman, Stephen Botein, and Edward C. Carter, II, *Beyond Confederation: Origins of the Constitution and American National Identity* (Chapel Hill: University of North Carolina Press, 1987).

Catherine Drinker Bowen, *Miracle at Philadelphia* (Boston: Little, Brown and Company, 1966).

Edward E. Cooke, *A Detailed Analysis of the Constitution*, 5th ed. (Savage, MD: Rowman & Littlefield Publishers, Inc., 1984).

Edward S. Corwin, *The "Higher Law" Background of American Constitutional Law* (Ithaca, NY: Cornell University Press, 1955).

Noble E. Cunningham, Jr., *The Pursuit of Reason: The Life of Thomas Jefferson* (Baton Rouge: Louisiana State University Press, 1987).

James A. Curry, Richard B. Riley, and Richard M. Battistoni, *Constitutional Government: The American Experiment*, 5th ed. (Dubuque, IA: Kendall Hunt, 2003).

Sue Davis and J. W. Peltason, *Corwin and Peltason's Understanding the Constitution*, 16th ed. (Belmont, CA: Wadsworth/Thomson Learning, 2004).

Max Farrand, *The Framing of the Constitution of the United States* (New Haven, CT: Yale University Press, 1913).

Max Farrand, *The Records of the Federal Convention of 1787*, 4 vols. (New Haven, CT: Yale University Press, 1966).

James Thomas Flexner, *Washington: The Indispensable Man* (Boston: Little, Brown and Company, 1974).

George J. Graham, Jr. and Scarlett G. Graham, *Founding Principles of American Government: Two Hundred Years of Democracy on Trial* (Chatham, NJ: Chatham House Publishers, 1984).

Alexander Hamilton, James Madison, and John Jay, *The Federalists Papers*, Clinton Rossiter, ed. (New York: New American Library, 1961).

Robert H. Horowitz, *The Moral Foundations of the American Republic*, 2nd ed. (Charlottesville: University Press of Virginia, 1979).

Harry V. Jaffa, *How to Think About the American Revolution: A Bicentennial Celebration* (Durham, NC: Carolina Academic Press, 1978).

Thomas Jefferson, *Notes on the State of Virginia* (New York: Harper & Row, 1964).

Merrill Jensen, *The Articles of Confederation* (Madison: University of Wisconsin Press, 1966).

Merrill Jensen, ed., *Constitutional Documents and Records, 17767–1787*, vol. I of *The Documentary History of the Ratification of the Constitution* (Madison: State Historical Society of Wisconsin, 1976).

Calvin C. Jillson, *Constitution Making: Conflict and Consensus in the Federal Convention of 1787* (New York: Agathon Press, Inc., 1988).

Michael Kammen, *A Machine That Would Go of Itself: The Constitution in American Culture* (New York: Alfred A. Knopf, 1987).

Joseph T. Kennan, *The Constitution of the United States: An Unfolding Story*, 2nd ed. (Chicago: The Dorsey Press, 1985).

Ralph Ketcham, *Framed for Posterity* (Lawrence: University Press of Kansas, 1993).

Johnny H. Killian, ed., *The Constitution of the United States of America: Analysis and Interpretation* (Washington, DC: U.S. Government Printing Office, 1973).

Philip B. Kurland and Ralph Lerner, *The Founders' Constitution*, 5 vols. (Chicago: The University of Chicago Press, 1987).

Leonard W. Levy, ed., *Essays on the Making of the Constitution* (New York: Oxford University Press, 1969).

John Locke, *Two Treatises of Government*, rev. ed., Peter Laslett, ed. (New York: New American Library, 1963).

Donald S. Lutz, *The Origins of American Constitutionalism* (Baton Rouge: Louisiana State University Press, 1988).

Pauline Maier, *American Scripture: Making the Declaration of Independence* (New York: Alfred A. Knopf, 1997).

Alpheus T. Mason and Gordon E. Baker, *Free Government in the Making: Readings in American Political Thought*, 4th ed. (New York: Oxford University Press, 1985).

Drew R. McCoy, *The Last of the Fathers: James Madison and the Republican Legacy* (Cambridge, England: Cambridge University Press, 1989).

Forrest McDonald, *Novus Ordo Seclorum: The Intellectual Origins of the Constitution* (Lawrence: The University Press of Kansas, 1985).

Charles H. McIlwain, *Constitutionalism: Ancient and Modern* (Ithaca, NY: Cornell University Press, 1947).

Marvin Meyers, ed., *The Mind of the Founder: Sources of the Political Thought of James Madison* (New York: The Bobbs-Merrill Company, Inc., 1973).

William L. Miller, *The Business of May Next: James Madison and the Founding* (Charlottesville: University Press of Virginia, 1992).

Thomas Paine, *Common Sense and Other Political Writings*, Nelson F. Adkins, ed. (New York: The Liberal Arts Press, 1953).

William Peters, *A More Perfect Union: The Making of the United States Constitution* (New York: Crown Publishers, 1987).

Jack N. Rakove, *Original Meanings: Politics and Ideas in the Making of the Constitution* (New York: Alfred A. Knopf, 1996).

John P. Reid, *Constitutional History of the American Revolution*, 3 vols. (Madison: The University of Wisconsin Press, 1987–1992).

Neal Riemer, *James Madison: Creating the American Constitution* (Washington, DC: Congressional Quarterly Inc., 1986).

David Brian Robertson, *The Constitution and America's Destiny* (New York: Cambridge University Press, 2005).

Clinton Rossiter, *1787: The Grand Convention* (New York: W.W. Norton, 1966).

Robert A. Rutland, ed., *James Madison: The Founding Father* (New York: MacMillan Publishing Company, 1987).

R. C. Simmons, ed., *The United States Constitution: The First 200 Years* (Manchester, England: Manchester University Press, 1989).

Shlomo Slonim, ed., *The Constitutional Bases of Political and Social Change in the United States* (New York: Praeger, 1990).

David G. Smith, *The Convention and the Constitution: The Political Ideas of the Founding Fathers* (New York: St. Martin's Press, 1965).

Winton U. Solberg, *The Federal Convention and Formation of the Union of the American States* (New York: The Liberal Arts Press, 1958).

Herbert A. Storing, *What the Anti-Federalists Were For: The Political Thought of the Opponents of the Constitution* (Chicago: The University of Chicago Press, 1981).

This Constitution (Washington, DC: Congressional Quarterly, Inc., 1986).

Francis N. Thorpe, ed., *The Federal and State Constitutions; Colonial Charters and Other Organic Laws of the States, Territories, and Colonies Now or Hetertofore Forming the United States of America* (Washington, DC: U.S. Government Printing Office, 1909).

John R. Vile, *The Constitutional Convention of 1787: A Comprehensive Encyclopedia of America's Founding*, 2 vols. (Santa Barbara, CA: ABC-CLIO, 2005).

John R. Vile, *History of the American Legal System: An Interactive Encyclopedia*, CD-ROM (Santa Barbara, CA: ABC-CLIO, 1999).

John R. Vile, *The United States Constitution: Questions and Answers* (Westport, CT: Greenwood Press, 1998).

Jon L. Wakelyn, *Birth of the Bill of Rights: Encyclopedia of the Antifederalists*, 2 vols. (Westport, CT: Greenwood Press, 2004).

Robert H. Webking, *The American Revolution and the Politics of Liberty* (Baton Rouge: Louisiana State University Press, 1988).

Morton White, *The Philosophy of the American Revolution* (New York: Oxford University Press, 1978).

Garry Wills, *Inventing America: Jefferson's Declaration of Independence* (New York: Doubleday, 1978).

Gordon S. Wood, *The Creation of the American Republic: 1776–1787* (Williamsburg: The University of North Carolina Press, 1969).

Gordon S. Wood, *The Radicalism of the American Revolution* (New York: Alfred A. Knopf, 1992).

Chapter 2

The Preamble and Article I: The Legislative Branch

The U.S. Constitution begins with an introductory paragraph, or preamble, which outlines the purposes of the new government. It continues with seven articles; the framers divided most of these into a number of sections. After examining the Preamble, this chapter focuses on Article I, which chiefly establishes and outlines the powers and limits of the legislative branch.

AMERICA'S WRITTEN CONSTITUTION

The U.S. Constitution is a written document. Citizens can carry a copy in their pockets, and authors can include the text in books. Americans often identify constitutionalism with a written constitution. Historically, however, a constitution may either be a single written document like that in America or a set of rules, practices, and principles, only some of which a nation commits to writing. Significantly, the British do not have a written constitution like that in the United States, which is superior to ordinary acts of legislation and unchangeable by ordinary legislative means. Although cultural constraints have prevented drastic changes, in theory the British Parliament is sovereign and can do anything that is not physically impossible. Fearing abuses like those of the British against the colonists, the American founders thought they could better secure their liberties by creating a written constitution that was paramount to, and foundational for, all other laws. By writing such a document, the delegates who met at the Constitutional Convention followed an example that the states had already taken individually in a surge of constitution-writing that had accompanied the start of the Revolutionary War.

THE PREAMBLE

> We the People of the United States, in Order to form a more perfect Union, establish Justice, insure domestic Tranquility, provide for the common defence, promote the general Welfare, and secure the Blessings of Liberty to ourselves and our Posterity, do ordain and establish this Constitution for the United States of America.

The Purposes of the Constitution

Scholars designate the opening paragraph of the U.S. Constitution as the Preamble. Judges rarely cite the Preamble as authority because it grants no specific powers to the national government. Instead, it describes the foundation and states the purposes or aspirations of those who wrote and ratified the Constitution.

The opening words are among the most elegant in the entire document. They assert the origins of the Constitution in "We the People" and identify this people as those who reside in the United States. Especially in the period leading up to the Civil War, both citizens and leaders debated whether the people of the nation as a whole, or the people of the states, exercised such power. Long after Abraham Lincoln led those who repudiated extreme notions of states' rights to victory, legitimate questions persist as to the relationship between the national government and the states.

The second phrase in the Constitution refers to its own antecedents. The founders created the Constitution "to form a more perfect Union." The less perfect union, which existed prior to the Constitution, was, of course, the Articles of Confederation. This "Union" was more a treaty, or League of Friendship, than a real government, and the economic, political, and diplomatic problems of this union led to the Convention that wrote the current Constitution.

The next provisions of the Preamble refer to the ideas of establishing justice, insuring domestic tranquility, providing for the common defense, and promoting the general welfare. These were precisely the concerns that had troubled leaders under the Articles of Confederation. Legislative majorities had sometimes jeopardized justice in the states by riding roughshod over the rights of minorities. In the winter of 1786–1787, Shay's Rebellion, like other disputes over taxation and state fiscal policies, had in turn threatened domestic tranquility. Congressional dependence on the states to provide troops and taxes had further jeopardized defense, while the internecine warfare over commerce had severely eroded the general welfare.

Ultimately, however, the framers of the Constitution sought to establish the "Blessings of Liberty." The one-time colonists had articulated their desire for liberty in the Declaration of Independence and further defined the term in their struggle with the British. Recognizing that liberty requires adherence to law, the founders distinguished liberty from license. The framers valued liberty enough to want to pass it down to posterity. To rephrase a popular song, the framers intended for the Constitution to last, "not just for an hour, not just for a day, but always." Written in 1787, ratified in 1788, and implemented in 1789, this document has now guided the U.S. government for more than two hundred years.

Article I, Section 1. All legislative Powers herein granted shall be vested in a Congress of the United States, . . .

THE SEPARATION OF POWERS AND THE STRUCTURE OF THE CONSTITUTION

Although the words of the Constitution do not employ the specific phrase, the structure of the document reflects the doctrine of separation of powers. The first three articles of the Constitution illustrate the doctrine of separation of powers in that each establishes a separate branch of the central, or national, government. Article I creates the legislative branch, Article II the executive branch, and Article III the judicial branch. This order is purposeful and instructive. Because they were creating a democratic, or representative, government that rested on what the Declaration of Independence called "the consent of the governed" and what the Constitution simply refers to as "We the People," the authors of the Constitution logically began with the two branches that the people elected and then proceeded to the branch that the president appointed and that the Senate confirmed.

The legislative branch had, in effect, been the only branch of government under the Articles of Confederation. It was the first branch that delegates discussed at any length at the Constitutional Convention, and most of the delegates thought that it would continue to be the most powerful. The framers, however, wanted to limit even the powers of this branch. They refused to entrust it, like the British Parliament, with complete sovereignty, but limited it to exercising legislative powers "herein granted." Although judges and legislatures have interpreted congressional designated powers broadly and supplemented them with implied powers, the other two branches still balance these powers.

By vesting "legislative powers" in Congress, the Constitution limited the powers that it could delegate to the other branches. *Schechter Poultry Corporation v. United States* (1935) provided one of the best examples of this limitation. Congress had, under the National Industrial Recovery Act of 1933, allowed individual industries to establish binding codes of fair competition subject only to presidential approval. The Supreme Court invalidated this massive delegation of powers. The Supreme Court has generally been more generous in upholding congressional delegations of power in the area of foreign affairs. In *United States v. Curtiss-Wright Export Corp.* (1936), it permitted the president to declare an arms embargo of a warring region in South America when, as per congressional stipulations, he thought it was in the nation's best interest to do so.

Article I, Section 1. ... which shall consist of a Senate and House of Representatives.

BICAMERALISM

Section 1 of Article I entrusts Congress with legislative powers and divided it into two houses, a Senate and a House of Representatives. This is the principle of bicameralism. Much like the division of government into three branches helps them check one another, bicameralism acts as an internal check on the Congress. When Thomas Jefferson—who had been serving during the Constitutional Convention as an ambassador to France—asked George Washington why the Convention had created two houses of Congress, Washington reputedly poured some coffee into his cup plate and blew over it to cool the liquid. He expected one house to cool the passions of the other much as he had cooled the liquid in his cup plate with his breath.

The British Parliament, the "mother of Parliaments" and the legislative branch, apart from the Confederal Congress, with which the colonists were most familiar, was bicameral. Significant differences existed between the House of Lords and House of Commons in England, and the Senate and House of Representatives under the U.S. Constitution. Most notably, the British House of Lords is largely hereditary, whereas the U.S. Senate is not.

THE U.S. HOUSE OF REPRESENTATIVES

Article I, Section 2. [1] The House of Representatives shall be composed of Members chosen every second Year by the People of the several States, and the Electors in each State shall have the Qualifications requisite for Electors of the most numerous Branch of the State Legislature.

[2] No person shall be a Representative who shall not have attained to the Age of twenty five Years, and been seven Years a Citizen of the United States, and who shall not, when elected, be an Inhabitant of that State in which he shall be chosen.

Terms of Office and Qualifications

Section 2 of Article I deals with the House of Representatives. As its name indicates, the framers designed it to be the most popular, or representative, house of the most popular branch. Members of the House serve for two-year terms, and all stand for election at once. The framers thereby enabled voters to keep members of the House on a short leash. Rather than set national voting qualifications at a time when such qualifications varied widely from one state to another, the framers simply specified that states would utilize the same qualifications as they did for state legislative elections. A number of constitutional amendments now further prohibit discrimination on the basis of race, sex, or age above eighteen.

The qualifications that paragraph 2 outlines for representatives are minimal. House members need only to be twenty-five years old, citizens for seven years, and inhabitants of the state that chooses them. Practice dictates that representatives also be living in the district that elected them, but this is an extra-constitutional development.

Article I, Section 2. [3] *Representatives and direct Taxes shall be apportioned among the several States which may be included within this Union, according to their respective Numbers, which shall be determined by adding to the whole Number of free Persons, including those bound to Service for a Term of Years; and excluding Indians not taxed, three fifths of all other Persons.* The actual Enumeration shall be made within three Years after the first Meeting of the Congress of the United States, and within every subsequent Term of ten Years, in such Manner as they shall by Law direct. The Number of Representatives shall not exceed one for every thirty Thousand, but each State shall have at

continued on next page

Least one Representative; and until such enumeration shall be made, the State of New Hampshire shall be entitled to chuse [sic] three, Massachusetts eight, Rhode-Island and Providence Plantations one, Connecticut five, New-York six, New Jersey four, Pennsylvania eight, Delaware one, Maryland six, Virginia ten, North Carolina five, South Carolina five, and Georgia three.

Representation and Taxation

The Articles of Confederation provided for equal state representation in Congress. Consistent with the interest of the large states and with more general conceptions of representational fairness, the delegates who introduced the Virginia Plan at the Constitutional Convention hoped to change this arrangement. They proposed representing states in both houses of this proposed national legislature according to population and/or tax contributions.

Although the delegates initially decided this issue in Virginia's favor, the issue of representation resurfaced as one of the most vexing that the delegates faced. William Paterson's New Jersey Plan proposed continuing to represent states equally in a unicameral, or one house, legislature similar to that under the existing Articles of Confederation. Ultimately, the delegates forged the Connecticut, or Great, Compromise. Under this plan, the delegates established a bicameral Congress, as the Virginians had proposed. In further accord with the Virginia Plan, the Connecticut Compromise apportioned the House of Representatives according to population. As in the proposed New Jersey Plan and the earlier Articles of Confederation, however, the Compromise accepted equal state representation in the Senate.

The Three-Fifths Clause

This paragraph of Section 2 also reflects another, less defensible, compromise that delegates made at the Constitutional Convention. Whereas the central question of representation divided the large states from the small states, the subsidiary issue of slavery divided the states of the North and the South. Northern and southern sentiments in 1787 were not what they became by 1860. At the time the framers wrote the Constitution, northerners were generally less concerned about the morality of slavery than they later became. For their part, southerners were more likely to defend the institution of slavery in 1787 much as people might today defend war or taxes, that is, as necessary evils rather than the positive good that southern spokesmen, like John C. Calhoun and George Fitzhugh, later claimed it to be.

Nonetheless, key differences of interest in the institution of slavery reinforced already diverging views of its morality. Northerners were eager to count slaves in assessing state tax contributions, but quite unwilling to count slaves in apportioning the number of congressional representatives each state should have. For their part, southerners wanted as many representatives as they could get, but they did not want states taxed on the numbers of slaves. The compromise, which the delegates embodied (like other superseded parts of the document throughout this book) in the italicized portion of Article I, Section 2, was to count slaves as three-fifths of a person for both purposes. Congress under the Articles of Confederation had previously formulated, albeit never implemented, this ratio.

The provision both recognized that slaves embodied an element of personhood and treated them as less than full persons. Significantly, the framers never employed the word "slave" in the Constitution; instead they used the words "all other Persons," in contrast to free persons, Indians, and those who were indentured servants. Noting the omission of the term "slave" in a document designed to secure the blessings of liberty, Abraham Lincoln said that the framers hid slavery within the Constitution "just as an afflicted man hides away a wen [cyst] or a cancer which he dares not cut out at once, lest he bleed to death" (Kammen, *A Machine That Would Go of Itself*, p. 102). The Union victory in the Civil War sounded the death knell to the three-fifths clause. The Thirteenth Amendment abolished slavery, and Section 2 of the Fourteenth Amendment allocated representation on the basis of "the whole number of persons in each State, excluding Indians not taxed."

Initial State Representation

Although they provided that censuses would establish future state allocations, the framers had to provide an initial scheme of representation in the House of Representatives, which they did by allocating to each state from one to ten representatives. The allocation reveals that they correctly believed Virginia, to which they assigned ten seats, was the most populous, and Rhode Island, to which they assigned one seat, was the least populous. The Constitution initially awarded New Jersey, which had so effectively represented the interests of the small states at the Constitutional Convention, four House seats.

There were sixty-five members in the first House of Representatives. As state populations grew, this number increased. In 1911, Congress capped membership in the house at 435. Congress reallocates seats to states after each decennial census. In *Department of Commerce v. U.S. House of Representatives* (1999), the Supreme Court ruled that Congress had to allocate such seats on an actual head count rather than on statistical samples designed to achieve more accurate results.

Article I, Section 2. [4] When vacancies happen in the Representation from any State, the Executive Authority thereof shall issue Writs of Election to fill such Vacancies.

[5] The House of Representatives shall chuse [sic] their Speaker and other Officers; and shall have the sole Power of Impeachment.

House Vacancies, the Speaker, and Impeachment

Paragraph 4 specifies that state executives will call elections to fill House vacancies. Such elections have not been as significant as the "by-elections" in Britain and other parliamentary democracies for two reasons. First, the two-year House terms are short enough to minimize the number of such vacancies. Second, because of the separation of powers, even a change in the party composition of one or both Houses of Congress does not bring down the president's government in the same way that a change of parties and a subsequent "vote of no confidence" brings down the prime minister in a parliamentary democracy.

The Constitution vests the House of Representatives with the prerogative of choosing its own Speaker. Members invariably choose a member of the majority party in one of the few straight party votes in this body, whose members otherwise demonstrate a great deal of independence. Because the party with the majority in the House is not necessarily the party that has captured the presidency, the House Speaker may be from a different party than the president and/or the Senate majority leader.

There have been some very powerful Speakers in House history, particularly Thomas Reed of Maine, who served from 1889 to 1891 and 1895 to 1899, and Joe Cannon of Illinois, who presided from 1903 to 1911. Democratic-minded reformers in the 1960s and 1970s undercut the power of modern Speakers by dispersing power more widely within Congress. At least for a time, Georgia Representative Newt Gingrich succeeded in bringing new visibility to this office after mobilizing his Republican colleagues around the Contract with America (a set of proposals that signers agreed to support if elected) in the election of 1994 and subsequently gaining control of the House for his party. Because the Constitution says so little about the office, its powers can clearly ebb and flow.

The Constitution vests the House of Representatives with the power of impeachment. The power to impeach is the power to bring charges. The Constitution vests the Senate with the power to try impeachments and requires a two-thirds vote for conviction.

The U.S. Senate

Article I, Section 3. [1] The Senate of the United States shall be composed of two Senators from each State, *chosen by the Legislature thereof*, for six Years, and each Senator shall have one Vote.

Representation, Voting, and Terms

Just as Section 2 deals with the lower house, the House of Representatives, Section 3 describes the upper house, the Senate. Whereas the House of Representatives reflects the scheme of representation in the Virginia Plan, the Senate embodies the plan of representation in the Articles of Confederation and the New Jersey Plan. Regardless of size, each state has two senators, each with a single independent vote. The Constitution specified that state legislatures would choose Senators, but the Seventeenth Amendment, which states ratified in 1913, provided for their direct popular election.

Whereas all members of the House of Representatives stand for election every two years, only one-third of the Senate seats are contested every two years, since senators serve for terms of six years rather than two. The framers designed this longer term to give the Senate greater stability so that it can oppose rash legislative measures of the House. Although the Twenty-second Amendment now limits presidents to two full terms, the Constitution does not limit the number of terms that representatives or senators can serve.

Given the high reelection rates of incumbents, particularly members of the House of Representatives, and the career orientation that this has fostered, some political leaders have proposed constitutional amendments mandating term limits. Critics argue, however, that this would restrict the people's current power of choice, diminish the legislature's institutional memory, and have other unintended consequences. In recent years, some states attempted to limit the number of terms their representatives could serve. In *U.S. Term Limits v. Thornton* (1995), however, the Supreme Court narrowly decided that existing qualifications in Article I, Section 3 are exclusive, unless and until such time as an amendment modifies them.

Article I, Section 3. [2] Immediately after they shall be assembled in Consequence of the first Election, they shall be divided as equally as may be

continued on next page

into three Classes. The Seats of the Senators of the first Class shall he vacated at the Expiration of the Second Year, of the second Class at the Expiration of the fourth Year, and of the third Class at the Expiration of the sixth Year, so that one third may be chosen every second Year; *and if Vacancies happen by Resignation, or otherwise, during the Recess of the Legislature of any State, the Executive thereof may make temporary Appointments until the next Meeting of the Legislature, which shall then fill such Vacancies.*

Staggered Senate Terms and Vacancies

This is a transition provision. The framers arranged the terms of new senators so that, at the end of the first six years, one-third of them would stand for election every two years. This provision invested state governors with the power to fill Senate vacancies when state legislatures were out of session. Governors may still make such temporary appointments. Under the terms of the Seventeenth Amendment, however, popular elections now determine who fills out such terms.

Article I, Section 3. [3] No person shall be a Senator who shall not have attained to the Age of thirty Years, and been nine Years a Citizen of the United States, and who shall not, when elected, be an Inhabitant of that State for which he shall be chosen.

Qualifications

Requirements for membership in the Senate are hardly onerous, but the age limit—thirty years instead of twenty-five—and the citizenship requirement—nine years rather than seven—indicate that the framers designed the Senate to be a more stable and mature body than the House of Representatives. Membership in the Senate is not, as in the British House of Lords, hereditary, nor do Senators serve for life. The differences between the U.S. House and Senate flow from differing terms and wider constituencies rather than from special wealth or privilege.

Article I, Section 3. [4] The Vice President of the United States shall be President of the Senate, but shall have no Vote, unless they be equally divided.

The Legislative Role of the Vice President

Although the Constitution embodies the theory of separation of powers, the framers did not establish a hermetic, or airtight, relationship among the branches, and they frequently share powers. Thus, the constitution designates the vice president, a member of the executive branch, as president of the Senate, with the power to cast tie-breaking votes. Because presidents often assign extra-constitutional duties to their vice presidents, most vice presidents do not spend much time in the Senate, and thus the Constitution also provides for a president pro tempore.

Article I, Section 3. [5] The Senate shall chuse [sic] their other Officers, and also a President pro tempore, in the Absence of the Vice President, or when he shall exercise the Office of President of the United States.

Other Senate Officers

As in the case of the House, the Constitution contains relatively little about the specific responsibilities of officers in the Senate, which selects its own leaders. While the Constitution vests the vice president and the president pro tempore with the task of presiding, the Senate can distribute other roles and functions relatively free of constitutional limitations. Like the House, the current Senate has both a majority and a minority leader, as well as whips, who try to rally votes by members of their respective parties.

Article I, Section 3. [6] The Senate shall have the sole Power to try all Impeachments. When sitting for that Purpose, they shall be on Oath or Affirmation. When the President of the United States is tried, the Chief Justice shall preside: And no Person shall be convicted without the Concurrence of two thirds of the Members Present.

[7] Judgment in Cases of Impeachment shall not extend further than to removal from Office, and disqualification to hold and enjoy any Office of honor, Trust or Profit under the United States: but the Party convicted shall nevertheless be liable and subject to Indictment, Trial, Judgment and Punishment, according to Law.

Trials of Impeachment

Paragraph 5 of Article I, Section 1 delineates the power of the House of Representatives to impeach. This power is similar to the power of a prosecutor to indict individuals for crimes. Whereas the House of Representatives impeaches public officials, the Senate tries impeachments. Conviction requires a two-thirds vote of the members present. The framers of the constitution specified this supermajority to limit convictions to cases of genuine wrongdoing rather than to mere partisan disagreements.

From 1799 through 2004, the House of Representatives has impeached two presidents, twelve federal judges, one senator, and a secretary of war. One judge (U.S. District Judge, George W. English, in 1926) resigned from office, and the Senate has convicted seven others; all other impeachments resulted in acquittals. Some politically motivated efforts at impeachment never lead to a congressional vote—during Earl Warren's controversial tenure as chief justice of the U.S. Supreme Court, right-wing organizations posted numerous roadside signs calling for his impeachment, but to no avail.

The late 1980s witnessed the convictions of three federal judges on impeachment charges. Each conviction was somewhat unusual. Congress impeached, convicted, and removed Judge Harry F. Claiborne from office in 1986 after he failed to resign after being convicted of felonies. Alcee Hastings' Florida district elected him to Congress even after Congress impeached, convicted, and removed him from his judgeship in 1988. The Senate removed Judge Walter L. Nixon, like Claiborne, in 1988 after he refused to resign his office after a perjury conviction.

Judge Nixon subsequently objected to the proceedings whereby the Senate conducted its initial investigation through a committee rather than in the chamber as a whole. In *Walter L. Nixon v. United States* (1993), the Court rejected Nixon's challenge. Speaking for the Court, Chief Justice William Rehnquist relied heavily on the language of Article I, Section 3 vesting the "sole" power to try impeachments in the Senate rather than in the courts to argue that the issue was a classic "political question" for the Senate to decide.

The House of Representatives has impeached two U.S. presidents, and one president resigned rather than face a full House vote and Senate removal. The U.S. House of Representatives, aggravated by his volatile temperament and unhappy with what it considered to be his overly lenient treatment of the states that had joined the Confederacy, impeached President Andrew Johnson, Abraham Lincoln's successor. Johnson catalyzed his impeachment when he attempted to remove his secretary of war, Edwin M. Stanton, contrary to a law—which most scholars now regard as unconstitutional—that Congress had adopted limiting such power. In 1867, the Senate fell a single vote shy of the necessary two-thirds needed to convict him.

From July 27 through July 30, 1974, the House Judiciary Committee approved three impeachment charges against President Richard Nixon, whose operatives had broken into the Democratic National Headquarters in the Watergate Building in Washington, D.C. By votes of 27 to 11, 28 to 10, and 21 to 17, the Judiciary Committee accused Nixon of: obstructing justice by impeding the investigation of the Watergate break-in; violating the rights of citizens through his use of the Internal Revenue Service, the Federal Bureau of Investigation, and other agencies; and failing to produce papers that the Committee had subpoenaed. The Committee rejected other accusations tied to his secret bombings of Cambodia and income tax matters. In response to the U.S. Supreme Court decision of July 24, 1974, in *United States v. Nixon* rejecting his broad claims of executive privilege, on August 5 Nixon released the so-called smoking-gun tape of a White House conversation with top aides that confirmed his participation in a cover-up. Nixon resigned at noon on August 9, 1974, after it became clear that even some of his long-time supporters would vote to convict if he were put on trial in the Senate, and, with his resignation, the House had no cause to vote on the charges that the Judiciary Committee had drafted.

The House impeached President Bill Clinton in late 1999 after a long-running investigation by Special Prosecutor Kenneth Starr. The attorney general originally commissioned Starr to look into a land deal, named Whitewater, in which the president and his wife, Hillary, had been involved. His investigation instead ultimately revealed that Clinton had engaged in a relationship with former White House aide Monica Lewinsky, and that he had attempted to conceal that relationship when attorneys deposed him in a civil case for sexual harassment that a former Arkansas employee, Paula Jones, had brought against him. The House voted 228 to 206 to indict Clinton for perjury before a federal grand jury, and 221 to 212 to indict him for obstruction of justice. In his trial before the Senate, over which Chief Justice William Rehnquist presided, Clinton's attorneys argued that his offenses did not rise to the level of "high crimes and misdemeanors," but were simple attempts to save his family and himself from embarrassment. The Senate subsequently voted 45 to 55 and 50 to 50 to convict, far short of the two-thirds majority required.

In and of itself, conviction on charges of impeachment results simply in removal from office and disqualification from other national offices. Courts may, however, punish individuals whom the Senate removes for crimes they committed while in office.

OTHER MATTERS INVOLVING CONGRESSIONAL OPERATIONS

Article I, Section 4. The Times, Places and Manner of holding Elections for Senators and Representatives, shall be prescribed in each State by the

continued on next page

Legislature thereof; but the Congress may at any time by Law make or alter such Regulations, except as to the Places of chusing [sic] Senators. The Congress shall assemble at least once in every Year, and such Meeting shall be on *the first Monday in December, unless they shall by Law appoint a different Day.*

Elections for Congress

Section 4 of Article I balances state and national powers by granting state legislatures the power to prescribe "the Times, Places and Manner of holding Elections" for members of Congress while also allowing Congress to "alter such Regulations, except as to the places of chusing [sic] Senators." This section also provides that Congress will assemble at least once yearly, with the first meeting set for the first Monday in December. The Twentieth Amendment later changed this provision to January 3, or some other time that the law designated.

Article I, Section 5. [1] Each House shall be the Judge of the Elections, Returns and Qualifications of its own Members, and a Majority of each shall constitute a Quorum to do Business; but a smaller Number may adjourn from day to day, and may be authorized to compel the Attendance of absent Members, in such Manner, and under such Penalties as each House may provide.

[2] Each House may determine the Rules of its Proceedings, punish its Members for disorderly Behaviour, and, with the Concurrence of two thirds, expel a Member.

[3] Each House shall keep a Journal of its Proceedings, and from time to time publish the same, excepting such Parts as may in their Judgment require Secrecy; and the Yeas and Nays of the Members of either House on any question shall, at the Desire of one fifth of those Present, be entered on the Journal.

[4] Neither House, during the Session of Congress, shall, without the Consent of the other, adjourn for more than three days, nor to any other Place than that in which the two Houses shall be sitting.

Housekeeping Provisions

While Section 4 discusses the election of members of Congress and when they shall meet, Section 5 addresses the routine housekeeping functions of Congress. The Constitution designates each house as the judge of disputed elections to it. The Constitution specifies that a majority of each house is necessary for a quorum, but lesser numbers may require the attendance of their colleagues. Each house of Congress sets its own rules and can punish its members "for disorderly Behaviour," but the Constitution requires a two-thirds vote to expel a member. Thus, in *Powell v. McCormack* (1969), the Supreme Court required Congress to seat representative Adam Clayton Powell of New York because he met the minimal qualifications, which the Constitution established.

Each house keeps a daily journal now called the *Congressional Record*, but, because Congress itself controls the content of the *Record*, it is often a better guide to what members of Congress wished they had said rather than what they actually did say. Section 5 specifies that one-fifth or more of those present in either house can ask for a recorded, or so called roll-call, vote. Neither house can adjourn for more than three days without notifying the other, nor can either meet other than in its designated place. The Founding Fathers had accused King George III in the Declaration of Independence of calling the legislature into session at untimely intervals and locations.

The amazing feature of this part of the Constitution is its relative absence of rules to govern the internal structure of each house. It does not mention the role of congressional committees or their chairs, require Congress to utilize a seniority system, mention the Senate filibuster, elaborate the role that political parties will play in either house, describe the job of the Speaker of the House or the president pro tempore of the Senate, or mention other functionaries like majority and minority leaders and whips. The framers wisely realized that Congress could best resolve such matters through experience; when Congress desires to make changes in such arrangements, the Constitution offers few obstacles.

Article I, Section 6. [1] The Senators and Representatives shall receive a Compensation for their Services, to be ascertained by Law, and paid out of the Treasury of the United States. They shall in all Cases, except Treason, Felony and Breach of the Peace, be privileged from Arrest during their Attendance at the Session of their respective Houses, and in going to and returning from the same; and for any Speech or Debate in either House, they shall not be questioned in any other Place.

Congressional Compensation and Privilege

Section 6 provides that the U.S. Treasury shall supply the salaries of members of Congress. In so doing, the framers cut off a source of state control that had sometimes embarrassed national power under the Articles of Confederation. In what might appear to violate the principle of checks and balances (a corollary to the doctrine of separation of powers), members of Congress, at least collectively, set their own salaries. However, members of Congress realize that their opponents will likely question any such raises when they run for reelection. Such arguments are often intense and can indeed sometimes torpedo the chances of an incumbent. Moreover, if the Twenty-seventh Amendment to the Constitution endures (and Chapter 12 describes its belated ratification), no new congressional pay raises will be able to go into effect without an intervening election.

The Constitution grants members of Congress certain privileges to ensure that they can participate without fear in robust debate. Thus, members of Congress can only be arrested in cases of "Treason, Felony and Breach of the Peace" while attending or commuting to or from work. Courts have interpreted this clause to include all criminal offenses, so that it only protects against arrests in civil suits, which governments no longer permit. The speech and debate clause is more important to understanding current congressional prerogatives. It prohibits anyone from questioning members of Congress about "any Speech or Debate" in which they participate in either house. Designed to remedy abuses by English Tudor and Stuart monarchs who prosecuted members of Parliament for positions they took in that body, the Supreme Court extended the protection of this provision in *Gravel v. United States* (1972) to congressional aides helping members of Congress with their work.

Article I, Section 6. [2] No Senator or Representative shall, during the Time for which he was elected, be appointed to any civil Office under the Authority of the United States, which shall have been created, or the Emoluments whereof shall have been encreased during such time; and no Person holding any Office under the United States, shall be a Member of either House during his Continuance in Office.

The Incompatibility Clause

The Constitution rarely recognizes a power or privilege without limiting it. Because Congress can create new offices and set the salaries of its members, this paragraph prohibits the appointment of members of Congress during their terms to any office whose "Emoluments," or salaries, were raised during this time. The clause does not, as some Antifederalists wanted, prohibit members of Congress from accepting such offices later.

In 1908, President (and later, Chief Justice) William Howard Taft nominated Senator Philander C. Knox to be secretary of state. Congress had raised the salary for this position from $8,000 to $12,000 during Knox's term of office. Taft persuaded Congress to roll the secretary's salary back so that it could confirm Knox to the office.

Congress has subsequently repeated this procedure. Scholars sometimes designate it as the "Saxbe Fix," after Senator William Saxbe, whom President Nixon appointed as attorney general in 1973 in a manner similar to Knox's appointment. Some scholars have questioned whether the mechanism, which clearly seems to fall outside the literal words of the emoluments clause, meets its spirit.

Just as the Constitution restricts members of Congress from accepting appointments to positions created during their tenures, so too, it limits them from simultaneously holding other civil offices. This "incompatibility clause" furthers the doctrine of separation of powers. In Great Britain and other parliamentary democracies, prime ministers choose members of their cabinets from Parliament, where they remain as cabinet officers, but if an American president appoints a member of Congress to office, that member must then resign from Congress. When President Jimmy Carter appointed Senator Edmund Muskie of Maine as secretary of state, for example, Muskie had to relinquish his Senate seat. Similarly, when Representative Jack Kemp of New York accepted a position as secretary of housing and urban development in the George H. W. Bush administration, he had to resign his seat in the House of Representatives.

Those who prefer parliamentary democracy, or at least strengthened relations between the legislative and executive branches, have frequently argued for changes in this part of the Constitution. In addition to those who support the provision because it upholds the idea of separation of powers, advocates of the current provision have argued that cabinet members already have enough to do without also representing a district or state constituency.

ARTICLE I, SECTION 7—PROCEDURES FOR PASSING LAWS

> **Article I, Section 7.** [1] All bills for raising Revenue shall originate in the House of Representatives; but the Senate may propose or concur with Amendments as on other Bills.

Revenue Bills

Sections 7 through 10 of Article I are especially important. The first specifies the procedures whereby bills, or proposals, become laws. This section provides that all bills for raising revenue must originate in the House. Clearly, the framers of the Constitution, who had once fought for "no taxation without representation," wanted to link the two. It made sense to vest special responsibility in members of the House of Representatives, who the people elect directly and frequently. Because Congress allows its members, including Senators, to add "riders" on revenue bills, however, this prohibition has not proven to be very effective.

Article I, Section 7. [2] Every Bill which shall have passed the House of Representatives and the Senate, shall, before it becomes a Law, he presented to the President of the United States; If he approve he shall sign it, but if not he shall return it, with his Objections to the House in which it shall have originated, who shall enter the Objections at large on their Journal, and proceed to reconsider it. If after such Reconsideration two thirds of that House shall agree to pass the Bill, it shall be sent, together with the Objections, to the other House, by which it shall likewise be reconsidered, and if approved by two thirds of that House, it shall become a Law. But in all such Cases the Votes of both Houses shall be determined by yeas and Nays, and the Names of the Persons voting for and against the Bill shall be entered on the Journal of each House respectively. If any Bill shall not he returned by the President within ten Days (Sundays excepted) after it shall have been presented to him, the Same shall be a Law, in like Manner as if he had signed it, unless the Congress by their Adjournment prevent its Return, in which Case it shall not be a Law.

Procedures for Lawmaking and Presidential Vetoes

Paragraph 2 of Section 7 demonstrates the founders' commitment to the doctrine of checks and balances. To become a law, both houses must approve a bill in identical language and present it to the president for approval. If the president signs the bill, it becomes law. If the president does nothing, after ten working days it becomes law. If the president returns a bill to Congress with his veto, however, Congress can override the veto by a two-thirds vote of both houses, with members required to go on record with their votes. Because of the supermajorities required, approximately 90 percent of presidential vetoes have succeeded.

In addition to the president's regular veto power, he may also exercise a pocket veto. This occurs when the president simply fails to sign a bill that Congress passes within ten days of its adjournment. Congress has no way to override such a veto. The pocket veto gives Congress an incentive to do its most important work before the last few days of a session.

Ambiguity remains as to whether a congressional recess can trigger a pocket veto in cases where Congress has designated an officer to receive veto messages. Lower court decisions suggest that such recesses do not give the president occasion to exercise such a veto, but, to date, the Supreme Court has not resolved the issue.

The Constitution requires Congress to present all laws to the president. Courts have made exceptions for internal housekeeping matters and for constitutional amendments. The Constitution already requires two-thirds majorities of both houses to propose the latter.

Beginning with Ulysses S. Grant in 1873, some presidents have advocated an item, or so-called line-item, veto similar to that which many state governors exercise. Such vetoes allow executives to void individual items within appropriations bills that legislatures present to them. An item veto would allow presidents to veto "riders" on subjects that are not otherwise germane to bills and might also help cut federal budget deficits.

Congress attempted to adopt a presidential item veto in the Balanced Budget and Taxpayer Relief Act of 1996. It allowed a president to rescind individual items of an appropriations bill within five days of signing such legislation. Congress could disapprove of such a veto, but the president could veto such disapproval, unless overridden by a two-thirds vote.

In *Clinton v. City of New York* (1998), the Supreme Court invalidated this law in a 6 to 3 decision, which Justice John Paul Stevens authored. Stevens argued that the presentment clause in Article I, Section 7 of the Constitution required a president to accept or reject a bill in full, not to accept some parts and reject others. Majority justices feared that an item veto threatened the constitutional separation of powers.

Article I, Section 7. [3] Every Order, Resolution, or Vote to which the Concurrence of the Senate and House of Representatives may be necessary (except on a question of Adjournment) shall be presented to the President of the United States; and before the Same shall take Effect, shall be approved by him, or being disapproved by him, shall be repassed by two thirds of the Senate and House of Representatives, according to the Rules and Limitations prescribed in the Case of a Bill.

The Presentment Clause

This passage of the Constitution reiterates the president's importance in lawmaking. It prevents Congress from evading the president's veto power by calling a law by another name. The Supreme Court relied on this provision in *Immigration and Naturalization Service v. Chadha* (1983) in rejecting a so-called legislative veto. Congress had delegated power to the attorney general to decide on exceptions to deportation orders while allowing a single house of Congress to counter this decision. Chief Justice Warren Burger decided that the legislative veto violated both the presentment clause and the bicameralism requirement. Although Congress removed a number of legislative veto provisions from some laws, it has continued to add them to still others. Congress has also substituted informal agreements with various agencies to replace earlier statutory mandates.

ARTICLE I, SECTION 8—POWERS GRANTED TO CONGRESS

As the word "constitution" implies, the document exists to "constitute," or, given the prior role of the Articles of Confederation, to "reconstitute," the polity. The U.S. Constitution grants and distributes powers. Americans also expect it to limit powers.

This dichotomy is evident in Article I, Sections 8 and 9. Section 8 lists the powers of Congress. Scholars call these granted, or enumerated, powers. Section 9, in turn, lists constitutional limits on the powers of Congress. These limits are a kind of internal bill of rights within the Constitution and indicate that, even before Antifederalists objected to the omission of such a bill of rights, the founders had sought to recognize and secure key liberties.

Article I, Section 8. The Congress shall have Power

[1] To lay and collect Taxes, Duties, Imposts and Excises, to pay the Debts and provide for the common Defence and general Welfare of the United States; but all Duties, Imposts and Excises shall be uniform throughout the United States;

[2] To borrow Money on the credit of the United States;

Taxing, Spending, and Borrowing

Altogether, eighteen paragraphs list the powers that the Constitution specifically delegates or grants to Congress. The founding fathers anticipated that Congress, and the national government more generally, would only exercise the powers (at least in domestic affairs) that the Constitution specifically enumerated or implied. Accordingly, many Federalists initially opposed a bill of rights. Since the Constitution did not grant the national government any power to regulate freedom of speech, religion, and the like, why should they add specific prohibitions against such laws? Antifederalists responded that expansive construction of powers would make such prohibitions necessary. Experience has arguably validated the Antifederalists' judgment. Provisions in the Bill of Rights continue to limit Congress's expansive claims under the general welfare, commerce, and necessary and proper clauses.

Significantly, the first power that this section of the Constitution delegates to Congress relates to taxes and duties. These powers are part of "the power of the purse." This power of appropriating or withholding money for the kings' wars initially led to the rise of the Parliament in England. The Constitution specifies that Congress may collect such taxes to pay for the debts, provide for defense, and promote the general welfare.

Fearing that the more expansive notion would undermine the value of enumerated powers, James Madison was among those who had argued that congressional spending and taxing powers must be tied to other specific grants of power that followed within Article I, Section 8 and elsewhere, but the more expansive view of this phrase that Alexander Hamilton championed has since prevailed (*United States v. Butler*, 1936). Accordingly, courts have interpreted the taxing and spending clause as an independent power. Congress has used this clause both to raise money and to impose regulations, by encouraging and discouraging certain activities. Moreover, when Congress appropriates money, it usually attaches conditions, giving it increased power. This is especially true of the categorical grants-in-aid programs by which Congress has funneled most federal aid to the states. Thus, Congress passed a law withholding a portion of federal highway funds from states that did not raise their legal drinking age to twenty-one. In upholding this law in *South Dakota v. Dole* (1987), the U.S. Supreme Court decided that the law met a four-fold test—Congress enacted it in pursuit of the "general welfare"; Congress had expressed its intentions unambiguously; the law was related to a legitimate federal interest; and the condition that Congress imposed did not conflict with another provision of the Constitution. Even in so-called block grants and revenue-sharing programs where Congress attaches fewer strings and permits greater state discretion, Congress usually insists that recipients follow certain general rules, like nondiscrimination.

The power to borrow is akin to the power of raising money. Paragraph 2 grants this power, and Congress has exercised it freely. Congress periodically circumvents old debt limits by adopting new limits, albeit often after rancorous debate or, as in two cases, after shutdowns of all nonessential governmental services. After years of unsuccessful attempts to limit deficit spending by legislation (the Gramm-Rudman-Hollings law, for example), some argue that only a constitutional amendment can achieve this objective. Others, however, have questioned the wisdom of incorporating such an economic policy within the Constitution. They have also raised concerns about whether courts could enforce such an amendment, most versions of which contain reservations to deal with war, recession, and inaccurate revenue projections.

[The Congress shall have Power]

[3] To regulate Commerce with foreign Nations, and among the several States, and with the Indian Tribes;

Power to Regulate Commerce

The Confederal Congress had no power to regulate interstate and foreign commerce. As a result, states that had fought in the Revolutionary War against a common foe began taxing one another's commerce, thus losing the potential benefit of a common commercial union. Contemporaries jokingly compared the state of New Jersey (which both New York and Pennsylvania taxed) to a cask with a tap at both ends. Paragraph 3 of Article I, Section 8 vested the power over commerce with foreign nations, Indian tribes, and among the states to Congress. Courts continue to define the contours of this clause by attempting to delineate the relationship between the intrastate powers that states can still exercise and the interstate powers that the Constitution entrusts to the Congress.

One of the earliest and most important decisions on the commerce clause, *Gibbons v. Ogden* (1824), justified the framers' concern over state rivalry. New York granted a monopoly to steamship owners Robert Fulton and Robert Livingston, who licensed Ogden to navigate the route between New York and New Jersey. This excluded those like Gibbons, who relied on a federal piloting license to transport passengers. Chief Justice John Marshall, the fourth chief justice of the U.S. Supreme Court, decided that the Constitution intended to define commerce broadly as "intercourse" rather than more narrowly as "traffic," and that congressional powers were inclusive enough to protect such commerce against all state legislation that would interfere with it. He thus voided New York's grant of a monopoly.

Courts have often based subsequent decisions on what scholars call the "dormant commerce clause." Cases have established that certain state laws impeding interstate commerce are illegal even when congressional laws do not specifically forbid them. Thus, for example, the Supreme Court struck down intrusive state regulations of the length of trains in *Southern Pacific Company v. Arizona* (1945) and laws prohibiting the importation of out-of-state hazardous wastes in *City of Philadelphia v. New Jersey* (1978), even though state laws did not conflict with specific congressional legislation on the subject. In *Cooley v. Board of Wardens* (1851), the Court recognized that, while some areas of commerce require a single uniform national rule, others—in this case, rules for navigating a dangerous harbor—just as necessarily demand accommodation to local laws and circumstances. The courts have played a major role in deciding which circumstances apply to a given area.

As the nation industrialized, Congress increasingly turned to the commerce power to justify its exercise of powers over economic activities that the Constitution did not otherwise address. During the period from roughly 1890 to 1937, the Supreme Court upheld laws, which Congress adopted under the commerce clause, regulating items like impure foods, colored oleomargarine, lottery tickets, and other items that the Court considered to be harmful or deceptive. It further struck down many other exercises of congressional power as interferences with state police powers. During this period, the Supreme Court thus voided the exercise of congressional power to restrict the shipment of goods produced by child labor in interstate commerce on the basis that such goods were not in and of themselves harmful (*Hammer v. Dagenhart*, 1918). Similarly, when it first confronted a case regulating monopolies under the Sherman Anti-Trust Act of 1890, the Court declared in *United States v. E. C. Knight* (1895) that this was a matter for state control. The Court thus enforced distinctions between matters that they thought were local as opposed to those that were national, between regulations of mining and manufacture and subsequent commerce, between matters that they thought had a "direct" and those that they thought only had an "indirect" effect on commerce, and between products that they thought were in the "throat" of commerce and those that were not.

The Supreme Court found these extra-constitutional distinctions extremely difficult to define and enforce, and it repudiated most of them in 1937. Today's Court takes a broader view of congressional power over commerce. It generally employs specific constitutional prohibitions (for example, the First Amendment would trump a law banning the interstate shipment of books) rather than judicial perceptions of harm or states' rights to serve as the primary limitation on the commerce power.

Congress and the Court have thus interpreted the power to regulate commerce very broadly. Congress created the first regulatory commission, the Interstate Commerce Commission (ICC), in 1887 to deal with railroad rates; it later widened this authority to include other forms of transportation. Congress also created the Federal Trade Commission (1915), Federal Power Commission (1920), Federal Communications Commission (1934), Securities and Exchange Commission (1934), National Labor Relations Board (1935), and Civil Aeronautics Board (1938) under authority of the commerce clause. Congress even based the Civil Rights Act of 1964, which prohibits discrimination on the basis of race in places of public accommodations, on the commerce clause. Courts have further upheld child labor laws and other regulatory legislation that Congress has passed under the authority of the commerce clause even though the states never ratified an amendment that Congress proposed to deal with child labor. In *Wickard v. Filburn* (1942), the U.S. Supreme Court upheld a penalty on excess wheat that a farmer had grown, even though he had grown it for home consumption, on the basis that such wheat, in conjunction with that of other farmers, overhung, and thus substantially effected, the broader market.

In recent decades the Supreme Court has again begun to question some broad exercises of congressional powers under the commerce clause. In *National League of Cities v. Usery* (1976), the Supreme Court interpreted the Tenth Amendment to limit the power of the national government to prescribe minimum wages for state employees. However, it overturned this decision in *Garcia v. San Antonio Metropolitan Transit Authority* (1985).

In 1995, however, the Court ruled in *United States v. Lopez* that the national government had exceeded its power under the commerce clause when it prohibited guns within 1,000 feet of a school zone. The Court decided that Congress had intruded into areas—criminal law and education—that the Constitution had left to the states. The Court said that the Constitution limited congressional regulatory powers over interstate commerce to cases where it was regulating the "channels" or the "instrumentalities" of such commerce, or where it was regulating an activity that "substantially affects" such commerce.

More recently, in *United States v. Morrison* (2000), the Supreme Court invalidated a part of the Omnibus Criminal Bill of 1994 designated as the Violence Against Women Act. It permitted victims of gender-motivated violent crimes to sue their attackers in federal courts. In a 5 to 4 decision that Chief Justice Rehnquist wrote, the Court thus rejected a suit by Christy Brzonkala, a former student at Virginia Tech who was suing two football players who had allegedly raped her on campus but had escaped serious punishment. In striking down the law under which she appealed, the Court majority questioned the adequacy of congressional findings of a significant effect on interstate commerce and argued that Congress had phrased the law so broadly that it usurped state control of criminal law. In so doing the law had obliterated the distinction between what was truly national and what was merely local. Rehnquist further argued that although the enforcement provision in Section 5 of the Fourteenth Amendment vested Congress with power over state discrimination, it did not give it unlimited authority over discrimination that private individuals practiced.

Dissenting justices argued that the Supreme Court had no business second-guessing the rationality of congressional findings like it had once done in the period before the Court's historic switch in decision-making in 1937. The dissenters further argued that the judiciary did not need to intervene in such matters because political processes adequately protected state federal interests.

In *Gonzales v. Raich* (2005), the U.S. Supreme Court struck down provisions of California Compassionate Use Act, which permitted noncommercial medical marijuana use. The Court found that federal law prohibiting such use was part of a comprehensive scheme of regulation of interstate commerce that trumped state laws to the contrary.

A Note on Native Americans

The commerce clause contains one of only two direct mentions of Native American Indians within the Constitution (the other occurs in the provision proportioning representation and direct taxes in Article I, Section 2—a clause that Section 2 of the Fourteenth Amendment later echoed). The commerce clause distinguishes Indians tribes both from states and from foreign nations, although the constitutional provisions relative to treaty-making also apply to them. In *Cherokee Nation v. Georgia* (1831), Chief Justice Marshall classified Indian tribes as domestic dependent nations. Marshall further decided in *Worcester v. Georgia* (1832) that the national government alone can enter into agreements with them. Congress must thus grant any powers that states exercise in regard to Native Americans who live on tribal lands. Congress has permitted tribes to exercise jurisdiction over most criminal matters involving Native-Americans on the reservations and has limited the rights of states to tax Indians there.

[The Congress shall have Power]

[4] To establish an uniform Rule of Naturalization, and uniform Laws on the subject of Bankruptcies throughout the United States;

Power Over Naturalization and Bankruptcies

The original Constitution does not specify which individuals are citizens. This silence nearly proved to be disastrous in the *Dred Scott* decision (1857), when the Supreme Court ruled (in a decision that the Fourteenth Amendment subsequently overturned) that blacks were not, and could not be, U.S. citizens. Paragraph 4 of Article I, Section 8, however, provides that Congress may establish "an uniform Rule of Naturalization." National rather than state laws thus govern the subject.

The Constitution also empowers Congress to deal with bankruptcies. Federal, rather than state, courts thus adjudicate such cases. Congress did not exercise its legislative power under this provision until 1898. Prior to this time, the Supreme Court allowed states to adopt their own legislation on the subject.

[The Congress shall have Power]

[5] To coin Money, regulate the Value thereof, and of foreign Coin, and fix the Standard of Weights and Measures;

[6] To provide for the Punishment of counterfeiting the Securities and current Coin of the United States;

Coining Money and Establishing Uniform Standards

As in the case of interstate commerce, the coining of money was a real problem under the Articles of Confederation. Without national uniformity, entering another state was somewhat akin to entering a foreign country. The Constitution accordingly vested Congress with the power to coin and regulate the value of money, a power akin to its authority to establish uniform weights and measures, and the power, which the Constitution specifies in the succeeding paragraph, to punish counterfeiting.

[The Congress shall have Power]

[7] To establish Post Offices and post Roads;

[8] To promote the Progress of Science and useful Arts, by securing for limited Times to Authors and Inventors the exclusive Right to their respective Writings and Discoveries;

Establishing a Post Office and Promoting Scientific Advances

The congressional power to establish a post office is allied with its authority to regulate interstate commerce. The Constitution also grants Congress the power to promote progress—the document's only mention of the subject—in the sciences and arts by establishing laws regulating copyrights and patents. Congress grants these limited monopolies for a number of years to encourage scholarly and scientific advances. In 1982, Congress combined the U.S. Court of Customs and Patent Appeals and the appellate division of the U.S. Court of Claims to create the Court of Appeals for the Federal Circuit and vested it with power to hear patent appeals.

In the *Trade Mark Cases* of 1879, the Supreme Court ruled that the power in this section did not extend power to Congress to grant trade marks. Congress subsequently legislated on the subject in the Lanham Act of 1946 and the Trademark Counterfeiting Act of 1984 under its authority to regulate interstate and foreign commerce.

[The Congress shall have Power]

[9] To constitute Tribunals inferior to the Supreme Court;

Establishing Lower Courts

Article I, Section 8, paragraph 9, vests Congress with the power to create courts inferior to the U.S. Supreme Court. Delegates to the Constitutional Convention deferred settling the issue of the precise organization of the federal courts, both because they found it difficult to agree on this configuration and because they realized that differing circumstances called for differing degrees of complexity. Certainly, a nation of 3 million inhabitants requires less complexity than a nation of close to 300 million. The current federal court system includes two levels of federal courts, designated as U.S. Courts of Appeals and U.S. District Courts, below the U.S. Supreme Court.

Members of courts that Congress has created under authority of Article III, so-called constitutional courts, serve "during good behavior," and have other constitutionally protected prerogatives. Members of Article I courts, designated "legislative courts," have no such constitutional protections. Such legislative courts—for example, the U.S. Court of Military Appeals—often serve administrative or quasilegislative duties.

[The Congress shall have Power]

[10] To define and punish Piracies and Felonies committed on the high Seas, and Offenses against the Law of Nations;

[11] To declare War, grant Letters of Marque and Reprisal, and make Rules concerning Captures on Land and Water;

[12] To raise and support Armies, but no Appropriation of Money to that Use shall be for a longer Term than two Years;

[13] To provide and maintain a Navy;

[14] To make Rules for the Government and Regulation of the land and naval Forces;

WAR POWERS

As the Preamble to the Constitution indicates, the framers were justifiably concerned about national defense. Paragraphs 10 through 14 of Article I, Section 8 accordingly relate to military powers. The Constitution entrusted Congress with the power to declare war. This power is one of the most awesome that Congress exercises, but presidents sometimes bypass this power, as Harry S. Truman did when he defended South Korea against a North Korean attack by calling his response a "police action" and justifying it under authority of the United Nations. Similarly, President Lyndon B. Johnson used the Gulf of Tonkin Resolution, which Congress adopted in response to a putative North Vietnamese attack on U.S. warships, as a substitute for a formal declaration of war in Vietnam. Congress declares wars, but presidents wage them, and the two branches often negotiate the boundaries of these specific responsibilities.

Nations issued letters of marque and reprisal in times when the line between piracy and defense of one's country was a fine one—witness Sir Francis Drake's role in English history and Jean Lafitte's help during the defense of New Orleans in the War of 1812. The Constitution thus vests Congress with this power. The Constitution also vests Congress with the right to define and punish piracies and felonies on the high seas, where its jurisdiction and international agreements, rather than state laws, prevail.

The framers of the Constitution limited military appropriations to two years as a way of addressing their concerns over the dangers of a "standing army" and navy. The effectiveness of this provision in an age when governments sometimes place orders for major weapons systems a decade in advance is questionable.

Readers should interpret congressional powers to "make Rules for the Governance and Regulation of the land and naval Forces" in conjunction with the Fifth Amendment's exemption of military personnel from grand jury indictment "in times of war or public danger." Given military exigencies, governments cannot always accord military personnel the same kinds of due process that civilians have. Congress has, indeed, set up an entire code, the Code of Military Justice, and a separate court system—albeit one subject to U.S. Supreme Court review—to deal with such personnel. This code governed the trials of U.S. military personnel for abuse of prisoners in Iraq during the second Gulf War.

[The Congress shall have Power]

[15] To provide for calling forth the Militia to execute the Laws of the Union, suppress Insurrections and repel Invasions;

continued on next page

> [16] To provide for organizing, arming, and disciplining, the Militia, and for governing such Part of them as may be employed in the Service of the United States, reserving to the States respectively, the Appointment of the Officers, and the Authority of training the Militia according to the discipline prescribed by Congress;

Calling the Militia

Article IV of the Constitution guarantees states a republican form of government and help against domestic insurrection. Paragraph 15 of Article I, Section 8, vests Congress with the responsibility of providing such protection. Congress has entrusted this role to the president, and the Supreme Court affirmed the president's authority to decide whether to send troops in the case of *Luther v. Borden* (1849). The Constitution also grants Congress power over the militia employed in U.S. service, along with the delegated power to determine their officers.

This section of the Constitution provides the basis for distinguishing state and national guards. The former automatically become members of the latter when presidents so designate them. Thus, President Eisenhower nationalized the Arkansas guard when Governor Orval Faubus called upon it to resist court-imposed desegregation at Central High School in Little Rock in 1957.

> [The Congress shall have Power]
>
> [17] To exercise exclusive Legislation in all Cases whatsoever, over such District (not exceeding ten Miles square) as may, by Cession of particular States, and the acceptance of Congress, become the Seat of the Government of the United States, and to exercise like Authority over all Places purchased by the Consent of the Legislature of the State in which the Same shall be, for the Erection of Forts, Magazines, Arsenals, dock-Yards, and other needed Buildings;

Governing the District of Columbia

New York and Philadelphia were the first two capital cities under the new Constitution, but framers worried about the impact that state policies could have on national affairs in such settings and provided for the establishment of an unspecified different site. Members of the first Congress settled on the location of the current capital through vote-swapping or "logrolling."

Southern representatives agreed to the federal assumption of state debts in exchange for the choice of the site on the Potomac River, which George Washington, who lived nearby, had especially favored.

Paragraph 17 deals with the governance of what is now the District of Columbia. Under the Articles of Confederation, militiamen seeking back pay had once threatened the Congress meeting in Philadelphia. Some founders feared that, without federal control over the seat of its own government, the national government might again fall prey to political squabbles and even physical intimidation. The result has been a continuing congressional tutelage over the District of Columbia that some residents, and their advocates, criticize as antidemocratic. The states, however, rejected an amendment that Congress proposed in 1978 to treat the District of Columbia as a state for purposes of representation. Although the District now has a "shadow" representative and senator (former presidential candidate Jesse Jackson was the first that the District elected to this post), these representatives have no formal rights, and questions remain as to the desirability of continuing federal control. Some think that as long as Congress maintains a federal enclave, it can make the rest of the District into a state through legislation. Alternatively, Congress might retrocede the inhabited part of the District to Maryland, as it previously retroceded other portions of the original district to Virginia.

The Constitution also vests Congress with power to purchase and control the location of military facilities. This control has been less controversial than its governance over the District of Columbia. However, representatives of some western states sometimes complain about the large tracts of land that Congress has obtained for this purpose.

And [The Congress shall have Power]

[18] To make all Laws which shall be necessary and proper for carrying into Execution the foregoing Powers, and all other Powers vested by this Constitution in the Government of the United States, or in any Department or Officer thereof.

Implied Powers

The last paragraph of Article I, Section 8 has become its most important and its most controversial. Often designated "the elastic," or "sweeping," clause, it grants Congress power "to make all Laws which shall be necessary and proper for carrying into Execution the foregoing Powers, and all other Powers vested by this Constitution in the Government of the United States."

Chief Justice John Marshall provided the most important explanation of this clause in the case of *McCulloch v. Maryland* (1819), in which he and his colleagues upheld the constitutionality of a national bank. The Constitution did not specifically authorize such a bank, but the Washington administration had created one, and the administration of James Madison, who had initially opposed the bank, had later recharted it after its first charter lapsed. Arguing that the bank was not an end in and of itself but a means to such ends, Marshall ruled that the necessary and proper clause gave Congress a choice of means of implementing its powers as long as it chose means consistent with the powers that the Constitution granted to Congress and not inconsistent with specific constitutional prohibitions. Observing that the Constitution had not employed the term "absolutely," as in other parts of the Constitution, to modify the words "necessary and proper," Marshall argued that the Constitution outlined varying degrees of necessity and that experience had demonstrated the propriety of a national bank. Marshall also noted that the Founding Fathers had provided context for the necessary and proper clause by placing it in a section of the Constitution, like Article I, Section 8, which granted, rather than limited, congressional powers.

Scholars sometimes designate the sum of congressional enumerated and implied powers as "resulting powers." Today's Congress passes antipollution laws, appropriates funds for building highways, ratifies consumer legislation, promotes agriculture, and regulates a variety of economic activities that the Constitution does not specifically mention. Congress justifies such laws by tying them to its powers over interstate commerce, over taxing and spending, and over war-making.

Congressional Investigations

Congressional committees conduct hearings and investigations. Without such investigative power, Congress would lack information it needs to legislate, oversee the operation of its progress and the conduct of government officials, and obtain necessary information about nominees to federal offices. Although the Constitution does not specifically delineate this power, courts have accepted it as an implied power.

Congressional hearings have probed into organized crime, health care, environmental issues, the conduct of presidents and their aides in scandals or alleged scandals, and the character and qualifications of nominees to the cabinet and the federal courts. Faced with abuses of power during the 1950s, the Supreme Court said in *Watkins v. United States* (1957) that Congress could not simply expose individuals for unpopular views or past associations; moreover, it had to tailor its questions to the subject it was investigating. The Court has otherwise been reluctant to limit this very important implied power.

ARTICLE I, SECTION 9—LIMITS ON CONGRESSIONAL POWERS

Whereas Article I, Section 8 of the Constitution grants broad powers to Congress, Article I, Section 9 limits such power to protect individual rights and preserve the federal system. The juxtaposition of these two sections illustrates the balance that the founding fathers attempted to achieve between creating an effective government and limiting its potential for abuse.

> **Article I, Section 9.** [1] The Migration or Importation of such Persons as any of the States now existing shall think proper to admit, shall not be prohibited by the Congress prior to the Year one thousand eight hundred and eight, but a Tax or duty may be imposed on such Importation, not exceeding ten dollars for each Person.

Slave Importation

Like the three-fifths clause, the first paragraph of Article I, Section 9 emerged from conflict between the North and the South over the issue of slavery. Delegates from some northern states wished to end the importation of slaves; some southerners, particularly in South Carolina and Georgia, wanted to continue the practice and thus keep slave prices down. As a compromise, the delegates delayed congressional control of the slave trade for twenty years. In the interim it allowed imposition of a maximum ten dollar tax per "Person"—significantly, the framers used this term rather than one merely designating chattel. Proponents and opponents of slavery later debated whether this clause, and or the interstate commerce clause, granted Congress the power to regulate or forbid the interstate sale of slaves.

> **Article I, Section 9.** [2] The Privilege of the Writ of Habeas Corpus shall not be suspended, unless when in Cases of Rebellion or Invasion the public Safety may require it.

The Writ of Habeas Corpus

This provision of Section 9 outlines the protection of the writ of habeas corpus, which the English call "The Great Writ." This Latin term literally means "you have the body." Under this provision, the government cannot suspend the privilege of defendants to require the government to specify the charges against them as a condition to incarceration, except in cases of rebellion or invasion.

Without such a clause, government officials could detain opponents without relief. Lincoln used his authority as commander in chief to detain suspected confederate sympathizers during the Civil War. Even those who believe that wartime exigencies justified Lincoln's actions recognize that they would have been unconstitutional in times of peace. The terrorist attacks on the United States on September 11, 2001, have raised further questions about the government's detention of suspected terrorists, but most such issues have focused on the rights of "enemy combatants" in the United States rather than on U.S. citizens.

Article I, Section 9. [3] No Bill of Attainder or ex post facto Law shall be passed.

Bills of Attainder and Ex Post Facto Laws

Article I, Section 9 also prohibits bills of attainder and ex post facto laws. Like the writ of habeas corpus, these technical legal terms are highly important. A bill of attainder is a legislative punishment without benefit of a trial. The British Parliament sometimes decreed a punishment for one of the king's ministers whom its members believed had committed a wrong. It thus deprived such defendants of the normal protections of due process that courts would have provided them. The founders hoped to prevent this abuse in America. In *Ex parte Garland* and *Cummings v. Missouri* (1867), the U.S. Supreme Court cited these provisions to invalidate state and federal laws that prohibited individuals from serving as lawyers unless they pledged that they had not aided the Confederacy.

In *Calder v. Bull* (1798), the U.S. Supreme Court defined an ex post facto law as a retroactive criminal law. It thus restricted the scope of this provision to criminal, as opposed to mere civil, matters. Drawing from English law, *Calder* identified four types of ex post facto laws: those punishing an act as criminal that government had not identified as criminal when it was committed; those classifying a crime as greater than when the individuals committed it; those inflicting a greater punishment of a crime than the government specified when individuals committed it; and those altering the legal rules of evidence, allowing lesser evidence in order to convict than the laws permitted when the crime was committed.

In *Carmell v. Texas* (2000), Justice John Paul Stevens applied the last of these categories to strike down the retroactive application of a Texas law that raised the age at which courts could accept unsupported testimony regarding sexual offenses from victims under the age of fourteen to victims under the age of eighteen. Fortunately, the decision affected only four of the fifteen convictions of the petitioner, who had committed sexual offenses against his stepdaughter over a four-year period, when she was between the ages of twelve and sixteen, and he remained in jail.

Article I, Section 9. [4] *No Capitation, or other direct, Tax shall be laid, unless in Proportion to the Census or Enumeration herein before directed to be taken.*

[5] No Tax or Duty shall be laid on Articles exported from any State.

[6] No Preference shall be given by any Regulation of Commerce or Revenue to the Ports of one State over those of another; nor shall Vessels bound to, or from, one State, be obliged to enter, clear, or pay Duties in another.

Protections for the States

Under the Articles of Confederation, states had exercised a good deal of sovereignty. Article I, Section 9 continues to recognize certain states' rights. Paragraph 4 limits capitation and direct taxes. The limit on capitation taxes protected southern slave interests by preventing Congress from arbitrarily taxing slaves. The Thirteenth Amendment abolition of slavery has alleviated this concern.

Unfortunately, the framers did not clearly define direct taxes. In *Hylton v. United States* (1796), the U.S. Supreme Court ruled that a national tax on carriages was not a direct tax and suggested that only taxes on persons and land would fit into the narrow category of prohibited taxes. In a much later decision in *Pollock v. Farmers' Loan & Trust Co.* (1895), the U.S. Supreme Court ruled that income taxes were direct taxes and hence unconstitutional. The Sixteenth Amendment overturned this decision and permitted Congress to apportion such taxes on the basis of wealth, or income, rather than population.

Paragraph 5 prohibits export taxes. Southerners, who especially insisted on this provision, depended heavily on agricultural exports for income. Paragraph 6 both protects against preference for ports in one part of the country over another and reinforces congressional control over commerce among the states by prohibiting states from enacting duties on vessels entering from other states.

> **Article I, Section 9.** [7] No Money shall be drawn from the Treasury, but in Consequence of Appropriations made by Law; and a regular Statement and Account of the Receipts and Expenditures of all public Money shall be published from time to time.

The Appropriation of Money

Paragraph 7 provides that Congress must legally appropriate all money it spends and requires the government to give regular accounts of its receipts and expenditures. Such records make it easier for the people to hold government officials accountable. Despite the forthright language of this provision, the U.S. government did not, until recently, publish the budget of the Central Intelligence Agency and other such intelligence-gathering operations. Moreover, in *United States v. Richardson* (1974), the Supreme Court denied standing to those who challenged this refusal.

> **Article I, Section 9.** [8] No Title of Nobility shall be granted by the United States: And no Person holding any Office of Profit or Trust under them, shall, without the Consent of the Congress, accept of any present, Emolument, Office, or Title, of any kind whatever, from any King, Prince, or foreign State.

Titles of Nobility

By contrast to the British House of Lords, the Senate consists of elected officials who serve for fixed terms rather than of people who inherit their positions and titles for life. Paragraph 8 reinforces this distinction by prohibiting the government from issuing titles of nobility and by requiring congressional consent to any titles that foreign nations confer on Americans.

In 1810, Maryland's Senator Philip Reed introduced, and Congress proposed, an amendment that would have further stripped any Americans who accepted titles of nobility from a foreign power of their citizenship and made them ineligible for other offices. Fears that the son of Napoleon's brother by an American socialite, Elizabeth Patterson, might one day attempt to establish himself as king apparently prompted this so-called phantom amendment, which the states did not ratify.

ARTICLE I, SECTION 10—LIMITS ON THE STATES

Article I, Section 8 grants powers to Congress, and Article I, Section 9 limits them. Article I, Section 10 further limits the powers of the states.

Article I, Section 10. [1] No State shall enter into any Treaty, Alliance, or Confederation; grant Letters of Marque and Reprisal; coin Money; emit Bills of Credit; make any Thing but gold and silver Coin a Tender in Payment of Debts; pass any Bill of Attainder, ex post facto Law, or Law impairing the Obligation of Contracts, or grant any Title of Nobility.

Powers Reserved to the National Government

In a federal system that divides power between a central government and constituent states, a constitution helps outline the respective powers of both governments. Article I, Section 10 indicates that a number of powers that Article I, Section 8 granted to Congress are exclusive powers that the states may not exercise concurrently. Thus, Article I, Section 10 prohibits states from engaging in treaty-making, matters concerned with war, coining money, and otherwise dealing in currency. Just as Article I, Section 9 limited such practices at the state level, so too, this section prohibits Congress from passing bills of attainder and ex post facto laws, or granting titles of nobility.

The Contract Clause

When they prohibited states from "impairing the obligation of contracts," the framers added a restriction to the states that they did not similarly apply to Congress. Why did the framers limit the latter and not the former? Under the Articles of Confederation, state governments passed class-based legislation benefiting those groups in power. This problem was particularly acute in Rhode Island, the single state that refused to send any delegates to the Constitutional Convention. Moreover, in arguing for a continental union, James Madison argued in *Federalist* No. 10 and elsewhere that minority and majority factions, or combinations of individuals out for their own self-interest, were more likely to prevail at the state than at the national level. Apparently, this provision reflects this view. The framers saw less need to limit the national government, which represented the interests of the whole, than to limit geographically smaller states where self-interested factions were more likely to prevail.

Early in the nation's history, the Supreme Court frequently relied on the contract clause to protect private property. The Court applied the clause in *Fletcher v. Peck* (1810) to prohibit a state from rescinding land grants, even though evidence suggested that bribes had influenced the legislators who had authorized the sale. In *Dartmouth College v. Woodward* (1819), the Court applied the contract clause even to contracts that parties had agreed to prior to the Constitution, in this case to a royal charter that the Crown had granted to Dartmouth College and that the New Hampshire legislature had subsequently sought to revise.

National expansion generated concern that an overly strict construction of the contract clause could hinder industrial progress. Thus, in the case of *Charles River Bridge Co. v. Warren River Bridge Co.* (1837), the Court, now headed by Chief Justice Roger Taney (whom President Andrew Jackson, a strong supporter of popular sovereignty, had appointed), said that it would interpret any ambiguity in the language of a contract to benefit the state. In this case, the Court refused to interpret a contract that the state had awarded a company to build a bridge as exclusive in the absence of specific language. Again, during the Great Depression of the twentieth century, the Supreme Court upheld a Minnesota Mortgage Moratorium law in *Home Building and Loan Association v. Blaisdell* (1934), extending the time for debt payments, on the basis that it was not a class-based law such as the contract clause intended to prevent (or an impairment of the "obligation" of contract), but a reasonable effort to preserve the economy, and thus the well-being, of the state as a whole. In *United Trust Co. of New York v. New Jersey* (1977), the Supreme Court decided that it would look closely at cases where governments attempted to alter contracts that they had created and thus voided an impairment of a contract by the New York and New Jersey Port Authority. Generally, however, the judiciary has paid less attention to economic rights in the twentieth century, and the justices' reduced reliance on the contract clause has reflected this.

Article I, Section 10. [2] No State shall, without the Consent of the Congress, lay any Imposts or Duties on Imports or Exports, except what may be absolutely necessary for executing it's inspection Laws: and the net Produce of all Duties and Imposts, laid by any State on Imports or Exports, shall be for the Use of the Treasury of the United States; and all such Laws shall be subject to the Revision and Controul of the Congress.

[3] No State shall, without the Consent of Congress, lay any Duty of Tonnage, keep Troops, or Ships of War in time of Peace, enter into any Agreement or Compact with another State, or with a foreign Power, or engage in War, unless actually invaded, or in such imminent Danger as will not admit of delay.

Other Limits on the States

Paragraph 2 of Article I, Section 10 prohibits state taxes on imports and exports except for what "may be absolutely necessary for executing its inspection laws." It thus employs the qualifying adjective "absolutely" that the elastic clause omits. The same paragraph reaffirms that other import and export taxes will go into national rather than state and local coffers.

Similarly, the third paragraph limits states from exercising other powers that the Constitution reserves for Congress. The section specifies that congress must approval attempts by states to keep troops in times of peace, to enter into agreements with foreign governments, or to agree to compacts among themselves. The Constitution does permit states to employ defensive forces when they are invaded and delay is impossible.

REFERENCES AND SUGGESTIONS FOR FURTHER STUDY

Cases

Calder v. Bull, 3 U.S. 386 (1798).

Carmell v. Texas, 120 S. Ct. 1620 (2000).

Charles River Bridge Co. v. Warren Bridge Co., 36 U.S. 420 (1837).

Cherokee Nation v. Georgia, 30 U.S. 1 (1831).

Chisholm v. Georgia, 2 U.S. 419 (1793).

City of Philadelphia v. New Jersey, 437 U.S. 617 (1978).

Clinton v. City of New York, 524 U.S. 417 (1998).

Cooley v. Board of Wardens, 53 U.S. 299 (1852).

Cummings v. Missouri, 72 U.S. 277 (1867).

Dartmouth College v. Woodward, 17 U.S. 518 (1819).

Department of Commerce v. U.S. House of Representatives, 525 U.S. 316 (1999).

Dred Scott v. Sandford, 60 U.S. 393 (1857).

Ex Parte Garland, 72 U.S. 333 (1867).

Fletcher v. Peck, 10 U.S. 87 (1810).

Garcia v. San Antonio Metropolitan Transit Authority, 469 U.S. 528 (1985).

Gibbons v. Ogden, 22 U.S. 1 (1824).

Gonzales v. Raich, 125 S. Ct. 2195 (2005).

Gravel v. United States, 408 U.S. 606 (1972).

Hammer v. Dagenhart, 247 U.S. 251 (1918).

Home Building & Loan Association v. Blaisdell, 290 U.S. 398 (1934).

Hylton v. United States, 3 U.S. 171 (1796).

Immigration and Naturalization Service v. Chadha, 462 U.S. 919 (1983).

Luther v. Borden, 48 U.S. 1 (1849).

McCulloch v. Maryland, 17 U.S. 316 (1819).

National League of Cities v. Usery, 426 U.S. 833 (1976).

Walter L. Nixon v. United States, 506 U.S. 224 (1993).
Pollock v. Farmers' Loan & Trust Co., 158 U.S. 601 (1895).
Powell v. McCormack, 395 U.S. 486 (1969).
Schechter Poultry Corporation v. United States, 295 U.S. 495 (1935).
South Dakota v. Dole, 483 U.S. 203 (1987).
Southern Pacific Company v. Arizona, 325 U.S. 761 (1945).
Trade Mark Cases, 100 U.S. 82 (1879).
U.S. Term Limits v. Thornton, 115 S. Ct. 1842 (1995).
United States Trust Co. of New York v. New Jersey, 431 U.S. 1 (1977).
United States v. Butler, 297 U.S. 1 (1936).
United States v. Curtiss-Wright Corporation, 299 U.S. 304 (1936).
United States v. E. C. Knight, 156 U.S. 1 (1895).
United States v. Lopez, 514 U.S. 549 (1995).
United States v. Morrison, 529 U.S. 598 (2000).
United States v. Richardson, 418 U.S. 166 (1974).
Watkins v. United States, 354 U.S. 178 (1957).
Wickard v. Filburn, 317 U.S. 111 (1942).
Worcester v. Georgia, 31 U.S. 515 (1832).

Books

Christopher J. Bailey, *The U.S. Congress* (New York: Basil Blackwell Ltd., 1989).

Sotorios Barber, *The Constitution and the Delegation of Congressional Power* (Chicago: The University of Chicago Press, 1975).

Boris I. Bittker, *Bittker on the Regulation of Interstate and Foreign Commerce* (Gaithersburg, PA: Aspen Law & Business, 1999).

Charles L. Black, Jr., *Perspectives in Constitutional Law* (Englewood Cliffs, NJ: Prentice-Hall, 1970).

Barbara H. Craig, *Chadha: The Story of an Epic Constitutional Struggle* (New York: Oxford University Press, 1988).

Robert A. Diamond, *Powers of Congress* (Washington, DC: Congressional Quarterly, Inc., 1976).

John H. Ely, *War and Responsibility: Constitutional Lessons of Vietnam and its Aftermath* (Princeton, NJ: Princeton University Press, 1993).

Max Farrand, *The Framing of the Constitution of the United States* (New Haven, CT: Yale University Press, 1913).

Louis Fisher, *Constitutional Conflicts Between the Congress and the President* (Princeton, NJ: Princeton University Press, 1985).

Louis Fisher, *The Politics of Shared Powers: Congress and the Executive*, 2nd ed. (Washington, DC: Congressional Quarterly Press, 1987).

Felix Frankfurter, *The Commerce Clause Under Marshall, Taney and Waite* (Chapel Hill: University of North Carolina Press, 1937).

Michael J. Gerhardt, *The Federal Impeachment Process: A Constitutional and Historical Analysis* (Princeton, NJ: Princeton University Press, 1996).

Robert A. Goldwin and Art Kaufman, eds., *Separation of Powers—Does It Still Work?* (Washington, DC: American Enterprise Institute for Public Policy Research, 1986).

Alexander Hamilton, James Madison, and John Jay, *The Federalist Papers*, Clinton Rossiter, ed. (New York: New American Library, 1961).

Michael Kammen, *A Machine That Would Go of Itself: The Constitution in American Culture* (New York: Alfred A. Knopf, 1987).

Thomas E. Mann, *A Question of Balance: The President, the Congress and Foreign Policy* (Washington, DC: The Brookings Institution, 1989).

John L. Moore, ed., *Guide to U.S. Elections*, 2nd ed. (Washington, DC: Congressional Quarterly, Inc., 1985).

Michael Nelson, ed., *Guide to the Presidency*, 3rd ed., 2 vols. (Washington, DC: Congressional Quarterly, Inc., 2002).

John E. O'Connor, "The Emoluments Clause: An Anti-Federalist Intruder in a Federal Constitution," *Hofstra Law Review* (Fall 1995), 24:89–178.

William H. Rehnquist, *Grand Inquests: The Historic Impeachments of Justice Samuel Chase and President Andrew Johnson* (New York: William Morrow & Company, 1992).

Randall B. Ripley, *Congress: Process and Policy*, 4th ed. (New York: W.W. Norton, 1988).

John R. Schmidhauser and Larry L. Berg, *The Supreme Court and Congress: Conflict and Interaction, 1945–1968* (New York: The Free Press, 1972).

Telford Taylor, *The Grand Inquest: The Story of Congressional Investigations* (New York: Simon and Schuster, 1955).

Laurence H. Tribe, *American Constitutional Law*, 3rd ed. (New York: Foundation Press, 2000).

John R. Vile, *Encyclopedia of Constitutional Amendments, Proposed Amendments, and Amending Issues: 1789–2002*, 2nd ed. (Santa Barbara, CA: ABC-CLIO, 2003).

Michael D. Wormser, *Guide to Congress*, 3rd ed. (Washington, DC: Congressional Quarterly, Inc., 1982).

Benjamin F. Wright, *The Contract Clause of the Constitution* (Cambridge, MA: Harvard University Press, 1938).

Chapter 3

Article II: The Executive Branch

The U.S. President is powerful. Although presidential power waxes and wanes with the personality of the individual who occupies the office and the circumstances of the time, much of it derives from the nature of the office itself. Just as Article I lists the powers and limits of the legislative branch of the national government, so too, Article II describes and limits the executive branch. The opening sentences of Articles I and II differ. Whereas Article I refers to "all powers herein granted," Article II refers less restrictively to "the executive Power." Traditionally, executives exercised prerogative powers that gave them greater leeway than the legislature.

A SINGLE EXECUTIVE

Article II, Section 1. The executive Power shall be vested in a President of the United States of America.

Some delegates to the Constitutional Convention, including some advocates of the Virginia Plan, favored a single executive. Others, generally supporting the New Jersey Plan, wanted a plural executive. The former group prevailed, and the delegates vested the "executive Power" in a single president who, along with a vice president, serves terms of four years.

Undoubtedly, the framers enlarged the power, and what the framers called the "energy" of this office, by vesting the presidency in one individual. As a single individual, the president's words are far more important, and the president's actions elicit far more attention, than if the president were but one member of an executive council or committee. The media give far more coverage to individual presidents than to members of Congress, with its 535 members, or the U.S. Supreme Court, with its nine.

The U.S. president is both the head of state and the head of government, thus combining the real and symbolic powers that England and other constitutional monarchies divide between the prime minister and the king or queen. A president has a unique capacity for performing both good and ill. Thus, Woodrow Wilson once noted that "The President is at liberty, both in law and conscience, to be as big a man as he can." Certainly presidents like George Washington, Andrew Jackson, Abraham Lincoln, Theodore and Franklin D. Roosevelt, and Ronald Reagan have validated the accuracy of Wilson's observation. A number of these individuals have radically changed the popular image and expectations of the presidency.

Article II, Section 1. [1] He shall hold his Office during the Term of four Years,

---

THE PRESIDENTIAL TERM

The Constitution sets the term of the president at four years, midway between the terms it established for members of the House of Representatives and the Senate. The president's term accentuates constitutional separation of powers. Although the Constitution provides that all member of the House face election in presidential election years, this does not guarantee that the people will elect a majority of the House from the president's own party. Moreover, the president's party almost invariably loses support in the midterm elections in the House two years later. With only one-third of the senators facing election in presidential election years, there is an even greater probability that a party other than the president's own will lead the Senate. Such a split in party dominance is impossible in most parliamentary systems, in which the prime minister heads the majority party or coalition.

During and immediately after the Revolutionary War, colonists feared executive abuses like those of George III. Experience under the Articles of Confederation and most state constitutions of the period demonstrated the problems connected with weak or nonexistent executive authority. The widespread belief among Convention Delegates that George Washington would be the nation's first chief executive undoubtedly eased their fears and made them more willing to invest real power in the office.

Article II, Section 1. [1] and, together with the Vice President, chosen for the same Term, be elected, as follows:

[2] Each State shall appoint, in such Manner as the Legislature thereof may direct, a Number of Electors, equal to the whole Number of Senators and Representatives to which the State may be entitled in the Congress: but no Senator or Representative, or Person holding an Office of Trust or Profit under the United States, shall be appointed an Elector.

[3] *The Electors shall meet in their respective States, and vote by Ballot for two Persons; of whom one at least shall not be an Inhabitant of the same State with themselves. And they shall make a List of all the Persons voted for, and of the Number of Votes for each; which List they shall sign and certify, and transmit sealed to the Seat of the Government of the United States, directed to the President of the Senate. The President of the Senate shall, in the Presence of the Senate and House of Representatives, open all the Certificates; and the Votes shall then be counted. The Person having the greatest Number of Votes shall be the President, if such Number be a Majority of the whole Number of Electors appointed; and if there be more than one who have such Majority, and have an equal Number of Votes, then the House of Representatives shall immediately chuse* [sic] *by Ballot one of them for President; and if no Person have a Majority, then from the five highest on the List the said House shall in like Manner chuse* [sic] *the President. But in chusing* [sic] *the President, the Votes shall be taken by States, the Representation from each State having one Vote; a quorum for this Purpose shall consist of a Member or Members from two thirds of the States, and a Majority of all the States shall be necessary to a Choice. In every Case, after the Choice of the President, the Person having the greatest Number of Votes of the Electors shall be the Vice President. But if there should remain two or more who have equal Votes; the Senate shall chuse [sic] from them by Ballot the Vice President.*

[4] The Congress may determine the Time of chusing [sic] the Electors, and the Day on which they shall give their Votes; which Day shall be the same throughout the United States.

PRESIDENTIAL SELECTION AND THE ELECTORAL COLLEGE

The problem of presidential selection was not easy. If the Constitution vested Congress with the power to elect and reelect the president, the president might attempt to bargain with, or corrupt, the legislature—a development that the colonists believed they had observed in Great Britain prior to the American Revolution. However appealing direct election may be today, the founding fathers feared that it might encourage demagoguery. Such an election also raised more practical questions, in an age long before computers and telecommunications, as to how state governments (each of which would have an incentive to inflate its own numbers) could accurately and quickly tally votes in a nation the size of the new Union. If the founders chose an indirect method of election, they had to decide—as in the earlier controversy over representation in Congress—how to represent individual states.

The delegates to the Constitutional Convention creatively responded by inventing the electoral college. Paragraphs 2 and 3 above describe its original structure. Under this system, the Constitution allocated to each state a number of electoral votes equivalent to its total number of senators and representatives (a minimum of three) established by the Connecticut Compromise. Electors from each state assembled only once after each election in the state capitals to choose the president and vice president and then dissolved into oblivion, obviating fears of presidential corruption.

Under the original electoral college scheme, the electors from each state cast two ballots for president. Each elector had to vote for at least one out-of-state resident—thus mitigating small state fears that the largest state would dominate the new system. States then transmitted these votes to the president of the Senate, who publicly counted the votes. The Senate awarded the presidency to the person getting a majority of the votes and the vice presidency to the runner-up. If no candidate received a majority or if two tied, the House of Representatives would choose one for president, voting by states from among the top five names. If the House of Representatives cast a tie vote for vice president, the Senate was to choose between them.

The U.S. Constitution nowhere mentions political parties, and the original electoral college neither fully anticipated them nor the practice of candidates running on a team ticket, where ties between the top two candidates would almost be inevitable. The election of 1800 best illustrated this dilemma. Thomas Jefferson and Aaron Burr, who both ran as Democratic-Republicans, garnered the same number of votes and sent the election to the U.S. House of Representatives. The states ratified the Twelfth Amendment, which addressed this problem, in 1804.

This Amendment still left open the possibility that a person could become president without winning the popular vote. Although such cases are rare, they are fairly dramatic. The presidential election of 2000, in which Republican candidate George W. Bush won the majority of the electoral college, and thus, the presidency, despite having fewer popular votes than Democrat Al Gore, highlighted this undemocratic feature of the current system.

Paragraph 4 requires Congress to establish a uniform day for national elections. It has established the first Tuesday after the first Monday in November of presidential selection years for individuals to vote. It further provided that electors would meet in their state capitals on the first Monday after the second Wednesday of the December of presidential election years to cast ballots that states would send to Congress to open in early January. For Congress to accept such results as conclusive, states have to choose such delegates prior to six days before this deadline. This "safe harbor" deadline factored into the Supreme Court's decision in *Bush v. Gore*, which ruled that inadequate time remained for a full vote recount.

> **Article II, Section 1.** [5] No Person except a natural born Citizen, or a Citizen of the United States, at the time of the Adoption of this Constitution, shall be eligible to the Office of President; neither shall any person be eligible to that Office who shall not have attained to the Age of thirty five Years, and been fourteen Years a Resident within the United States.

PRESIDENTIAL QUALIFICATIONS

The Constitution limits eligibility to the presidency to those who were citizens when the states ratified the Constitution or who were subsequently natural born. The framers thereby sought to prevent people not thoroughly acculturated to American ideals from running for the office. This requirement also helped quash rumors, circulating at the time of the Constitutional Convention, that the delegates intended to install a foreign king.

The Constitution established a minimum age of thirty-five for presidents. This age is five years higher than the Constitution required for members of the Senate and ten years higher than it required for members of the House, but it is still fairly minimal. In an attempt to ensure familiarity with national ideals, this section also provides that a person who has not resided in the United States for a minimum of fourteen years cannot be president. From time to time critics have proposed that the Constitution should permit foreign-born naturalized U.S. citizens like Madeline Albright, the first woman secretary of state, or Arnold Schwarzenegger, the populist governor of California, who have lived in the nation for a specified number of years, to run. The nation would first have to adopt a constitutional amendment.

> **Article II, Section 1.** [6] *In Case of the Removal of the President from Office, or of his Death, Resignation, or Inability to discharge the Powers and Duties of the said Office, the Same shall devolve on the Vice President, and the Congress may by Law provide for the Case of Removal, Death, Resignation or Inability,*
>
> *Continued on next page*

> *both of the President and Vice President, declaring what Officer shall then act*
> *as President, and such Officer shall act accordingly, until the Disability be*
> *removed, or a President shall be elected.*

THE VICE PRESIDENT AND PRESIDENTIAL DISABILITY

Although the role has become increasingly institutionalized over the past few decades, the Constitution does not list extensive duties for the vice president. Indeed, the office largely emerged from the Constitutional Convention as a byproduct of the selection procedure of the electoral college, which required each elector to cast two votes. Even more than serving as president of the Senate, the vice president's main constitutional responsibility is to serve as a kind of president-in-waiting in case a president dies, resigns, or is disabled. To date, Richard Nixon is the only president who resigned. Others have, however, died of natural causes or been assassinated. Cases of presidential disability have also occurred, but, absent the greater clarification that the Twenty-fifth Amendment later provided, this part of the Constitution offered vice presidents little guidance as to their powers in such circumstances.

In 1841, Vice President John Tyler became the first vice president to assume the reigns of office when President William Henry Harrison died in office of natural causes. Tyler set the precedent, which successors have followed, of serving not simply as an "acting," or interim president, but as a president fully exercising all the prerogatives of his predecessors. The language of paragraph six suggests, but does not conclusively establish, that the framers may have anticipated a new election in such circumstances.

> **Article II, Section 1.** [7] The President shall, at stated Times, receive for his Services, a Compensation, which shall neither be increased nor diminished during the Period for which he shall have been elected, and he shall not receive within that Period any other Emolument from the United States, or any of them.

THE PRESIDENTIAL SALARY

Subject to time restrictions that the Twenty-seventh Amendment now imposes, members of Congress collectively set their own salaries. If Congress could raise or lower the salary of the president, it might employ this power to undercut executive independence. The Constitution accordingly prohibits Congress from so adjusting presidential pay during the president's term of office. Similarly, the Constitution prohibits the president from accepting any other "Emolument[s]" from the nation or the states. This provision has not kept former presidents from cashing in on their offices by accepting lucrative speaking and/or publication fees after leaving office.

The first Congress set the salary of early U.S. presidents at $25,000. This salary was increased to $50,000 in 1873, to $75,000 in 1909, to $100,000 in 1949, and to $200,000 in 1969. Since 2001, the president receives $400,000 a year.

Article II, Section 1. [8] Before he enter on the Execution of his Office, he shall take the following Oath or Affirmation:—"I do solemnly swear (or affirm) that I will faithfully execute the Office of President of the United States, and will to the best of my Ability, preserve, protect and defend the Constitution of the United States."

THE PRESIDENTIAL OATH

Many Americans view judges as the primary defenders of the Constitution, but the presidential oath puts this responsibility in some perspective. In addition to pledging to execute the office of president, the chief executive also pledges to "preserve, protect and defend the Constitution of the United States." Citing this pledge, a number of presidents have defended their own views of the Constitution against rival interpretations by the judicial branch. Thus, for example, Andrew Jackson vetoed a bank bill even though the U.S. Supreme Court had earlier ruled that the bank was constitutional. Abraham Lincoln believed the provision of the Missouri Compromise banning slavery from the territories had been constitutional, even after the U.S. Supreme Court said otherwise.

The Constitution enables the president either to swear or affirm this pledge. With a sensitivity to religious beliefs that the First Amendment later reaffirmed, the framers thus accommodated those with religious convictions against swearing. The Constitution does not require presidents to use the words "so help me God," which most repeat after their oath.

PRESIDENTIAL DUTIES

> **Article II, Section 2.** [1] The President shall be Commander in Chief of the Army and Navy of the United States, and of the Militia of the several States, when called into the actual Service of the United States;

Commander in Chief

Article II, Section 2 lists presidential duties. The first duty is actually an office rather than a function and may well be the most important. It vests the president with what scholars calls "the power of the sword." It provides that the president is commander in chief of the army and navy and of state militia called into national service. Thus, the Constitution embodies the principle of civilian control of the military that Jefferson cited in the Declaration of Independence. Although some generals, like George Washington, William Henry Harrison, and Dwight D. Eisenhower, have become president, a president is the nation's highest military official regardless of prior military training and service or lack of it. This provision has enabled the nation to avoid the bloody coups that have marked the history of many other nations, including those in the western hemisphere. The controversy between President Harry Truman and General Douglas MacArthur during the Korean War was a classic example of the conflict that sometimes occurs between the president and the military brass, but the Constitution clearly weighs in on the side of civilian control.

Conflicts between the president and Congress in the area of foreign affairs are necessarily more complex since the Constitution divides power between them. It grants Congress the power to declare war and authorize appropriations for it and leaves the president to wage it. In an insightful concurring opinion in *Youngstown Sheet & Tube Co. v. Sawyer* (1952), Justice Robert Jackson explained that presidential war powers are strongest when presidents are pursuing congressional policies, weakest when they conflict with these policies, and in an intermediate "zone of twilight" when congress has neither sanctioned nor condemned such actions.

The perpetual state of cold war that existed from the end of World War II in 1945 until shortly after the fall of the Berlin Wall in late 1989, like the current conflict with international terrorism, heightened concerns that presidential powers could threaten civil liberties. An example occurred when the Supreme Court, in *Korematsu v. United States* (1944), sanctioned the exclusion of Japanese-Americans from large areas of the West Coast. The United States had incarcerated more than 100,000 Japanese-Americans, most of whom were U.S. citizens, without trial during World War II on the basis of an executive order that Franklin Roosevelt issued and justified on the basis of a perceived threat to national security. In a decision the U.S. Supreme Court chose not to reverse, lower federal courts ruled in the 1980s that this judgment had been mistaken, and Congress subsequently adopted a law giving $20,000 to each living Japanese-American who had been interned during World War II.

Other decisions have also limited executive powers. *Ex Parte Milligan* (1866) thus invalidated the conviction of a civilian by a military court in Indiana during the Civil War, at a time when the South had not invaded the state and the regular courts were still operating. Similarly, the ruling in *Youngstown Sheet & Tube Co. v. Sawyer* (1952) during the Korean War invalidated the president's attempt to seize U.S. steel mills in order to avoid a threatened strike.

Responses to terrorist attacks on the United States in September, 2001, have raised questions of individual rights, especially of foreign nationals, in times of war. In *Hamdi v. Rumsfeld* (2004), the U.S. Supreme Court ruled both that the United States had legally detained a U.S. citizen whom it had captured in Afghanistan and that he also had the legal right to seek release. In *Rasul v. Bush* (2004), it ruled that aliens the United States was holding at a navy base in Guantanamo Bay, Cuba, had the right to a federal judicial hearing as to their continuing confinement.

After widespread complaints about presidential abuses of power during the Vietnam War, Congress passed the War Powers Resolution of 1973 over President Nixon's veto. The law required presidents to consult with Congress and notify it within forty-eight hours that the president was engaging American troops in hostile actions. It also provided that the president could only commit troops for sixty days—with a thirty-day extension possible— unless Congress approved an extension. John Hart Ely has noted that "presidential defiance, congressional irresolution, and judicial abstention" (Ely, *War and Responsibility*, p. 49) have complicated the implementation of the War Powers Resolution. Not only does the law contain a legislative veto mechanism like that which the U.S. Supreme Court invalidated in the *Chadha* case, but the consultation and reporting provisions of the law are so ambiguous that presidents sometimes bypass the law by refusing to submit a report that will trigger the sixty-day limit. Although some presidents have evaded the law, it has heightened their awareness of the need to seek congressional support when undertaking foreign policy initiatives. Thus, President George H. W. Bush sought and received support from Congress for his attack on Iraqi troops that had invaded Kuwait. Under congressional pressure, President Clinton subsequently established deadlines for troops committed to peace-keeping assignments in Somalia (an action George H. W. Bush initiated),

Haiti, and Bosnia, and George W. Bush sought and received congressional authorization to depose Iraq's Saddam Hussein.

Article II, Section 2. [1] he may require the Opinion, in writing, of the principal Officer in each of the executive Departments, upon any Subject relating to the Duties of their respective Offices,

---

Getting Advice from the Cabinet

As chief executive, the president oversees the heads of government agencies, which Americans collectively designate as the cabinet. The Constitution authorizes the president to call upon these heads for written advice connected with their duties. In an early example, President Washington asked his secretary of treasury, Alexander Hamilton, his secretary of state, Thomas Jefferson, and his attorney general, Edmund Randolph, for their opinions on the constitutionality of the bank. As often happens in such cases, they gave conflicting advice. The Constitution does not require a president to take votes in cabinet meetings or accept the cabinet's judgment. Congress approves cabinet appointments, but they serve at the president's pleasure. As the nation's top elected official, the president is ultimately responsible for executing the powers of this office.

Article II, Section 2. [1] and he shall have Power to grant Reprieves and Pardons for Offenses against the United States, except in Cases of Impeachment.

Power to Pardon and Reprieve

The Constitution grants the president power to issue reprieves and pardons for offenses against the United States. This power mirrors that of most state governors. The president's pardon power is broad, but it neither extends to offenses against individual states nor allows the president to intervene in civil suits. In *Ex Parte Grossman* (1925), the Supreme Court ruled that the president can pardon individuals convicted of contempt of Congress. The pardon power also allows presidents to issue general amnesties, such as the one President Jimmy Carter extended to Vietnam era draft evaders.

Although the Supreme Court once ruled that a pardon was invalid unless its intended recipient accepted it, in *Biddle v. Perovich* (1927) Justice Oliver Wendell Holmes, Jr. ruled that a pardon was "not a private act of grace from an individual happening to possess power" but "a part of the Constitutional scheme." Accordingly, Holmes said that a president could extend a pardon, as the judge had imposed an original punishment, "without regard to the prisoner's consent and in the teeth of his will, whether he liked it or not, [since] the public welfare, not his [a prisoner's] consent, determines what shall be done." In *Schick v. Reed* (1974), the Court recognized a president's power to issue a conditional pardon.

Shortly after assuming his office, President Gerald Ford pardoned former President Richard Nixon—who had resigned after the Watergate scandal— for all crimes he may have committed while in office. Ford hoped this pardon would help heal the wounds of Watergate and allow the nation to tackle other matters. Instead, the pardon stirred intense criticism and probably worked against Ford's reelection. Still, in *Murphy v. Ford* (1975), a district court judge ruled that the pardon was constitutional.

Article II, Section 2. [2] He shall have Power, by and with the Advice and Consent of the Senate, to make Treaties, provided two thirds of the Senators present concur;

Negotiation and Ratification of Treaties

The Constitution vests the president with responsibility for making and ne-gotiating treaties. Such treaties do not become law of the land, under Arti-cle VI, however, until the Senate approves them by a two-thirds vote. This can disadvantage a president in reaching agreement with heads of nations that do not require such approval. At least since the Senate failed to approve the League of Nations that Woodrow Wilson had helped to create, members of Congress have introduced amendments to reduce the majority needed for such affirmation in the Senate, albeit sometimes also involving the House of Representatives in such votes. Congress has not, however, proposed any such amendment by the required majority and presidents have continued to worry about Senate approval—President Jimmy Carter thus proved unable to get approval for the SALT (Strategic Arms Limitation Talks) Treaty that he had negotiated with the Soviet Union. Presidents often make agreements with foreign governments, called executive agreements, that deal with matters, particularly ones that they do not think require formal approval through treaties.

In a number of cases, the Supreme Court has upheld the validity of such executive agreements. In *United States v. Belmont* (1937), for example, the Court upheld the executive agreement under which President Franklin

Roosevelt recognized the government of the Soviet Union. Similarly, in *Dames & Moore v. Regan* (1981), the Court validated an executive agreement with Iran that President Reagan issued effectively ratifying an earlier order whereby President Carter had frozen Iranian assets and transferred them to the Federal Reserve Bank of New York, pending negotiations to settle differences between the two nations.

In a further complication, Congress sometimes authorizes through joint congressional resolution what the Senate might otherwise accomplish through a treaty. The United States so entered into its agreement with Canada to build the St. Lawrence Seaway. Congress also used this mechanism to adopt the controversial North American Free Trade Agreement (NAFTA) with Canada and Mexico that President Clinton signed in 1994.

The Constitution does not specify who has the power to terminate treaties. Clearly congressional adoption or ratification of a new conflicting law voids an earlier one, but the lines of authority are otherwise fuzzy. After the United States recognized the People's Republic of China, President Jimmy Carter terminated a defense treaty with Taiwan. In *Goldwater v. Carter* (1979), a majority of the Supreme Court sidestepped the issue of his authority to do so by declaring that the issue was not "ripe" for review, but some justices said they thought that Carter had authority to take this action.

Article II, Section 2. [2] and he shall nominate, and by and with the Advice and Consent of the Senate, shall appoint Ambassadors, other public Ministers and Consuls, Judges of the supreme Court, and all other Officers of the United States, whose Appointments are not herein otherwise provided for, and which shall be established by Law: but the Congress may by Law vest the Appointment of such inferior Officers, as they think proper, in the President alone, in the Courts of Law, or in the Heads of Departments.

Presidential Appointment and Removal Powers

The president's appointment power is one of his most important. The current method is a compromise between two proposals at the Constitutional Convention. The Virginia Plan proposed vesting appointment power in Congress; the New Jersey Plan proposed vesting it in the executive branch. The resulting compromise granted the president the power to appoint ambassadors, ministers, judges, and other constitutional offices subject to senatorial "Advice and Consent," or confirmation. The president's role in appointing ambassadors reaffirms his role as the nation's chief diplomat.

Because presidents appoint members to the judicial branch for life terms, these are also especially important.

This method of selection almost ensures that most appointees will have a "political" dimension. Especially in the case of judges, however, presidents have found that they cannot always predict accurately how the judges will rule. Referring to Earl Warren and William Brennan, President Eisenhower once said that his "two biggest mistakes" were "both on the Supreme Court." All three of the justices that President Nixon appointed who participated in *United States v. Nixon* (1974) joined their brethren in rejecting his claim of executive privilege.

The Senate has taken its role of advice and consent seriously, often rejecting presidential nominees and sometimes using filibusters (literally talking a nomination to death) to delay consideration of, or avoid votes on, nominees. In May 2005, the Senate narrowly avoided a vote, which Republicans spearheaded, to eliminate this option in such cases, after a bipartisan group of lawmakers agreed to up-or-down votes on a number of nominees to U.S. Circuit courts that George W. Bush had made but that the Senate had delayed. Confirmation fights can be extremely partisan, but they fulfill an essential role, especially in the case of judges who hold their positions for life.

The Constitution does not specify who can remove officers who do not serve life terms. Some interpreters argued that in areas where the Constitution required Senate advice and consent to appointment, it should also require such agreement for dismissal. The first Congress rejected this view and vested removal power in the president. During Reconstruction, Congress changed its mind, but this new view has not subsequently prevailed. Chief Justice William Howard Taft, a former president, affirmed in *Myers v. United States* (1926) that as the official responsible for the execution of laws, the president alone should have such removal power. The Supreme Court somewhat limited presidential removal powers in *Humphrey's Executor v. United States* (1935) and *Wiener v. United States* (1958) to protect appointees who were in quasijudicial positions requiring independence, rather than in executive positions where the president exercises ultimate responsibility for the outcome.

The Constitution designates the president, the Courts, or department heads to appoint other inferior officers. Apart from limited cases in which Congress appoints its own officers, it cannot make appointments. Thus in *Buckley v. Valeo* (1976), the Supreme Court invalidated a scheme that had authorized key congressional leaders to appoint some members of a Federal Election Commission.

In *Bowsher v. Synar* (1986), the Supreme Court decided that the comptroller general of the United States was not an executive officer because

Congress had retained the power to remove him. The Court therefore ruled that the comptroller had no authority to recommend budget cuts to the president under the Balanced Budget and Emergency Deficit Control Act, or Gramm-Rudman-Hollings law. More recently, the Supreme Court in *Morrison v. Olson* (1988) upheld the appointment of a special prosecutor, an executive official, by members of the judicial branch. Chief Justice William Rehnquist said that because the special prosecutor was an "inferior" officer, the president did not need to appoint him directly and that the law granted the attorney general sufficient control over the office so that the president could continue to exercise his constitutional duties. In dissent, Justice Antonin Scalia's argued that vesting the appointment of such an officer within the executive branch violated the doctrine of separation of powers, and that politics made it extremely difficult for the attorney general to fire a prosecutor conducting an ongoing investigation. When Special Prosecutor Kenneth Starr's investigation of President Clinton continued for years and extended far beyond its original mandate—eventually leading to impeachment of the president—some observers argued that Scalia's arguments had proven prescient. Starr himself did not think that the attorney general had adequately protected his office against presidential criticisms. In the face of such criticism, Congress chose not to renew the special prosecutor statute.

In *Mistretta v. United States* (1989), the Supreme Court upheld the constitutionality of a U.S. Sentencing Commission, which Congress created to establish binding sentencing guidelines. The Commission consisted of seven members, three of whom were judges that the president could only remove for cause. The president appointed members from a list that the Judicial Conference of the United States supplied. Evoking the little-used doctrine of excessive delegation of legislative power in his dissent, Justice Scalia compared the commission to "a sort of 'junior varsity' Congress" that, unlike Congress itself, was unaccountable to the people.

Article II, Section 2. [3] The President shall have Power to fill up all Vacancies that may happen during the Recess of the Senate, by granting Commissions which shall expire at the End of their next Session.

Interim Presidential Appointments

When the Senate is in recess, presidents can issue commissions that will end, unless confirmed, at the end of the next Senate session. This power was important when Congress met for only a few months of the year, but it is far less important in an age where Congress meets for most of the year.

Presidents generally inform the Senate of key recess appointments before-hand so as not to antagonize those who will be subsequently voting on them. Presidents often find it especially useful to make recess appointments to courts where vacancies could otherwise retard judicial business.

> **Article II, Section 3.** He shall from time to time give to the Congress Information of the State of the Union, and recommend to their Consideration such Measures as he shall judge necessary and expedient;

The State of the Union Address

The first paragraph of Article II, Section 3 provides the constitutional basis of the State of the Union Addresses, once simply called annual messages, that presidents deliver each January. Modern presidents give these speeches in person, but the Constitution does not require this. Woodrow Wilson, who was especially enamored with the potentially beneficial effects of presidential rhetoric, reinstituted the practice of presenting the speeches in person, which Thomas Jefferson and his successors had discontinued.

Although Congress must make the laws, presidents have initiated major legislation to further their election platform. Because of the visibility of their office, presidents have a unique ability to focus public attention on such laws. In part because of the president's veto power, members of Congress, especially those from the president's party, generally give the president's wishes great weight.

> **Article II, Section 3.** he may, on extraordinary Occasions, convene both Houses, or either of them, and in Case of Disagreement between them, with Respect to the Time of Adjournment, he may adjourn them to such Time as he shall think proper;

Power to Convene and Adjourn Congress

Like most state governors, the president can convene one or both houses of Congress in special session. Thus Franklin D. Roosevelt convened both houses of Congress for a special session the day after the Japanese attacked Pearl Harbor on December 7, 1941. Whereas this power is important at the state level, where legislatures often meet for only a few months of the year, it is not especially important at the national level because Congress now meets most of the year. Similarly, modern presidents have not needed to exercise their power to reconcile differences between the two branches of Congress over times of adjournment.

Article II, Section 3. [1] he shall receive Ambassadors and other public Ministers;

The President as Chief Diplomat

This provision points to the president's wide power over foreign affairs. As the nation's chief diplomat, the president receives foreign ambassadors and public ministers. The president serves as both the actual and symbolic head of the executive branch. In England, by contrast, the prime minister heads the government while the monarch is the symbolic head of state.

Article II, Section 3. he shall take Care that the Laws be faithfully executed,

---

Power to Execute the Laws and Executive Privilege

Consistent with the idea of separation of powers, political scientists often say that Congress makes the laws, the president enforces them, and the judges and justices interpret them. Thus, the Constitution vests the president with the duty to see "that the Laws be faithfully executed." Such a power requires presidents to exercise sound discretion.

In the case of *In Re Neagle* (1890), the Court upheld the president's authority to assign a U.S. Marshal to defend a U.S. Supreme Court justice despite the lack of specific statutory authorization for him to do so. The Court thereby recognized that the president, like Congress, has certain inherent powers to accomplish the tasks that the Constitution assigns to him.

Activist presidents have argued that, especially in foreign affairs, they should be able to exercise certain inherent powers, that is, powers that the Constitution does not state or imply but that derive from, or inhere in, their office. Even some presidential proponents of strict constitutional construction have exercised expansive powers once they were in office. Thus, Thomas Jefferson construed his powers broadly in embargoing goods to Great Britain and in purchasing the Louisiana Territory from France without specific constitutional authorization. Some presidents have further asserted claims of "executive privilege" to withhold certain sensitive information from congressional committees or from other investigatory bodies.

President Richard Nixon asserted a bold claim of executive privilege when he tried to withhold certain Watergate tape recordings that he had made of conversations in the Oval Office from a special prosecutor, Leon Jaworski. Officially recognizing for the first time that a president has a special need for maintaining the confidentiality of conversations with subordinates, in *United States v. Nixon* (1974) a unanimous Supreme Court nonetheless rejected Nixon's claim to withhold the tapes. The Court argued that it was particularly critical for a grand jury to hear evidence in cases involving possible criminal wrongdoing where national security was not involved. That decision provided the evidence that drove Nixon from office. During Special Prosecutor Kenneth Starr's investigation of the truthfulness of President Clinton's testimony regarding his relationship with Monica Lewinsky, the Secret Service also failed to get the courts to recognize a special privilege that would keep its agents from testifying about possible wrongdoing they had observed while on duty.

Lawsuits could hamstring presidents. In *Nixon v. Fitzgerald* (1982), the Supreme Court accordingly extended immunity to presidents in connection with lawsuits resulting from their official acts—in this case, former President Nixon's concurrence in the dismissal of a whistle-blowing civilian employee of the Air Force. Courts may summon presidents to testify in trials; Clinton thus testified in the 1996 Whitewater trial involving former business associates, Jim and Susan McDougal. In such cases, courts generally accommodate presidents' schedules and allow them to testify via videotape.

To date, the Supreme Court has not decided whether presidential privileges should insulate a sitting president against criminal indictments. During the Nixon presidency, Solicitor General Robert Bork argued that prosecutors could not indict a sitting president. Special Prosecutor Leon Jaworski was uncertain enough that he asked the jury in the Watergate case to name President Nixon as an "un-indicted coconspirator."

In 1997, Paula Jones, a former Arkansas state employee, brought a civil suit against President Bill Clinton for alleged sexual advances that he had made when he was governor of Arkansas. Clinton argued that she could not sue him and that opposing attorneys should not be able to continue to collect evidence (the process of discovery) while he was in office. Justice John Paul Stevens wrote the Supreme Court's majority decision allowing the case to proceed while Clinton remained president. Stevens argued that courts could dismiss frivolous suits and accommodate the president's schedule; he further noted that delay could harm claimants. Justice Stephen Breyer's concurring opinion raised the possibility that such cases could unduly burden the presidency.

Decisions from the Nixon era restricted the president's growing use of "impoundment," whereby he refused to spend money that Congress appropriated for certain purposes. The Congressional Budget and Impoundment Control Act of 1974 has since distinguished rescissions, or outright refusals to spend monies, from deferrals or mere delays. After lower courts voided this law because of a legislative veto mechanism, Congress subsequently limited such deferrals to fairly routine matters.

> **Article II, Section 3.** and shall Commission all the Officers of the United States.

Commissioning of Military Officers

Finally, Section 3 entrusts the president with authority to commission all officers of the United States. Because the president is also commander in chief, this duty obviously extends to military officials. Whereas officers in some dictatorships pledge personal allegiance to their leaders, American officers, like the president himself, pledge first and foremost to uphold the Constitution of the United States. In this way, they affirm that the rule of law is superior to the rule of a human leader.

> **Article II, Section 4.** The President, Vice President and all civil Officers of the United States, shall be removed from Office on Impeachment for, and Conviction of, Treason, Bribery, or other high Crimes and Misdemeanors.

PRESIDENTIAL IMPEACHMENT

Section 4 subjects the president, like other officeholders, to impeachment and conviction. To prevent Congress from using this tool in a merely partisan fashion, the Constitution specifies and limits the grounds of impeachment to cases of "Treason, Bribery or other high Crimes and Misdemeanors." The first two terms have a fairly precise meaning; indeed, the Constitution specifically defines treason in Article III, Section 3. The expression "high Crimes and Misdemeanors" is more ambiguous, but it clearly encompasses more than an unpopular stance on a political issue. A committee that investigated this phrase noted:

> [T]hat Congress may properly impeach and remove a President only
> for conduct amounting to a gross breach or serious abuse of power,

and only if it would be prepared to take the same action against any President who engaged in comparable conduct in similar circumstances (Committee on Federal Legislation, *The Law of Presidential Impeachment*, p. 6).

Thus, the charges that the House Judiciary Committee finally accepted against President Nixon included obstructing justice, abuse of power, and contempt of Congress. Similarly, the impeachment charges that the House of Representatives brought against President Clinton focused on possible perjury and obstruction of justice rather than on his sexual indiscretions.

The U.S. Constitution does not give Congress to power to take a "vote of no confidence" to force a new presidential election prior to the end of a president's regular four-year term. This guarantee of presidential tenure enhances presidential power by assuring the president greater independence of Congress. It may also leave an unresponsive president, in whom the nation no longer has confidence, in control. Those who have opposed proposed amendments to allow the U.S. president to serve for a single six-year term have cited the fear of saddling the nation with a president for a more extended period of time.

REFERENCES AND SUGGESTIONS FOR FURTHER STUDY

Cases

Biddle v. Perovich, 274 U.S. 480 (1927).
Bowsher v. Synar, 478 U.S. 714 (1986).
Buckley v. Valeo, 424 U.S. 1 (1976).
Clinton v. Jones, 525 U.S. 820 (1998).
Dames & Moore v. Regan, 453 U.S. 654 (1981).
Ex Parte Grossman, 267 U.S. 87 (1925).
Ex Parte Milligan, 71 U.S. 2 (1866).
Goldwater v. Carter, 444 U.S. 996 (1979).
Hamdi v. Rumsfeld, 542 U.S. 507 (2004).
Humphrey's Executor v. United States, 295 U.S. 602 (1935).
Immigration and Naturalization Service v. Chadha, 462 U.S. 919 (1983).
In Re Neagle, 135 U.S. 1 (1890).
Korematsu v. United States, 323 U.S. 214 (1944).
Mistretta v. United States, 488 U.S. 361 (1989).
Morrison v. Olson, 487 U.S. 654 (1988).
Murphy v. Ford, 390 F. Supp. 1372 (1975).
Myers v. United States, 272 U.S. 52 (1926).
Nixon v. Fitzgerald, 457 U.S. 731 (1982).

Rasul v. Bush, 542 U.S. 466 (2004).
Schick v. Reed, 419 U.S. 256 (1974).
Trade Mark Cases, 100 U.S. 82 (1879).
United States v. Belmont, 301 U.S. 324 (1937).
United States v. Nixon, 418 U.S. 683 (1974).
U.S. Term Limits v. Thornton, 514 U.S. 779 (1995).
Walter L Nixon v. United States, 506 U.S. 204 (1993).
Wiener v. United States, 357 U.S. 349 (1958).
Youngstown Sheet & Tube Co. v. Sawyer, 343 U.S. 579 (1952).

Books

Henry J. Abraham, *Justices, Presidents, and Senators: A History of the U.S. Supreme Court Appointments from Washington to Clinton*, rev. ed. (Lanham: Rowman & Littlefield Publisher, Inc., 1999).

Raoul Berger, *Executive Privilege: A Constitutional Myth* (Cambridge, MA: Harvard University Press, 1974).

Raoul Berger, *Impeachment: The Constitutional Problem* (Cambridge, MA: Harvard University Press, 1973).

Robert E. Di Clerico, ed., *Analyzing the Presidency*, 2nd ed. (Guilford, CT: The Dushkin Publishing Group, Inc., 1990).

Committee on Federal Legislation, *The Law of Presidential Impeachment* (New York: Harper & Row, n.d.).

Edward S. Corwin, *The President, Office and Powers* (New York: New York University Press, 1940).

John Hart Ely, *War and Responsibility: Constitutional Lessons of Vietnam and Its Aftermath* (Princeton, NJ: Princeton University Press, 1993).

Louis Fisher, *The Politics of Shared Power: Congress and the Executive*, 3rd ed. (Washington, DC: Congressional Quarterly Press, 1993).

Richard Hofstader, *The Idea of a Party System: The Rise of Legitimate Opposition in the United States; 1780–1840* (Berkeley: University of California Press, 1972).

Charles O. Jones, *The Presidency in a Separated System* (Washington, DC: The Brookings Institution, 1994).

Barbara Kellerman and Ryan J. Barilleaux, *The President as World Leader* (New York: St. Martin's Press, 1991).

Louis W. Koenig, *The Chief Executive*, 4th ed. (New York: Harcourt Brace Jovanovich, 1980).

Harvey C. Mansfield, Jr., *Taming the Prince: The Ambivalence of Modern Executive Power* (New York: The Free Press, 1989).

Christopher N. May, *In the Name of War: Judicial Review and the War Powers Since 1918* (Cambridge, MA: Harvard University Press, 1989).

Forrest McDonald, *The American Presidency: An Intellectual History* (Lawrence: University Press of Kansas, 1994).

Michael Nelson, ed., *Guide to the Presidency*, 3rd ed., 2 vols. (Washington, DC: Congressional Quarterly, Inc., 2002).

Michael Nelson, ed., *The Presidency: A History of the Office of the President of the United States from 1789 to the Present* (New York: Smithmark, 1996).

Richard E. Neustadt, *Presidential Power* (New York: John Wiley & Sons, 1980).

Benjamin I. Page and Mark P. Petracca, *The American Presidency* (New York: McGraw Hill, 1983).

Clinton Rossiter, *The American Presidency* (New York: Harcourt, Brace and World, rev. ed., 1960).

Clinton Rossiter, expanded with additional text by Richard P. Longaker, *The Supreme Court and the Commander in Chief* (Ithaca, NY: Cornell University Press, 1976).

Mark J. Rozell, *Executive Privilege: The Dilemma of Secrecy and Democratic Accountability* (Baltimore, MD: The Johns Hopkins University Press, 1994).

Susan Schmidt and Michael Weisskopf, *Truth at Any Cost: Ken Starr and the Unmaking of Bill Clinton* (New York: HarperCollins, 2000).

Robert Scigliano, *The Supreme Court and the Presidency* (New York: The Free Press, 1971).

Jean E. Smith, *The Constitution and American Foreign Policy* (St. Paul, MN: West Publishing Company, 1989).

Robert J. Spitzer, *The Presidential Veto: Touchstone of the American Presidency* (Albany: State University of New York Press, 1988).

Jeffrey K. Tulis, *The Rhetorical Presidency* (Princeton, NJ: Princeton University Press, 1987).

Woodrow Wilson, *Constitutional Government in the United States* (New York: Columbia University Press, 1961).

Donald Young, *American Roulette: The History and Dilemma of the Vice Presidency* (New York: The Viking Press, 1974).

Chapter 4

Article III: The Judicial Branch

Articles I and II of the U.S. Constitution respectively structure and limit the powers of the legislative and executive branches. The people select both. By contrast, Article III deals with the judicial branch. The president appoints its members, and the U.S. Senate confirms them. Article III is the briefest of the first three articles. It mentions only the U.S. Supreme Court, and it allows Congress to establish other inferior courts at its discretion.

ORGANIZATION AND GUIDELINES

> **Article III, Section 1.** The judicial Power of the United States, shall be vested in one supreme Court, and in such inferior Courts as the Congress may from time to time ordain and establish.

The U.S. Supreme Court and Other Inferior Courts

Ever since Congress adopted the Judiciary Act of 1789, it has arranged the federal constitutional courts into three tiers, each with distinct functions (albeit with courts in the middle tier originally being composed of panels of judges from the tiers above and below it). There are currently ninety-four U.S. district courts on the bottom tier. These are trial courts that empanel juries and hear cases. Congress has established one to four such courts in each state. Above the district courts is a second tier of courts composed of thirteen circuit courts of appeal that include eleven numbered circuits covering distinct geographical regions (the Ninth Circuit, for example, covers the far Western states) and a District of Columbia and Federal Circuit Court, both located in the nation's capital. They chiefly hear appeals from the district courts. The U.S. Supreme Court, which Article III mentions, constitutes the top tier of this hierarchy.

In addition to overseeing the U.S. District and Circuit Courts, the Supreme Court can, where substantial federal issues are involved, hear appeals from state court systems. Most state court systems are structured like the national system, with a supreme court, or its equivalent, at the top and one or more rungs of lower courts. The major difference is that many states either elect judges or combine a system of initial appointment with electoral confirmation. It is thus more accurate to refer to the fifty-one judicial systems in the United States than to one.

Article III, Section 1. The Judges, both of the supreme and inferior Courts, shall hold their Offices during good Behaviour,

---

Judicial Tenure

Whereas some states elect their judges to fixed terms of office, Article II, Section 2 [2] provides for the president to appoint all members of federal constitutional courts, with the advice and consent of the Senate. Article III further specifies that federal judges hold their offices "during good Behaviour." In effect, these judges therefore serve for life rather than at the pleasure of the people or the other elected branches. The only way that judges leave office is through death, resignation, retirement, or, in rare cases, after the U.S. House of Representatives impeaches and the U.S. Senate convicts them according to constitutional guidelines. The framers wanted to insulate judges from day-to-day political pressures so that they could decide legal cases without fear or favor. In 1980, Congress did adopt the Judicial Councils Reform and Judicial Conduct and Disability Act, which allows for a council of judges to discipline, albeit not remove, lower court judges engaged in conduct short of impeachable offenses.

Judicial Qualifications

The Constitution does not outline specific requirements for age, residency, and citizenship of judges as it does for members of the two elected branches.

The framers probably thought they had less cause to fear that the president would appoint, and the Senate confirm, incompetent people than that the people would elect them. Alternatively, they may have expected legal education to screen out those who were unfit for office.

Presidents have increasingly considered the race, gender, religion, and geographical origins of judges and justices that they have appointed. The Constitution does not require such balance, and some scholars argue that objective merit, however elusive, should be a president's primary concern. "Senatorial courtesy," an unwritten convention rather than a constitutional mandate, permits a senator from a president's party to block the nomination of a judge from his state to which the senator objects and about whom the president has not first consulted the senator. Debates during the Administration of George W. Bush focused on the extent to which senators should use the filibuster (talking a nomination to death) and other tactics, some of which Republicans had previously employed, to deny judicial candidates an up-or-down vote.

Article III, Section 1. and shall, at stated Times, receive for their Services, a Compensation, which shall not be diminished during their Continuance in Office.

Judicial Compensation

Subject to restrictions of timing that the Twenty-seventh Amendment now mandates, the Constitution permits members of Congress collectively to set their own salaries and prevents Congress from increasing or decreasing presidential pay during the executive's term. By contrast, Article III permits Congress to raise but not lower the pay of judges during their tenure. Because the framers favored judicial independence, they did not want Congress to lower judicial salaries on the basis of specific decisions the judges had made. Those who wrote the Constitution further realized that in extended inflationary times, only wealthy judges (who might perpetuate aristocracy) could continue in office without raises. By preventing cuts and permitting raises, the framers hoped to provide adequate salaries while minimizing excessive partisanship in the determination of such salaries.

The Number of Justices

Because the Constitution does not specify the number of judges and justices, Congress can make needed alterations. Congress has exercised this power fairly freely with respect to creating new federal judicial districts and circuits and appointing additional judges to lower federal courts. Since 1869, however, Congress has fixed the number of Supreme Court justices at nine, with eight associate justices and one chief justice. Franklin D. Roosevelt launched the last serious effort to change this number in his so-called court-packing plan of 1937, which proposed adding one justice for every sitting justice over age seventy up to a total of fifteen. Critics rightly criticized this proposal as a partisan plan to change the direction of a Court that been invalidating many New Deal programs. Congress accordingly rejected the proposal. In light of this history, future presidents proposing similar changes in the number of justices would have to show that they were offering their proposals in the nation's best interest rather than seeking partisan advantage. The number nine has thus almost come to be an unwritten constitutional rule that Congress is unlikely to change except under the most extraordinary circumstances.

Supreme Court Decisions

The Constitution does not require judicial unanimity. The Supreme Court determines the outcomes of cases by majority vote, and it sometimes decides important cases by a 5 to 4 margin. The justices usually sign majority opinions, but the Court will sometimes issue unsigned per curiam opinions. In addition to the majority opinion, justices often write concurring and dissenting opinions. In the former, justices vote with the majority but add their own explanations or otherwise qualify their votes. In the latter, justices indicate why they cannot vote with the majority and appeal to the judgment of history. By custom, the chief justice of the Supreme Court writes or assigns opinions when voting with the majority; otherwise, the ranking member of the majority exercises this responsibility.

JURISDICTION

Article III, Section 2. [1] The judicial Power shall extend to all Cases, in Law and Equity, arising under this Constitution, the Laws of the United States, and Treaties made, or which shall be made, under their Authority;—to all Cases affecting Ambassadors, other public Ministers and Consuls;—to all Cases of admiralty and maritime Jurisdiction;—to Controversies to which the United States shall be a Party;—to Controversies between two or more States;—*between a State and Citizens of another State*;—between Citizens of different States;—between Citizens of the same State claiming Lands under Grants of different States, *and between a State, or the Citizens thereof, and foreign States, Citizens or Subjects.*

Cases Based on Subject Matter and Parties to the Suit

Americans justly pride themselves in their written constitution. By hearing or overseeing all cases that arise under this Constitution, the federal judicial branch provides relatively uniform interpretations of this document throughout the nation. U.S. courts hear cases in both law and equity. English law separated these areas. The first utilizes fairly traditional remedies like fines and imprisonment to punish past conduct, and the second provides more flexible remedies like orders and injunctions designed to prevent initial harm.

Section 2 of the Constitution further divides the cases that federal courts hear into two groups. Federal courts hear some cases on the basis of their subject matter and others based on the parties to the case. Article III vests exclusive subject-matter jurisdiction in the courts in four instances. These include all cases: (1) arising under the Constitution, or involving (2) federal laws, (3) federal treaties, or (4) admiralty and maritime law. This jurisdiction assures that federal, rather than state courts, will hear cases involving a substantial federal question.

Article III assigns cases to federal courts based on the character of the parties to the suits in seven instances. These include the following: (1) all cases affecting ambassadors, public ministers, and consuls; (2) controversies involving the United States; (3) cases, like boundary disputes, involving two or more states; (4) cases involving a state and citizens of another state; (5) cases between citizens of different states, called diversity of citizenship cases; (6) controversies between state citizens who claim land under land grants from other states; and (7) cases that arise between a state and its citizens and citizens of foreign states. The Eleventh Amendment altered, or clarified, this jurisdiction by forbidding federal courts from hearing disputes that citizens of other states or nations instituted, but this jurisdiction has otherwise remained unchanged from the time the Constitution was written to the present.

In some cases where Article III does not refer "all" cases within a given category to federal courts, state and federal courts exercise concurrent jurisdiction. Thus, Congress has specified that in certain instances, for example, diversity of citizenship cases below a certain minimum monetary amount, litigants may pursue their cases in either state or federal courts. Generally, the Supreme Court will not review cases in which state courts based their judgments solely on interpretations of the state constitution. Where important federal issues are involved, however, attorneys can file writs (for example, the writ of habeas corpus) to transfer cases from a state court—usually the state's highest, or supreme, court—to the U.S. Supreme Court for review. Because the U.S. system is federal and includes both state and national systems, courts adhere to principles of comity, or mutual restraint, deference, and respect, to ease friction between the two systems. Generally more deferential to state judgments, especially in the area of criminal procedures, than some previous Courts, the Rehnquist Court has significantly limited the cases it will accept for review from the states, especially in cases involving capital punishment.

Article III, Section 2. [2] In all Cases affecting Ambassadors, other public Ministers and Counsuls, and those in which a State shall be Party, the supreme Court shall have original Jurisdiction. In all the other Cases before mentioned, the supreme Court shall have appellate Jurisdiction, both as to Law and Fact, with such Exceptions, and under such Regulations as the Congress shall make.

Cases of Original and Appellate Jurisdiction

Just as the Constitution assigns jurisdiction to the courts based both on the subject matter and the parties to the suits, so too, it divides cases that reach the Supreme Court into cases of original and cases of appellate jurisdiction. The first narrow category, which Article III limits to cases involving ambassadors and public ministers and cases in which the states are parties, begins and ends in the Supreme Court. Even in these cases, the Constitution does not require federal jurisdiction to be exclusive. In the other cases specified earlier, the large majority of cases it hears, the Constitution vests the Court with appellate jurisdiction only. In these cases, the Court hears cases that litigants appeal from lower federal courts, from administrative agencies, or from state supreme courts. In such cases, the Supreme Court focuses on issues of law rather than on findings of fact.

Limits on the Judicial Branch

Article III's focus on cases is significant. In defending the judicial branch in *Federalist* No. 78, Alexander Hamilton argued that it would exercise neither the power of the purse nor the sword, "neither FORCE nor WILL." Hamilton argued that it would simply exercise the power of "judgment." Whereas the legislative and executive branches can initiate legislation and other changes in governmental practices, the judicial branch more passively waits for cases to come before it. Parties before the courts must establish "standing," that is, a clear stake in the outcome. Similarly, they must convince the court that the case is "justiciable," or capable of judicial resolution. Typically, American courts refuse to hear "friendly" suits where the parties involved are not really at loggerheads or cases where the result will be "moot." Moreover, by long-standing practice, which they base on Article III's "case or controversy" requirement, U.S. courts do not issue so-called advisory opinions, or opinions about what they might do in hypothetical cases.

Although Congress has granted the Supreme Court wide discretion to choose the cases it will review, it must still accept cases the way they are, and not necessarily the way it would like to frame them. Whereas interest groups directly lobby members of the elected branches, lobbyists can only appeal directly to courts by bringing suits or filing amicus curiae, or "friend of the court," briefs. In choosing which writs of certiorari (as courts designate such petitions for review of lower court judgments) to accept, the Supreme Court currently operates by "the rule of four," and accepts no cases unless four justices agree to do so.

Because Americans are litigious, most controversial issues eventually reach the courts. Given their inability to frame cases as they might want to hear them, however, there is still a difference in degree, and arguably in kind, between the broad role that the elected branches play in initiating policies and the more restricted role that the judicial branch plays in reacting to them. Moreover, most judges preserve legal stability by operating according to the principle of stare decisis and adhering to past precedents. Although courts sometimes deviate from this doctrine, most of their decisions initiate only incremental changes.

JUDICIAL POWERS

Statutory Interpretation and Judicial Review

Scholars refer to the power of courts to interpret laws as the power of statutory construction. Judicial judgments on such matters are not necessarily final since legislatures may reverse such decisions by more clearly stating their intentions. Thus, for example, Congress overturned the Supreme Court's decision in *Tennessee Valley Authority v. Hill* (1978). The Court had enjoined construction of the Tellico Dam on the Little Tennessee River on the basis that Congress had, in the Endangered Species Act of 1973, intended to stop the construction even of ongoing projects in cases where such construction threatened species, in this case a three-inch relative of the perch known as a snail-darter. Congress waited until it adopted the Curt Flood Act of 1998 before it modified another case of statutory interpretation, *Flood v. Kuhn* (1972), in which the Supreme Court decided that, unlike other major-league sports, Congress had chosen to exempt baseball from provisions of the Sherman Anti-Trust Act.

The courts' power of judicial review has become even more important and controversial than the power of statutory construction. Courts exercise judicial review when they decide whether laws or executive actions applicable to cases before them are constitutional and valid, or unconstitutional and hence void. Article III does not specifically vest courts with judicial review, but many of those who wrote and ratified the Constitution anticipated that courts would exercise it, and supporters argue that this and other parts of the Constitution reasonably imply it. Courts exercised this power over state laws soon after states ratified the U.S. Constitution. This power over unconstitutional state laws is arguably essential to a federal system in which individual states cannot determine national law, but the power of unelected judges to void federal laws remains more controversial in a democracy because it sometimes elevates such judges over at least the short-term judgments of the people's own elected representatives.

Scholars often trace judicial review to the case of *Marbury v. Madison* (1803). In that case, Chief Justice John Marshall cogently argued that the power of judicial review was implicit in the nature of a written constitution serving as a fundamental expression of the will of the people, and in the power that the Constitution granted to the Court to decide cases and controversies that arose under the Constitution. Who could better enforce the Constitution than an educated body that neither made nor enforced the law?

Marbury v. Madison was one of the most fascinating and important cases that the Supreme Court considered in its early years. The outgoing Federalist administration of John Adams stacked the judiciary with fellow Federalists prior to the time that the newly elected Democratic-Republican Party under the leadership of Thomas Jefferson took control. To this end, Adams signed and sealed a commission appointing William Marbury to a newly created position as a justice of the peace in the District of Columbia. When Jefferson and his secretary of state, James Madison, arrived in their offices, they discovered that the outgoing secretary of state, who just happened to be John Marshall himself, had failed to deliver Marbury's commission to him, and they refused to do so. Marbury asked the court to issue a writ of mandamus—an order directed to an executive official—requiring them to do this.

Jefferson and Madison were still chaffing at Federalist attempts to "pack" the judiciary. Marshall, who was serving as chief justice of the U.S. Supreme Court and wanted to strengthen its power, knew that they were politically powerful enough to expose the weakness of the Court by simply disregarding any order he issued to them. Marshall also observed that Marbury had brought his case directly to the Supreme Court, rather than on appeal from a lower court. Marshall further observed that Article III of the Constitution did not vest the Supreme Court with original jurisdiction in cases such as this.

Thus, while he castigated Madison and Jefferson for failing to do their duty, he ruled that the Court could not issue the writ of mandamus that Marbury had requested because the law, a section of the Judiciary Act of 1789 purporting to give the Supreme Court such original jurisdiction, unconstitutionally violated Article III's allocation of jurisdiction.

More than two hundred years of practice have confirmed Marshall's decision in *Marbury v. Madison*. Politicians and scholars still debate the principles that judges should employ when they interpret the Constitution, and this debate often spills over into confirmation hearings for judges and justices. Some participants phrase this debate in terms of judicial activism or judicial restraint; the former emphasize the vigorous assertion of judicial power and the latter emphasize deference to legislative judgments. Other participants couch the debate as one between interpretivists and noninterpretivists; the former insist that judges should firmly base their decisions on the constitutional text and/or on the intentions of the framers and the latter encourage judges to resort to broader natural law principles or the spirit of the Constitution as a whole.

Judicial Review in Practice

Courts have emphasized different kinds of issues and diverse principles of interpretation in successive periods of American history. Throughout the first hundred years or so, the Supreme Court's most important decisions clarified the relationship between state and national powers and the respective powers of each branch of government. The Court also emphasized property rights, focusing in early years on the contract clause and then on the due process clauses of the Fifth and Fourteenth Amendments in the period after the Civil War until about 1937. During this time, the Court often struck down economic legislation that it considered to be class-based. The Court argued that, in addition to their protections of procedure, both due process clauses had a substantive dimension (the notion of "substantive due process") limiting or prohibiting governmental interferences with the natural laws of the market place and freedom of contract. In *Lochner v. New York* (1905), for example, the Supreme Court struck down a state law regulating the hours of bakers.

After Roosevelt threatened to pack the Court, it made an apparent turnabout in *West Coast Hotel v. Parrish* (1937) and in *N.L.R.B. v. Jones & Laughlin Steel Corporation* (1937). Drawing from a popular proverb, scholars sometimes playfully call this "the switch [rather than the stitch] in time that saved nine [justices rather than stitches]." Shortly thereafter, Justice Harlan Fiske Stone authored a famous footnote—number four—in an otherwise obscure case called *United States v. Carolene Products Company*

(1938). The case dealt with the transportation of filled milk, or skimmed milk with fats other than milk or cream. Although Stone deferred to congressional regulation of such matters, he argued that the Court might have less cause to defer to legislative judgments in three specific areas. The first consisted of enforcement of explicit prohibitions, such as those that the Constitution lists in the Bill of Rights and the Fourteenth Amendment. The second dealt with legislation that "restricts those political processes which can ordinarily be expected to bring about repeal of undesirable legislation." The third concerned the protection of racial, religious, and other minorities, which political majorities might not otherwise protect. Although the Court has in recent years directed renewed attention to issues of federalism and separation of powers, the issues that Stone outlined continue to dominate much of its current agenda.

Over time, the Court has articulated its differential review by formulating three basic standards. In examining most laws, especially those that deal with the kind of economic regulation that so engaged the Court's attention before the New Deal, the Court now generally applies the "rational basis" test. When applying this test, the Court upholds those laws that legislatures adopt in pursuit of a legitimate state interest and that are reasonably related to such interests. When dealing with so-called suspect classes like race, alienage, and national origin or with fundamental rights like voting rights, the right to travel, and freedom of speech, the Court requires governments to carry a much heavier burden. They must demonstrate that they adopted such legislation in pursuit "of a compelling state interest" and that the laws they adopted were substantially related to this interest. Finally, the Court has developed an intermediate test, which it most frequently employs in the area of gender discrimination, in which it applies "heightened scrutiny," without requiring governments to show a "compelling state interest."

By its very nature, judicial review often brings the judiciary into conflict with the elected branches of government. At times courts ease this conflict when they reverse or modify their own judgments, sometimes in the wake of political pressures. The Eleventh, Fourteenth, Sixteenth, and Twenty-sixth Amendments have overturned or modified Supreme Court decisions. Usually, though, Supreme Court interpretations of the Constitution stand, sometimes with dramatic consequences.

Given the difficulty of the amending process, some critics of the courts have sought shortcuts to reversing judicial judgments. The provision in Article I, Section 2, which grants jurisdiction to the Supreme Court "with such Exceptions, and under such Regulations as the Congress shall make," seems to offer the possibility of such a shortcut. Scholarly opinion and judicial decisions—compare, for example, *ExParte McCardle* (1869) and *United States v. Klein* (1872)—differ sharply over the extent of this congressional power. Numerous members of Congress have issued calls from the 1950s to the present to withdraw controversial issues like school busing, prayer in schools, flag-saluting, and abortion from the Court's agenda. In addition to threatening some existing rights, withdrawing jurisdiction from the Supreme Court might also result in a cacophony of opinions in the lower courts.

PROTECTIONS

> **Article III, Section 2.** [3] The Trial of all Crimes, except in Cases of Impeachment, shall be by Jury; and such Trial shall be held in the State where the said Crimes shall have been committed; but when not committed within any State, the Trial shall be at such Place or Places as the Congress may by Law have directed.

Trial by Jury

The third paragraph of Section 2 demonstrates that the founding fathers valued human rights even before they added the Bill of Rights to the Constitution. This paragraph specifies that juries will try crimes other than impeachment, where the Senate serves this function. It further provides that such trials shall take place within the states where the individuals committed the crimes—federal law specifies the trial venue for crimes that were committed outside the states. The origins of a jury trial go far back into English law, and Thomas Jefferson condemned George III in the Declaration of Independence for suspending such rights.

> **Article III, Section 3.** Treason against the United States, shall consist only in levying War against them, or in adhering to their Enemies, giving them Aid and Comfort. No Person shall be convicted of Treason unless on the Testimony of two Witnesses to the same overt Act, or on Confession in open Court. The Congress shall have Power to declare the Punishment of Treason, but no Attainder of Treason shall work Corruption of Blood, or Forfeiture except during the Life of the Person attainted.

Treason

The Constitution lists treason as one of three stated offenses for which members of Congress may be arrested to and from work. If rulers defined treason too broadly, they could squelch legitimate democratic opposition. Thus, the Constitution narrowly defines treason as "levying War" against the United States, or "in adhering to their Enemies, giving them Aid and Comfort." With a similar desire to restrain excessive prosecutions under this clause, the Constitution forbids convicting a person of treason without the person's own confession or that of two witnesses "to the same overt Act." This stiff evidentiary requirement eventually led the courts to acquit Aaron Burr of treason during the Jefferson Administration.

The Constitution grants Congress the power to decide on the punishment for treason, but it limits such punishments by prohibiting "Corruption of Blood, or Forfeiture except during the Life of the Person attainted." This clause prevents the government from prohibiting descendants from inheriting property from individuals convicted of treason, as England and some European nations had previously done.

THE NATURE OF ARTICLE III

Article III is short, but it serves as the basis for one of the world's most powerful judiciaries. More than in the case of the other two branches, the framers created an outline and allowed Congress to fill in structures and powers as necessity required. Although the framers assured judges considerable independence from day-to-day political pressures by granting them tenure "during good behavior" and prohibiting Congress from cutting their salaries, the system of judicial appointment and confirmation, and the possibility that congressional and state majorities can reverse judicial decisions through constitutional amendments, continue to subject judges to checks and balances.

REFERENCES AND SUGGESTIONS FOR FURTHER STUDY

Cases

Ex Parte McCardle, 71 U.S. 2 (1869).
Flood v. Kuhn, 407 U.S. 258 (1972).
Garcia v. San Antonio Metropolitan Transit Authority, 469 U.S. 528 (1985).
Lochner v. New York, 198 U.S. 45 (1905).
Marbury v. Madison, 5 U.S. 137 (1803).
N.L.R.B. v. Jones & Laughlin Steel Corp., 301 U.S. 1 (1937).
National League of Cities v. Usery, 426 U.S. 833 (1976).
Tennessee Valley Authority v. Hill, 437 U.S. 153 (1978).
United States v. Carolene Products Co., 304 U.S. 144 (1938).

United States v. Klein, 80 U.S. 128 (1872).
United States v. Lopez, 514 U.S. 549 (1995).
West Coast Hotel v. Parrish, 300 U.S. 379 (1937).

Books

Henry J. Abraham, *The Judicial Process: An Introductory Analysis of the Courts of the United States, England, and France*, 7th ed. (New York: Oxford University Press, 1998).

Henry J. Abraham, *The Judiciary: The Supreme Court in the Governmental Process*, 10th ed. (New York: New York University Press, 1996).

Henry J. Abraham, *Justices, Presidents, and Senators: A History of the U.S. Supreme Court Appointments from Washington to Clinton*, 3rd ed. (Lanham, MD: Rowman & Littlefield Publishers, Inc., 1999).

Akhil Reed Amar, *America's Constitution: A Biography* (New York: Random House, 2005).

Alice E. Bartee, *Cases Lost, Causes Won: The Supreme Court and the Judicial Process* (New York: St. Martin's Press, 1984).

Lawrence Baum, *American Courts: Process and Policy*, 2nd ed. (Boston: Houghton Mifflin Company, 1990).

Alexander M. Bickel, *The Least Dangerous Branch: The Supreme Court at the Bar of Politics*, 2nd ed. (New Haven, CT: Yale University Press, 1968).

Benjamin N. Cardozo, *The Nature of the Judicial Process* (New Haven, CT: Yale University Press, 1949).

Robert L. Clinton, *Marbury v. Madison and Judicial Review* (Lawrence: University Press of Kansas, 1989).

Phillip Cooper and Howard Ball, *The United States Supreme Court: From the Inside Out* (Upper Saddle River, NJ: Prentice-Hall, 1996).

Archibald Cox, *The Court and the Constitution* (Boston: Houghton Mifflin Company, 1987).

Peter G. Fish, *The Office of Chief Justice of the United States: Into the Federal Judiciary's Bicentennial Decade* (Charlottesville, VA: White Burkett Miller Center of Public Affairs, 1984).

Fred W. Friendly and Martha J. H. Elliott, *The Constitution, That Delicate Balance: Landmark Cases That Shaped the Constitution* (New York: Random House, 1984).

Richard Y. Funston, *Constitutional Counter-Revolution? The Warren Court and the Burger Court: Judicial Policy Making in Modern America* (Cambridge, MA: Schenkman Publishing Company, Inc., 1977).

John A. Garraty, ed., *Quarrels That Have Shaped the Constitution*, rev. ed. (New York: Harper & Row, 1987).

Leslie G. Goldstein, *In Defense of the Text: Democracy and Constitutional Theory* (Savage, MD: Rowman & Littlefield Publishers, Inc., 1991).

Kermit Hall, ed., *The Oxford Companion to the Supreme Court of the United States* (New York: Oxford University Press, 1992).

Stephen C. Halpern and Charles M. Lamb, *Supreme Court Activism and Restraint* (Lexington, MA: Lexington Books, 1982).

Alexander Hamilton, James Madison, and John Jay, *The Federalist Papers*, Clinton Rossiter, ed. (New York: New American Library, 1961).

Eugene W. Hickok and Gary L. McDowell, *Justice vs. Law: Courts and Politics in American Society* (New York: The Free Press, 1993).

J. Woodford Howard, Jr., *Courts of Appeals in the Federal Judicial System: A History of the Second, Fifth, and District of Columbia Circuits* (Princeton, NJ: Princeton University Press, 1981).

Peter Irons, *The Courage of Their Convictions: Sixteen Americans Who Fought Their Way to the Supreme Court* (New York: Penguin Books, l990).

Peter Irons and Stephanie Guitton, eds., *May It Please the Court* (New York: The New Press, 1993).

Herbert Jacob, *Justice in America: Courts, Lawyers, and the Judicial Process* (Boston: Little, Brown and Company, 1984).

Paul Kens, *Judicial Power and Reform Politics: The Anatomy of Lochner v. New York* (Lawrence: University Press of Kansas, 1990).

Edward Keynes and Randall Miller, *The Court vs. Congress: Prayer, Busing, and Abortion* (Durham, NC: Duke University Press, 1989).

Jethro K. Lieberman, *The Evolving Constitution: How the Supreme Court Has Ruled on Issues from Abortion to Zoning* (New York: Random House, 1992).

Suzy Maroon, *The Supreme Court of the United States* (New York: Thomasson-Grant & Lickle, 1996).

Alpheus T. Mason, *The Supreme Court from Taft to Burger*, 3rd ed. (Baton Rouge: Louisiana University Press, 1979).

Alpheus T. Mason and Donald G. Stephenson, Jr., *American Constitutional Law: Introductory Essays and Selected Cases*, 14th ed. (Upper Saddle River, NJ: Pearson/Prentice-Hall, 2005).

John Massaro, *Supremely Political: The Role of Ideology and Presidential Management in Unsuccessful Supreme Court Nominations* (Albany: State University of New York Press, 1990).

Robert G. McCloskey, *The American Supreme Court*, 2nd ed. (Chicago: The University of Chicago Press, 1994).

Daniel J. Meador, *American Courts* (St. Paul, MN: West Publishing Co., 1991).

Joseph F. Menez and John R. Vile, *Summaries of Leading Cases on the Constitution*, 14th ed. (Lanham, MD: Rowman & Littlefield Publishers, Inc., 2004).

Walter F. Murphy, *Congress and the Court* (Chicago: University of Chicago Press, 1962).

Walter F. Murphy and C. Herman Pritchett, *Courts, Judges, and Politics: An Introduction to the Judicial Process*, 5th ed. (Boston: McGraw Hill, 2002).

R. Kent Newmyer, *The Supreme Court Under Marshall and Taney* (New York: Thomas Y. Crowell Company, 1968).

David M. O'Brien, *Storm Center: The Supreme Court in American Politics*, 7th ed. (New York: W.W. Norton, 2005).

Barbara A. Perry, *The Priestly Tribe: The Supreme Court's Image in the American Mind* (Westport, CT: Praeger, 1999).

C. Herman Pritchett, *Congress Versus the Supreme Court, 1957–1960* (Minneapolis: University of Minnesota Press, 1961).

C. Herman Pritchett, *Constitutional Law of the Federal System* (Englewood Cliffs, NJ: Prentice-Hall, 1984).

Jeremy Rabkin, *Judicial Compulsions: How Public Law Distorts Public Policy* (New York: Basic Books, Inc., 1989).

William H. Rehnquist, *The Supreme Court: How It Was, How It Is* (New York: William Morrow & Company, 1987).

Ralph A. Rossum and G. Alan Tarr, *American Constitutional Law: Cases and Interpretation*, 6th ed. (Belmont, CA: Wadsworth, 2003).

David G. Savage, *Turning Right: The Making of the Rehnquist Court* (New York: John Wiley & Sons, 1992).

John R. Schmidhauser, *Judges and Justices: The Federal Appellate Judiciary* (Boston: Little, Brown and Company, 1979).

Bernard Schwartz, *Decision: How the Supreme Court Decides Cases* (New York: Oxford University Press, 1996).

Elliott E. Slotnick, ed., *Judicial Politics: Readings from Judicature*, 3rd ed. (Washington, DC: Congressional Quarterly Press, 2005).

Otis H. Stephens, Jr. and John M. Scheb, II, *American Constitutional Law*, 3rd ed. (Belmont, CA: Thompson/West, 2003).

Stephen L. Wasby, *The Supreme Court in the Federal Judicial System*, 3rd ed. (Chicago: Nelson-Hall Publishers, 1988).

William M. Wiecek, *Liberty Under Law: The Supreme Court in American Life* (Baltimore, MD: The Johns Hopkins University Press, 1988).

Elder Witt, *A Different Justice: Reagan and the Supreme Court* (Washington, DC: Congressional Quarterly, Inc., 1986).

Elder Witt, ed., *Guide to the U.S. Supreme Court*, 2nd ed. (Washington, DC: Congressional Quarterly, Inc., 1990).

Christopher Wolfe, *Judicial Activism: Bulwark of Freedom or Precarious Security?* (Pacific Grove, CA: Brooks/Cole Publishing Company, 1991).

Tinsley E. Yarbrough, *The Rehnquist Court and the Constitution* (New York: Oxford University Press, 2000).

Chapter 5

Article IV: The Federal System

Whereas the first three articles of the Constitution distribute powers horizontally among the legislative, executive, and judicial branches of the national government, Article IV divides power vertically between the central or national government and the states. States had been practically sovereign under the Articles of Confederation, and many delegates to the Constitutional Convention remained quite jealous of state powers. Most could hardly imagine a system in which states did not maintain their separate existence. Moreover, many framers believed that a government that divided powers between two sets of governments was more likely to preserve liberty and provide for regional diversity in such a large nation. Still, many delegates to the Constitutional Convention realized that the Articles had overemphasized state powers and that they needed to strengthen the national government.

THREE FORMS OF GOVERNMENT

When classifying the relationship between central and peripheral authorities, political scientists have identified three types of governments—confederal, unitary, and federal. Political scientists designate the form of government under the Articles of Confederation, like that of the later Confederate States of America, as confederal. In such a system, states retain their own existence, and the central government must operate—as in allocating taxes and raising troops—through these sovereign states. By contrast, unitary governments, like that of Britain or France, have no permanent, or sovereign, subunits. The national authority may create or destroy such political subdivisions at will.

The federal government of the U.S. Constitution fits into a third category that the American founders created and nations such as Canada, Mexico, Switzerland, India, and Australia have since copied. Such federal governments blend elements of the two other forms. Like confederal systems, federal governments maintain states that are sovereign in the sense that the national government cannot destroy them. As in unitary systems, however, the national authorities in federal systems can operate directly on individual citizens, as when they collect taxes or muster individuals for military service.

One key purpose of a written constitution in a federal system is to outline the division of power between the national government and the states and the responsibilities that such governments owe one another. This is the primary function of Article IV of the Constitution. Other federal provisions in the U.S. Constitution include the assignment of congressional representatives to states in Article I; the specification of congressional powers and limitations on state powers in Article I, Sections 8 and 10; the creation of an electoral college for selecting the president in Article II; and the formulation of the Supremacy Clause in Article VI of the Constitution. Further provisions that have refined and altered federalism include the mention of reserved powers in the Tenth Amendment, the limitation on federal jurisdiction in the Eleventh Amendment, and provisions limiting the states in the post-Civil War Amendments, especially the Fourteenth Amendment, and amendments relative to voting rights.

LAYER CAKE OR MARBLE CAKE?

Scholars have likened the traditional view of the relationship among national, state, and local governments in the United States to a layer cake in which the rights and powers of each layer of government are as distinctive as the layers of the cake. Prior to the New Deal, the Supreme Court often based its rulings on the idea that the Constitution created a system of "dual federalism" with clear divisions. Political scientist Morton Grodzins has argued that the reality of modern federalism is considerably more complex—what Grodzins has called a marble cake and what others have designated as "cooperative federalism." Frequently, state and national governments share powers rather than divide them clearly between themselves. As issues have become more complex, fewer and fewer issues have remained purely state and local. Although state and national authorities sometimes clash, more frequently both governments work for the common good on projects as diverse as education, highways, and health and safety regulations.

OBLIGATIONS OF STATES TO ONE ANOTHER

> **Article IV, Section 1.** Full Faith and Credit shall be given in each State to the public Acts, Records, and judicial Proceedings of every other State; And the Congress may by general Laws prescribe the Manner in which such Acts, Records and Proceedings shall be proved, and the Effect thereof.

The Full Faith and Credit Clause

Section 1 of Article IV begins by defining an obligation that states owe to one another to recognize, or give "Full Faith and Credit," to "public Acts, Records, and judicial Proceedings" of other states, subject to congressional regulation. This provision requires states to recognize marriages, contracts, wills, legal awards, and other transactions that have taken place in other states. Because the United States does not have a uniform civil code, questions sometimes arise as to the validity of divorces recognized in some states but not in others.

In 2000, Vermont approved a domestic partners act that gave committed homosexual couples most of the same legal rights as heterosexual married couples, and (in a decision that the state might in time reverse through constitutional amendment) the Massachusetts Supreme Court subsequently ruled that its state constitution granted gay couples equal rights to marry. A number of states have passed laws or adopted referenda indicating that they would not recognize such unions. The second half of the first sentence in Article IV, Section 2 grants Congress power to pass general laws relative to such matters, and in 1996 it adopted the Defense of Marriage Act (DOMA), allowing states to reject same-sex marriages. As homosexual couples move from states approving such unions to those that do not, they will undoubtedly challenge the constitutionality of this law.

> **Article IV, Section 2.** [1] The Citizens of each State shall be entitled to all Privileges and Immunities of Citizens in the several States.

The Privileges and Immunities Clause

Article IV, Section 2 outlines additional obligations that states owe to one another. The first provision uses a clause that the Fourteenth Amendment later repeated. It guarantees state citizens "all Privileges and Immunities of Citizens in the several States." Although scholars still debate whether the framers intended for this clause to recognize additional substantive rights, it most clearly requires that states treat visitors from other states as they do their own residents. Courts have also interpreted this provision to bar states from denying employment opportunities to outsiders, from denying them access to courts, or from preventing them from making property purchases. Courts do not require states to charge the same college tuition or license fees to out-of-state residents, who have not been paying taxes in the state to support schools and public lands, or to extend the right to vote in state elections to nonresidents. In *Saenz v. Roe* (1999), the Supreme Court did use this clause as support for a right to travel.

Article IV, Section 2. [2] A Person charged in any State with Treason, Felony, or other Crime, who shall flee from Justice, and be found in another State, shall on Demand of the executive Authority of the State from which he fled, be delivered up, to be removed to the State having Jurisdiction of the Crime.

Extradition

The second paragraph of Section 2 deals with the process of extradition. Under this provision, if a crime suspect in one state flees to another, the governor of the state from which the fugitive fled may request the fugitive's return. Until fairly recently, courts interpreted this as a moral rather than a legally enforceable duty, thus permitting some governors to evade their responsibility. Since the Supreme Court's decision in *Puerto Rico v. Branstad* (1987), however, judges may order a governor to fulfill this duty.

Article IV, Section 2. [3] *No Person held to Service or Labour in one State, under the Laws thereof, escaping into another, shall, in Consequence of any Law or Regulation therein, be discharged from such Service or Labour, but shall be delivered up on Claim of the Party to whom such Service or Labour may he due.*

The Fugitive Slave Clause

This paragraph addresses another issue related to slavery. Avoiding direct mentions of the institution, the paragraph asserts that persons "held to Service or Labour" in one state and escaping to another shall be returned upon presentment of a claim by "the Party to whom such Service or Labour may be due." Beginning in 1793, Congress adopted fugitive slave laws. Such laws led abolitionist William Lloyd Garrison to denounce the Constitution as "a covenant with death and an agreement with hell." They became an increasingly bitter source of controversy in the years prior to the Civil War (federal legislation on the subject was part of the historic Compromise of 1850). Northerners often translated strong moral compunctions about returning slaves into captivity into personal liberty laws that impeded slave captures, and southerners searching for runaways were not always scrupulous about the rights of free blacks. Because the Thirteenth Amendment abolished slavery, this clause is, happily, only of historic interest.

> **Article IV, Section 3.** [1] New States may be admitted by the Congress into this Union; but no new State shall be formed or erected within the Jurisdiction of any other State; nor any State be formed by the Junction of two or more States, or Parts of States, without the Consent of the Legislatures of the States concerned as well as of the Congress.

THE ADMISSION OF NEW STATES

Article IV, Section 3 is one of the most far-sighted provisions of the Constitution. It provides for the admission of new states into the Union without discriminating, as some delegates to the Constitutional Convention wanted to do, between new and old states. Without such a provision, the United States might have exercised colonial authority over its own West, which could have fostered rebellion.

In *Coyle v. Smith* (1911), the Supreme Court upheld Oklahoma's decision to move its state capital to Oklahoma City once the United States had granted that territory statehood, even though the legislation admitting the state had provided that the capital would remain at Guthrie. The Court wisely ruled that new states enter the Union on an equal basis with the old. It thus assured that they would not be states in name and colonies in fact.

Congress cannot carve new states from existing states without their consent, and separate states cannot join without the consent of all parties. Congress created Vermont, Maine, Kentucky, and Tennessee from previous states that consented. Congress carved West Virginia, whose residents overwhelmingly opposed slavery, from Virginia in a more irregular procedure during the Civil War.

> **Article IV, Section 3.** [2] The Congress shall have Power to dispose of and make all needful Rules and Regulations respecting the Territory or other Property belonging to the United States; and nothing in this Constitution shall be so construed as to Prejudice any Claims of the United States, or of any particular State.

GOVERNING THE TERRITORIES

Section 3 grants Congress the power to govern territories. The extent of this power was a key issue prior to the Civil War. As early as the Northwest Ordinance, which the Confederal Congress enacted in 1787, and continuing through the Missouri Compromise of 1820 and beyond, the national government prohibited slavery in some of the territories. In the *Dred Scott* decision of 1857, the Court ruled that this prohibition violated the Fifth Amendment. Chief Justice Roger Taney ruled that slaves were chattels, or property, rather than persons, and that the law deprived slave owners of their property without due process of law. The Thirteenth and Fourteenth Amendments overturned this decision.

In the twentieth century, Article IV, Section 3 provided authority for the national government to establish and maintain a system of national parks.

OBLIGATIONS OF THE NATION TO THE STATES

> **Article IV, Section 4.** The United States shall guarantee to every State in this Union a Republican Form of Government, and shall protect each of them against Invasion; and on Application of the Legislature, or of the Executive (when the Legislature cannot be convened) against domestic Violence.

The Guarantee Clause

Whereas Section 1 of Article IV focuses on the obligations that states owe to one another, Section 4 focuses on the obligations that the national government owes to the states. The section actually contains two separate provisions, but courts often interpret them together. The first provision obligates the national government to guarantee each state a "Republican Form of Government." Consistent with usage at the time the framers wrote the Constitution, most scholars agree that a republican government is a representative government; Congress considered all thirteen of the original states to have such governments.

In guaranteeing only a republican "form" of government to the states, the national Constitution left them free to change their existing constitutions or even to adopt completely new ones as long as they remained consistent with "republican" principles. Many states have responded by altering or completely changing their constitutions on a number of occasions.

Congress recognizes that a state government is republican when it seats its members. In the 1840s, Dorr's Rebellion in Rhode Island pitted two rival governments against one another. In resolving the case of *Luther v. Borden* (1849), which resulted when owners of a house sued agents of one government who had entered the house of a member loyal to the other for trespass, the Court designated the issue of whether a state government is republican as a "political question," which the Constitution entrusted to the other two branches. This precedent remains good law.

Clearly related to, albeit arguably separate from, the guarantee clause is the provision that mandates the national government to protect the states against invasion or domestic violence. In the latter case, the clause provides for the state legislative or executive branches first to request help. In the winter of 1786–1787, the government under the Articles of Confederation had responded lethargically to Shay's Rebellion in Massachusetts. The framers formulated this provision with this Rebellion in mind.

REJECTED DOCTRINES OF FEDERALISM

However much the writers of the Constitution attempted to formalize and clarify the relationship between the national government and the states, it has generated controversy throughout most of American history. Questions of state versus national power have influenced discussions of such diverse issues as slavery, tariffs, economic regulation, and even civil rights.

Interposition

An early dispute arose over the passage of the Alien and Sedition Acts in 1798. Federalists, who feared the rising popularity of Jefferson's Democratic Republican Party, which eventually ousted them from office in the fateful election of 1800, authored the laws. The Alien law made it more difficult for immigrants, who disproportionately sided with Jefferson, to become citizens. The Sedition Act, in turn, made it a crime for individuals to criticize the government or the president, Federalist John Adams, who was not a wholehearted supporter of the new laws.

In opposing these laws, the second of which conflicted with the First Amendment, the Democratic Republicans had to formulate a strategy that took account of existing Federalist dominance in Congress. They accordingly introduced the Virginia and Kentucky resolutions (which James Madison and Thomas Jefferson secretly authored) in the two state legislatures. It called for other states to "interpose" themselves against this act. However much many citizens from other states opposed the Federalist legislation in question, others refused to heed Virginia and Kentucky's plea for interposition. This specific controversy ended with Jefferson's election in 1800 and the termination of the Sedition Act.

Nullification

In time, proponents of states' rights formulated even more expansive doctrines. The most dramatic development came with the tariff controversies of the 1820s and 1830s. Northern representatives favored high tariffs to protect the nascent industries in their region from foreign competition. Southerners, who exported agricultural goods and imported manufacturing products, generally opposed such tariffs, which Congress nonetheless levied over their protests. In defending their economic interests, leading southerners—most notably Vice President, and later Senator, John C. Calhoun of South Carolina—developed the doctrine of nullification. By this theory, when states confronted laws that they believed to be unconstitutional, they had the right to "nullify" such laws within their jurisdiction and appeal to other states for a constitutional convention; in the meantime, federal powers would remain in abeyance unless the necessary number of states ratified an amendment granting this disputed power to Congress.

Such a theory would have nearly prostrated national powers at the feet of a small minority of states. In describing two famous toasts from the time period, Paul Angle has observed that as against Calhoun's views that "the Union" was "next to our liberty [that is, to states' rights] most dear," President Andrew Jackson affirmed that "Our Union . . . must be preserved." Fortunately, Congress resolved the standoff between these two men and the views they represented with a compromise tariff, but the conflict sowed seeds for the even more radical doctrine of secession. The doctrine was neither completely new nor completely southern because representatives of New England States who had met at the Hartford Convention in 1815 in protest of the U.S. embargo and the War of 1812 had discussed a similar idea, which had largely doomed the Federalist Party.

Secession

According to this doctrine of secession, which southern states sought to implement at the time of the Civil War, the Constitution had created a voluntary compact among the states who were free, singly or in a group, to leave the government when they thought it no longer served their interests or when the national government assumed inappropriate powers. The southern states that joined the Confederacy resurrected some features of the earlier Articles of Confederation and attempted to secede after the election of Abraham Lincoln. Lincoln denied their legal authority to do so and, like Jackson, asserted that his oath required that he seek to preserve the Union.

After the Union defeated the seceding states, the Supreme Court affirmed in *Texas v. White* (1869) that the United States Constitution "looks to an indestructible Union, composed of indestructible states." Although the war and this decision renounced doctrines like interposition, nullification, and secession, conflicts between state and national powers have continued. Southern governors like George Wallace of Alabama and Orval Faubus of Arkansas were among those who resurrected the doctrine of state sovereignty in fighting civil rights advances in the 1950s and 1960s, but modern advocates of states' rights could just as easily use the doctrine to defend freedom as to oppose it.

THE STATUS OF LOCAL GOVERNMENTS

Neither Article IV nor any other provision of the Constitution deals specifically with local governments. The framers probably omitted these entities on purpose. While Americans often value local governments, these governments derive their powers from state governments rather than from the national Constitution. For legal purposes, federal courts treat local governments as state subdivisions, subject to their governance and control. State control over the boundaries and governance of local subdivisions allows them to adopt to the ever-changing dynamics of population growth and industrialization.

REFERENCES AND SUGGESTIONS FOR FURTHER STUDY

Cases

Coyle v. Smith, 221 U.S. 559 (1911).
Dred Scott v. Sandford, 60 U.S. 393 (1857).
Luther v. Borden, 48 U.S. 1 (1849).
Puerto Rico v. Branstad, 483 U.S. 219 (1987).
Saenz v. Roe, 526 U.S. 489 (1999).
Texas v. White, 74 U.S. 700 (1869).

Books

Paul M. Angle, *By These Words: Great Documents of American Liberty Selected and Placed in Their Contemporary Setting* (New York: Rand McNally & Company, 1954).

Samuel H. Beer, *To Make a Nation: The Rediscovery of American Federalism* (Cambridge, MA: Belknap Press, 1993).

The Book of the States: 2004–2005 Edition (Lexington, KY: Council of State Governments, 2004).

John C. Calhoun, *A Disquisition on Government and Selections From the Discourses*, C. Gordon Post, ed. (Indianapolis, IN: The Bobbs-Merrill Company, Inc., 1953).

David J. Elazar, *American Federalism: A View From the States* (New York: Thomas Y. Crowell Company, 1966).

Robert A. Goldwin, ed., *A Nation of States*, 2nd ed. (Chicago: Rand McNally & Company, 1974).

Morton Grodzins, *The American System: A New View of Government in the United States* (Chicago: Rand McNally & Company, 1966).

Alpheus T. Mason, *The States Rights Debate: Antifederalism and the Constitution*, 2nd ed. (New York: Oxford University Press, 1972).

David C. Nice, *Federalism: The Politics of Intergovernmental Relations* (New York: St. Martin's Press, 1987).

Laurence J. O'Toole, Jr., ed., *American Intergovernmental Relations: Foundations, Perspectives, and Issues* (Washington, DC: Congressional Quarterly Inc., 1985).

John R. Schmidhauser, *The Supreme Court as Final Arbiter in Federal-State Relations 1789–1957* (Chapel Hill: The University of North Carolina Press, 1958).

Lindsay Swith, ed., *The Great Debate Between Robert Young Hayne of South Carolina and Daniel Webster of Massachusetts* (Boston: Houghton Mifflin Company, 1898).

M.J.C. Vile, *The Structure of American Federalism* (Plymouth, England: Oxford University Press, 1961).

William J. Watkins, Jr., *Reclaiming the American Revolution: The Kentucky and Virginia Resolutions and their Legacy* (New York: Palgrave, 2004).

Leonard D. White, *The States and the Nation* (Baton Rouge: Louisiana University Press, 1956).

William M. Wiecek, *The Guarantee Clause of the U.S. Constitution* (Ithaca, NY: Cornell University Press, 1972).

Elder Witt, *Guide to the U.S. Supreme Court*, 2nd ed. (Washington, DC: Congressional Quarterly, Inc., 1990).

Deil S. Wright, *Understanding Intergovernmental Relations: Public Policy and Participants' Perspectives in Local, State, and National Governments* (North Scituate, MA: Duxbury Press, 1978).

Joseph F. Zimmerman, *Contemporary American Federalism* (New York: Praeger, 1992).

Chapter 6

Articles V–VII: The Amending Provision and Miscellaneous Matters

If Americans could have found a peaceful way to preserve what they believed to have been their prior constitutional arrangement with Great Britain, they might have averted the Revolutionary War. Absent such a peaceful mechanism, the colonists thought they had little choice but to revolt. Similarly, the provision that required unanimous consent of the state legislatures to amend the Articles of Confederation proved to be a critical weakness that the delegates to the Constitutional Convention of 1787 circumvented. In designing the U.S. Constitution, the framers hoped to avoid the problems they perceived with a constitution like that of Great Britain, which Parliament could change through ordinary means, or like that under the Articles of Confederation, which was too rigid. The U.S. framers hoped to establish an amendable, yet stable, constitution.

Article V. The Congress, whenever two thirds of both Houses shall deem it necessary, shall propose Amendments to this Constitution, or, on the Application of the Legislatures of two thirds of the several States, shall call a Convention for proposing Amendments, which, in either Case, shall be valid to all Intents and Purposes, as Part of this Constitution, when ratified by the Legislatures of three fourths of the several states, or by Conventions in three fourths thereof, as the one or other Mode of Ratification may be proposed by the Congress;

AMENDING PROCEDURES

The Most Common Route for Proposal and Ratification

In *Federalist* No. 43, James Madison praised the amending process as guarding "equally against that extreme facility, which would render the Constitution too mutable; and that extreme difficulty, which might perpetuate its discovered faults." To serve these ends, the framers created two mechanisms to propose amendments and two mechanisms to ratify them.

Congress can propose amendments either by voting on them by a two-thirds majority in both houses or, in a mechanism that the following section outlines, by calling a constitutional convention for this purpose at the behest of the states. To date, two-thirds majorities in both Houses of Congress have proposed thirty-three amendments. The states have ratified twenty-seven of these.

Article V allows Congress to specify whether state legislatures or state conventions will ratify individual amendments. State legislatures have ratified twenty-six amendments. Following the alternative ratification mechanism that Article V outlined, Congress specified that the states should ratify the Twenty-first Amendment, which overturned the national prohibition of alcohol, through special conventions that the states called for this purpose. Not only did such ratifying conventions more closely approximate the method that the framers employed to ratify the Constitution, but such conventions are arguably more accountable because the people elected those who serve in such conventions to deal with a single issue.

Congress proposes amendments by the same two-thirds majority that the Constitution requires to override a presidential veto. Perhaps as a consequence, the Constitution does not specifically require the president to sign amendments before they become part of the Constitution. In *Hollingsworth v. Virginia*, 1798, the Supreme Court affirmed this understanding.

The Unused Convention Mechanism

Delegates to the Constitutional Convention included an alternate method for proposing amendments in order to prevent Congress from monopolizing the process. It requires Congress to call a convention for proposing amendments when two-thirds of the states petition it to do so. Although many more states than this have so applied to Congress for conventions, two-thirds of the states have not submitted petitions on similar or identical issues in a time span that represents the kind of contemporary consensus that the Court has deemed desirable in other matters involving amendments. Calls for a convention to reverse the Supreme Court decisions on state legislative apportionment in the 1960s and, more recently, to propose a balanced budget amendment approached the required number, but the validity of some state petitions was questionable.

Congress has never adopted a law to regulate the calling of such a convention, and many issues related to such a convention are necessarily speculative unless and until the states call for one. Scholars disagree over whether Congress or the states could limit such a convention or whether it could set its own agenda (perhaps even completely rewriting the Constitution), subject to eventual state ratification of its proposals. State representation would pose another thorny issue. Possible alternatives include a system like that of the Constitution Convention of 1787 that granted each state one vote, representation based solely on population, or a compromise solution similar to that which the Connecticut Compromise and electoral college embody granting each state a number of delegates equal to its current number of U.S. Representatives and Senators.

RESCISSIONS AND TIME LIMITS

Although the Constitution is silent on the issue, Congress currently permits states to ratify amendments that they previously rejected. The issue of whether they should be able to rescind ratification of amendments that Congress has proposed but that states have not yet ratified remains controversial. Existing precedents are inconclusive.

The Constitution also does not specify how long states have to ratify amendments. In *Dillon v. Gloss* (1921) the Supreme Court ruled that such ratifications should reflect a contemporary consensus. In *Coleman v. Miller* (1939), however, it decided that this determination was a "political question" for Congress to decide.

Congress has included clauses within some amendments designating the time, typically seven years, that states have to ratify them. Congress placed its seven-year deadline for the Equal Rights Amendment in the authorizing resolution rather than in the text of the amendment and later extended it by three years and three months. Because the required number of states still failed to ratify the amendment, the constitutionality of this extension is still uncertain. More recently, Congress voted to accept state ratification of the Congressional Pay Amendment almost 203 years after Congress first proposed it.

IS THE AMENDING PROCESS EXCLUSIVE?

Are there other ways of amending the Constitution besides those that Article V specifies? In one sense, the answer is obvious. Every time the Supreme Court issues a constitutional decision, it interprets, and to some extent, thus "amends" the Constitution. Over time, congressional and presidential practices also give life to the document. However, it would be odd to list them at the end of the Constitution along with the twenty-seven other formal amendments.

In recent years, two scholars, both from Yale University, have argued for still other methods of constitutional change. Akhil Reed Amar has suggested that Article V only limits agencies of government in proposing and ratifying amendments and argues that the people could propose and/or ratify amendments through popular vote. Similarly, Bruce Ackerman has contended that major "constitutional moments" in American history, most notably the writing of the Constitution, the period following the Civil War, and the New Deal period, all departed from strict constitutional procedures. He says that periods of "higher lawmaking" typically involve four steps—a signaling phase, a proposal, mobilized popular deliberation, and a period during which the Supreme Court codifies the new understandings. He believes such extra-constitutional moments could recur. Scholars argue vigorously over whether Ackerman's description is accurate or whether changes that institutions bring about in an extra-constitutional fashion such as he and Amar describe really qualify as amendments.

Article V. Provided that no Amendment which may be made prior to the Year One thousand eight hundred and eight shall in any Manner affect the first and fourth Clauses in the Ninth Section of the first Article; and that no State, without its Consent, shall be deprived of its equal Suffrage in the Senate.

UNAMENDABLE PROVISIONS

The amending provision contains two entrenchment clauses, or unamendable provisions. The framers designed the first to guarantee the compromise reached in regard to slave importation and direct taxes. The second restriction is practically, if not theoretically, unalterable because it provides that Congress cannot deprive any state of its equal representation in the Senate without its consent. The clause further demonstrates both the importance of the Connecticut Compromise and the irrevocable commitment of delegates to the Constitutional Convention to maintain the continuing integrity and viability of the states.

Scholars have speculated as to whether the Constitution implies any additional limitations on the constitutional amending process. Early in the twentieth century conservative legal commentators and lawyers argued that such implicit limitations invalidated Amendments 15 through 19. The

Supreme Court dismissed these arguments. More recently, liberal scholars have argued that certain rights like freedom of speech and equal protection of the laws are also unamendable.

Such scholars seek to extend yet another level of protection to the nation's most cherished freedoms. Critics fear, however, that judicial attempts to enforce such limits might unwisely transfer power, or sovereignty, from the people acting through Article V to the unelected judicial branch. The Court would undoubtedly find it difficult both to define such limits and to enforce them against the supermajorities that successfully propose and ratify amendments

THE HISTORY OF AMENDMENTS
IN THE UNITED STATES

State constitutions come and go—Louisiana alone has had eleven. Many states also amend their constitutions frequently. By contrast, the U.S. Constitution remains as it was in 1787, albeit with twenty-seven alterations and additions. The remaining chapters of this book detail the various amendments that the people have added to the Constitution.

The first Congress heeded the advice of Connecticut's Roger Sherman and agreed to append such amendments to the end of the Constitution rather than integrating them into its text, as James Madison had advocated. It is therefore much easier to trace constitutional history than it would otherwise be. To date, members of Congress have proposed more than 11,500, mostly redundant, amendments. Congress itself remains the central hurdle to formal constitutional change. Thus, of the thirty-three amendments that it has proposed by the necessary two-thirds majorities, the states have ratified twenty-seven by the required three-fourths majorities.

The people proposed and ratified the first ten of these amendments—which they designated as the Bill of Rights—so close to constitutional ratification that a Supreme Court justice commented in *The Slaughterhouse Cases* (1873) that "they were practically contemporaneous with the adoption of the original." Two other amendments—the Eighteenth and the Twenty-first, respectively mandating and repealing the national prohibition of alcohol—negate one another. The U.S. adopted Amendments 13 through 15 and 16 through 19 within relatively short time periods. The states ratified the last amendment—the Twenty-seventh—in 1992.

Although the amending process has not been as wooden as the mechanism under the Articles of Confederation, it has been extremely resistant to change. The difficulty of enacting formal constitutional change has increased pressures on the courts and other institutions of government to adapt the Constitution to changing times. Although many such efforts have been highly creative, constitutional amendments remain the only mechanism to enact and secure some changes.

ARTICLE VI

Because Article VI is a kind of catch-all, it is more difficult to label than the other articles. Coming just before an article that addressed constitutional ratification, Article VI served as a repository for provisions that did not handily fit elsewhere in the Constitution.

> **Article VI.** [1] All Debts contracted and Engagements entered into, before the Adoption of this Constitution, shall be as valid against the United States under this Constitution, as under the Confederation.

The Continuing Validity of Debts

Paragraph 1 obligated the new government to assume the debts that the Articles of Confederation owed, thus allaying the fears of government creditors. This provision did not, however, eliminate subsequent partisan controversy between Democratic-Republicans and Federalists. The former generally wanted to pay original bond-holders whereas the latter wanted to pay those—most usually speculators—who had subsequently purchased the bonds, often at substantial discounts. Congress eventually adopted the Federalist position.

> **Article VI.** [2] This Constitution, and the Laws of the United States which shall be made in Pursuance thereof; and all Treaties made, or which shall be made, under the Authority of the United States, shall be the supreme Law of the Land; and the Judges in every State shall be bound thereby, any Thing in the Constitution of Laws of any State to the Contrary notwithstanding.

The Supremacy Clause

Scholars designate Paragraph 2 of Article VII as the Supremacy Clause. This clause, which originated in the New Jersey Plan, signaled a departure from the state sovereignty that the Articles of Confederation had embodied. The Supremacy Clause provides that the Constitution and federal laws and treaties will be "the supreme Law of the Land." It further binds state judges to the U.S. Constitution, "any Thing in the Constitution or Laws of any State to the Contrary notwithstanding."

This clause has served as a key support for judicial review, especially of state legislation, and for federal preemption of state laws and constitutional provisions that conflict with the U.S. Constitution. When state judges take their oaths to support the federal Constitution, they pledge to honor it above any conflicting provisions within their own states' constitutions.

The Supremacy Clause also provides for the supremacy of U.S. treaties over conflicting state legislation. *Crosby, Secretary of Administration and Finance of Massachusetts v. National Foreign Trade Council* (2000) provides an example of a case in which the U.S. Supreme Court overturned a state law barring state entities from buying or selling from companies that did business in Burma (Myanmar). The Court decided that the Massachusetts law, which the legislature adopted to express the state's concerns about human rights abuses in that nation, was void because it conflicted with a more comprehensive scheme of regulation that Congress subsequently adopted.

Scholars have raised serious questions about the status of federal treaties under the supremacy clause. The language—as well as the opinion of at least one Supreme Court decision, *Missouri v. Holland* (1920), dealing with the constitutionality of a migratory bird treaty with Great Britain—appears to suggest that, whereas Congress must adopt laws in pursuance of the Constitution in order for them to be valid, the president needs only to negotiate and the Senate needs only to ratify treaties "under the Authority of the United States" for them to have this status. By such logic, the U.S. government might evade constitutional protections of rights through treaties rather than ordinary laws.

More recent court decisions have indicated, however, that the framers included the peculiar language of Article VI relative to treaties not to exclude them from the reach of the Constitution, but rather to affirm the validity of existing treaties, such as the treaty that ended the Revolutionary War, which the Articles of Confederation had approved. Accordingly, approved treaties can no more violate the written Constitution than can other laws. Thus, in *Reid v. Covert* (1957), the Court invalidated an executive agreement with Japan that violated the constitutional guarantees of trial by jury by permitting the trial of civilian dependents of American service personnel abroad by court martial.

Article VI. [3] The Senators and Representatives before mentioned, and the Members of the several State Legislatures, and all executive and judicial Officers, both of the United States and of the several States, shall be bound by Oath or Affirmation, to support this Constitution; but no religious Test shall ever be required as a Qualification to any Office or public Trust under the United States.

Oaths of Office and Prohibition of Religious Tests

Article VI binds all members of Congress, state legislators, and all other state and federal officials to support the Constitution by oath or by affirmation. This paragraph also prohibits religious tests as qualifications for federal offices. This provision applied specifically to federal qualifications and thus initially left existing state religious tests in place. However, in *Torasco v. Watkins* (1961), the Supreme Court used the free exercise clause of the First Amendment to void a Maryland law requiring all officeholders to declare that they believed in God.

ARTICLE VII

Article VII. The Ratification of the Conventions of nine States, shall be sufficient for the Establishment of this Constitution between the States so ratifying the Same.

Ratification of the Constitution

The provision of the Articles of Confederation that required states to ratify amendments unanimously proved to be a weakness. No amendments passed through this difficult gauntlet prior to the Constitutional Convention. Since Rhode Island had refused even to send delegates to this gathering, it seemed unlikely that states would initially ratify the Constitution unanimously. The delegates accordingly provided for the new Constitution to go into effect among ratifying states when nine or more states joined. This extra-legal, or even illegal, provision succeeded. Once nine states signed, the others feared the consequences of staying outside the new Union.

The Constitution further bypassed the requirement under the Articles of Confederation for state legislative assent and instead called upon the states to convene special ratifying conventions to approve the new document. The framers thought that state legislatures would be more reluctant to give up their status as representatives of sovereign states than would delegates to conventions who had no such personal interests. Moreover, influenced by the successful examples of state conventions, many framers equated the actions of such popular conventions with the actions of the sovereign people themselves.

The framers anticipated that the Constitution would achieve greater legitimacy if special conventions ratified it than if state legislative bodies, which the people had not specifically elected for this purpose, sought to do so. Ratification by special convention affirmed the commitment to "We the People" that the framers had made in the opening words of the Constitution's preamble.

> [D]one in Convention by the Unanimous Consent of the States present the Seventeenth Day of September in the Year of our Lord one thousand seven hundred and Eighty seven and of the Independence of the United States of America the Twelfth In witness whereof We have hereunto subscribed our Names.

The Convention Resolution

Many, but not all, versions of the U.S. Constitution append the resolution by which the Convention adopted the Constitution. It indicates that the delegates signed the document on September 17, 1787. Significantly, they chose to date this event as twelve years from the nation's independence that they believed they were furthering. The resolution further indicates that the delegates adopted the document "by the Unanimous Consent of the States present." The signatures of thirty-nine delegates from twelve states follow.

Although it was technically accurate, the resolution, which Gouverneur Morris apparently wrote and Benjamin Franklin introduced at the Constitutional Convention, downplayed two facts. First, since Rhode Island had refused to send delegates, only twelve of the thirteen states were present, and Alexander Hamilton, who thus signed only on his own behalf, was the only one of three New York delegates who remained. Second, while a majority from each remaining state's delegation signed the new Constitution, the delegates were not themselves unanimous. Of the fifty-five men who had attended convention proceedings, only forty-two (including John Dickinson, who had left a proxy vote) remained by September 17. Many had, of course, left because of business and personal reasons rather than because they disagreed with the way that proceedings were going. Of those who remained, however, three delegates refused to sign. They were Elbridge Gerry of Massachusetts, and Edmund Randolph and George Mason of Virginia. Their concerns about states' rights and the absence of a bill of rights helped fuel the debate that followed as citizens decided whether to accept this new charter of government.

REFERENCES AND SUGGESTIONS FOR FURTHER STUDY

Cases

Coleman v. Miller, 307 U.S. 433 (1939).
Crosby v. National Foreign Trade Council, 530 U.S. 363 (2000).
Dillon v. Gloss, 256 U.S. 368 (1921).
Hollingsworth v. Virginia, 3 U.S. 379 (1798).

Missouri v. Holland, 252 U.S. 416 (1920).

Reid v. Covert, 354 U.S. 1 (1957).

Slaughterhouse Cases (Butchers' Benevolent Association v. Crescent City Live-Stock Landing & Slaughter-House Co.), 16 Wallace 36 (1873).

Torasco v. Watkins, 367 U.S. 488 (1961).

Books

Bruce Ackerman, *We the People: Foundations* (Cambridge, MA: The Belknap Press of Harvard University Press, 1991).

American Bar Association, *Special Constitutional Convention Study Committee, Amendment of the Constitution by the Convention Method Under Article V* (Chicago: American Bar Association, Public Service Division, 1979).

Herman Ames, *The Proposed Amendments to the Constitution of the United States During the First Century of its History* (New York: Burt Franklin, 1970; reprint of 1896 edition).

George Anastaplo, *The Amendments to the Constitution: A Commentary* (Baltimore, MD: The Johns Hopkins University Press, 1995).

Richard B. Bernstein with Jerome Agel, *Amending America* (New York: Times Books, 1993).

Mary Frances Berry, *Why ERA Failed: Politics, Women's Rights, and the Amending Process of the Constitution* (Bloomington: Indiana University Press, 1986).

Steven R. Boyd, *Alternative Constitutions for the United States: A Documentary History* (Westport, CT: Greenwood Press, 1992).

Russell L. Caplan, *Constitutional Brinkmanship: Amending the Constitution by National Convention* (New York: Oxford University Press, 1988).

Patrick T. Conley and John P. Kaminski, eds., *The Constitution and the States: The Role of the Original Thirteen in the Framing and Adoption of the Federal Constitution* (Madison, WI: Madison House, 1988).

Wilbur Edel, *A Constitutional Convention: Threat or Challenge?* (New York: Praeger, 1981).

Jonathan Elliott, ed., *The Debates in the Several State Conventions on the Adoption of the Federal Constitution*, 5 vols., 2nd ed. (Philadelphia: J.B. Lippincott, 1861–63).

Michael Allen Gillespie and Michael Lienesch, eds., *Ratifying the Constitution* (Lawrence: University Press of Kansas, 1989).

Alan P. Grimes, *Democracy and the Amendments to the Constitution* (Lexington, MA: Lexington Books, 1978).

Kermit L. Hall, Harold M. Hyman, and Leon V. Sigal, *The Constitutional Convention as an Amending Device* (Washington, DC: American Historical Association and American Political Science Association, 1981).

Alexander Hamilton, James Madison, and John Jay, *The Federalist Papers*, Clinton Rossiter, ed. (New York: New American Library, 1961).

John J. Jameson, *A Treatise on Constitutional Conventions: Their History,*

Powers, and Modes of Proceedings (New York: Da Capo Press, 1972; reprint of 1887 edition).

Sanford Levinson, ed., *Responding to Imperfection: The Theory and Practice of Constitutional Amendment* (Princeton, NJ: Princeton University Press, 1995).

Jane J. Mansbridge, *Why We Lost the ERA* (Chicago: University of Chicago Press, 1986).

Lester B. Orfield, *The Amending of the Federal Constitution* (Ann Arbor: The University of Michigan Press, 1942).

Kris E. Palmer, *Constitutional Amendments, 1789 to the Present* (Detroit, MI: Gale Group, 2000).

Donald L. Robinson, *Reforming American Government: The Bicentennial Papers of the Committee on the Constitutional System* (Boulder, CO: Westview Press, 1985).

U.S. Senate, Subcommittee on the Constitution, Committee on the Judiciary, *Amendments to the Constitution: A Brief Legislative History* (Washington, DC: U.S. Government Printing Office, 1985).

John R. Vile, *The Constitutional Amending Process in American Political Thought* (New York: Praeger, 1992).

John R. Vile, *Constitutional Change in the United States* (Westport, CT: Praeger, 1994).

John R. Vile, *Contemporary Questions Surrounding the Constitutional Amending Process* (Westport, CT: Praeger, 1993).

John R. Vile, *Encyclopedia of Constitutional Amendments: Amendments, Proposed Amendments, and Amending Issues: 1789–2002*, 2nd ed. (Santa Barbara, CA: ABC-CLIO, 2003).

John R. Vile, *Rewriting the United States Constitution: An Examination of Proposals from Reconstruction to the Present* (New York: Praeger, 1991).

John R. Vile, *The Theory and Practice of Constitutional Change in America: A Collection of Original Source Materials* (New York: Peter Lang, 1993).

John R. Vile, ed. *Proposed Amendments to the U.S. Constitution, 1787–2001*, 3 vols. (Clark, NJ: Lawbook Exchange, 2003).

Clement Vose, *Constitutional Change: Amendment Politics and Supreme Court Litigation Since 1900* (Lexington, MA: DC Heath, 1972).

Paul J. Weber and Barbara A. Perry, *Unfounded Fears: Myths and Realities of a Constitutional Convention* (New York: Praeger, 1989).

Chapter 7

The Bill of Rights—The First Three Amendments

The first ten amendments to the Constitution constitute the Bill of Rights. Congress proposed these amendments in 1789, and the required number of states ratified them in 1791. In addition to protecting civil liberties, these amendments provide further insight into the values of those who wrote the Constitution and the controversies surrounding its ratification.

BACKGROUND

Almost as soon as the convention sent the Constitution to the states for approval, the nation split into two camps. Federalists supported the new Constitution, and Antifederalists opposed it. Antifederalists feared that the new national government was too strong and would abuse personal rights. Federalists argued that the structure of the new national government would restrain it from acting oppressively and that it could only exercise the powers the Constitution delegated to it. Despite such assurances, Antifederalists continued to insist on binding the new national government, as they had bound their own state governments, by additional written restraints. Even individuals like Thomas Jefferson, who did not oppose the Constitution, argued in letters that he wrote from France to James Madison that a bill of rights might help secure liberties and could certainly do no harm.

Eventually, prominent Federalists agreed to support a bill of rights if the states ratified the Constitution. James Madison, who represented Virginia in the U.S. House of Representatives, took the lead in shaping the Bill of Rights and getting it through the first Congress. Madison sought to guarantee individual rights without diluting the strength of the new national government. By contrast, some Antifederalists used fears that the government would abuse individual rights as a smokescreen for their more prominent concern that the new government would undercut the rights of the states.

APPLICATION OF THE BILL OF RIGHTS

The provisions of the Bill of Rights originally applied to the national government rather than to the states. The opening word of the First Amendment, which provides that "*Congress* [a branch of the national government] shall make no law," evidences this intention. Most states that ratified the U.S. Constitution already had their own bills of rights. In *Federalist* No. 10, James Madison argued that factions or groups of factions were more likely to dominate in smaller states than at the larger national level. However, he and other authors of the Bill of Rights designed its guarantees to placate the Antifederalists who chiefly feared the actions of the national government. Thus, the same Congress that proposed the Bill of Rights rejected an amendment that Madison proposed to limit the states in regards to matters of conscience.

Altogether, Congress sent twelve amendments to the states for ratification. They ratified all but two. One amendment, which the states did not ratify, related to the size of Congress. The other, which states belatedly ratified as the Twenty-seventh Amendment in 1992, prohibited Congress from enacting congressional pay raises before an election transpired. In his last major decision from the bench in *Barron v. Baltimore* (1833), Chief Justice Marshall affirmed that the Bill of Rights applied only to the national government, and few judges questioned this decision until the states ratified the Fourteenth Amendment in 1868.

Among other provisions, Section 1 of this amendment prohibited any state from denying a person's "life, liberty, or property" without "due process of law." Some congressmen who proposed this language hoped and believed that it, or the corresponding "privileges and immunities clause," would overturn *Barron v. Baltimore* and enable judges to apply the guarantees in the Bill of Rights to the states. Initially, at least, the courts rejected this interpretation. In *Hurtado v. California* (1884), for example, the Supreme Court refused to read the Fifth Amendment provision for a grand jury indictment into the due process clause of the Fourteenth Amendment. It pointed out that, if it so interpreted the due process clause of the Fourteenth Amendment, then the identical clause in the Fifth Amendment would be redundant.

In *Chicago, Burlington & Quincy Railroad Co. v. Chicago* (1897), however, the U.S. Supreme Court applied the takings clause of the Fifth

Amendment to the states via the Fourteenth Amendment. In *Gitlow v. New York* (1925), the Court further applied free speech guarantees to the states and began increasingly to look to provisions in the Bill of Rights to interpret the due process clause. By 1937, the Court had "incorporated" or "absorbed" a number of these rights into the due process clause.

Some observers hoped that it might soon reverse *Hurtado* and simply apply all these guarantees to the states. In *Palko v. Connecticut* (1937), however, Justice Benjamin Cardozo's majority decision rejected this idea of "total incorporation" (the position that Justice Hugo Black soon forcefully and consistently advocated). Instead, he said that the Court would selectively apply only those provisions of the Bill of Rights that it considered most fundamental; in *Palko*, it decided that the Fifth Amendment provision against double jeopardy was not so fundamental. The Court allowed the state to execute Palko despite the fact that an earlier trial (in which the jury had improperly convicted him of second-degree, rather than first-degree, murder) had sentenced him to a life term. Closely related to the selective incorporation doctrine is a case-by-case approach, whose most prominent spokesman was Supreme Court Justice Felix Frankfurter. This approach focuses on whether proceedings in each case were consistent with a "fair trial."

Advocates of total incorporation lost individual battles but essentially won the war. By 1969, when the Court incorporated the right to a jury trial in cases involving possible imprisonment, it had applied all but five such guarantees to the states. These were: the Second Amendment's right to bear arms, the Third Amendment's provision against quartering troops in private homes, the Fifth Amendment's grand jury requirement, the Seventh Amendment's right to a petit jury in civil cases, and the Eighth Amendment's prohibitions against excessive bail and fines. By then, some justices had gone even beyond Justice Black's view by arguing that, in addition to specific guarantees in the Bill of Rights, the due process clause incorporated other rights as well—a view scholars call "total incorporation plus." Still other justices advocated "selective incorporation plus," whereby they would incorporate the most important provisions of the Bill of Rights and other key rights as well.

THE BILL OF RIGHTS: A FLOOR OR A CEILING?

Federal judges and justices have often interpreted and applied the provisions of the Bill of Rights quite expansively. With the transition from the Warren Court to those that have followed, however, the Supreme Court has been more reluctant to expand individual rights against the government. When Supreme Court decisions were almost invariably more liberal than those of comparable state courts, civil libertarians regarded them as a benchmark, or ceiling, beyond which it would be difficult to advance. As state judges have interpreted provisions within their constitutions more expansively than comparable provision in the U.S. Constitution, advocates of civil liberties have increasingly viewed federal judicial interpretations of the guarantees in the Bill of Rights and elsewhere in the Constitution as a floor rather than as a ceiling. In some states, lawyers have more successfully expanded individual rights through their own state constitutions than through the national constitution.

The framers originally borrowed most of the guarantees in the Bill of Rights from existing state bills or declarations rights. The increased attention to state constitutions shows that federalism continues to enhance human rights. States can try new approaches and serve as what Justice Louis Brandeis once called "laboratories."

THE IDEA OF RIGHTS

The framer's decision to designate the first ten amendments to the Constitution as the Bill of Rights requires attention. Americans claimed their rights against England in the controversies that led to the War for Independence. When the colonies declared their independence, they justified their actions as a way of preserving more universal rights to "life, liberty, and the pursuit of happiness," which they believed individuals created government to protect.

Rights are legitimate moral claims, or entitlements. Jefferson identified the rights of "life, liberty, and the pursuit of happiness" as human rights because he believed that they were the birthright of individuals as human beings, whom their Creator had endowed with special dignity. When laws grant such rights against the government, they become civil, or legal, rights. American colonists considered the freedom from taxation without representation to be an essential right of Englishmen. Governments sometimes create certain legal entitlements—for example, the right to receive royalty money from oil drilled on public lands within a state—that might go beyond that which mere personhood requires.

Leaders of many nations fail to honor basic human rights. Recognition and protection of rights is a hallmark of democratic governments that respect their citizens. Americans express pride in the Bill of Rights because it guarantees expanded recognition to, and protection of, such rights and helped clarify the nation's distinctiveness.

Scholars generally agree that rights imply duties, although the U.S. Constitution is relatively silent about them. At a minimum, one's exercise of such rights as freedom of speech and religion requires a negative duty not to interfere with such rights for others. One can further argue that individuals' desire to have the right to a jury trial might obligate them to serve on a jury, and citizens' desires for the right to due process should encourage them to abide by the rule of law.

The framers phrased most rights in the first ten amendments in fairly broad terms. The freedom to believe what one wants may be one of the few important absolute rights. It is absolute because it remains internal. Those who exercise other rights generally find that if they push them beyond their natural limits, they end up harming others. An old adage states that one's right to shadow box ends where another's nose begins. The framers of the Bill of Rights, and subsequent interpreters, have often distinguished liberty from license.

The twenty-seven different rights that the first ten amendments to the Constitution guarantee are political rights. Twentieth-century constitutions directed increased attention to social and economic rights. The constitutions of Mexico and the former Soviet Union, for example, granted such rights as a minimum wage, the right to an education, and guaranteed paid vacations. With these guarantees, such constitutions tend to be significantly longer than that of the United States. Some advocates of such rights have convincingly argued that political rights will mean little to people who are starving, suffering severe economic deprivation, or who lack adequate education. At the same time, written guarantees of such economic rights mean little if the society offering them does not have the will or the wherewithal to finance them, and not all nations that include protections for such economic rights actually protect them. Societies in which governments take on too many obligations are often less productive than those that rely more heavily on private enterprise.

THE PLACEMENT OF THE FIRST AMENDMENT

The First Amendment has a special place in the American mind. The provisions of the First Amendment are first through happenstance, namely, the states' initial failure to ratify the first two proposals. The resulting placement of such cherished values in the First Amendment has nonetheless played an important symbolic, almost mystical, value in the popular mind. The Supreme Court itself has sometimes said that the guarantees in this amendment enjoy a "preferred position" within the Constitution.

Amendment 1. Congress shall make no law respecting an establishment of religion, or prohibiting the free exercise thereof;

THE ESTABLISHMENT AND FREE EXERCISE CLAUSES

Although the Declaration of Independence refers on several occasions to God, the only reference that the U.S. Constitution makes to the Deity is the oblique mention of "the Year of our Lord" in the convention's authorizing resolution that sometimes accompanies the document. Still, especially by comparison to citizens of West European nations, Americans are a highly religious people, and the first two provisions of the First Amendment both relate to the subject of religion.

The initial clause prohibits Congress from making laws "respecting an establishment of religion." Although it might be more accurate to call this the disestablishment, or nonestablishment, clause, most commentators call it the establishment clause. The accompanying free exercise clause forbids Congress from prohibiting "the free exercise of religion." Whatever myriad controversies these two clauses have generated, including the difficulty of defining religion itself, their central aims are clear. The Constitution prohibits a state church and extends wide freedom to individuals to practice their religious beliefs.

Judges and scholars continue to debate the relationship between the establishment and free exercise clauses and differ as to which clause governments should favor in cases where the clauses appear to conflict. Some argue that the framers designed both clauses chiefly to ensure religious liberty and thus advocate keeping this goal paramount. Others think entanglements between church and state pose the central danger and accordingly emphasize the establishment clause.

The Three-Part Lemon Test and the Wall of Separation

In interpreting the establishment clause, the Supreme Court has developed a three-pronged test, which it calls the Lemon Test, and which it first fully articulated in a case involving aid to parochial schools called *Lemon v. Kurtzman* (1971). This controversial test requires that laws must: (1) have a clear secular, or nonreligious, legislative purpose; (2) have a primary, or central, effect that neither advances nor inhibits religion; and (3) avoid excessive entanglement between church and state. The Supreme Court relied primarily on the first and second of these three tests in *Wallace v. Jaffree* (1985) to strike down a newly amended Alabama law specifying that students could use a one-minute moment of silence at the beginning of the public school day for prayer. The Court in turn used the third prong of the Lemon Test in *Walz v. Tax Commission* (1970) to justify a state's decision to continue to exempt church property from taxation.

Thomas Jefferson, who was a strong advocate of disestablishment within his own state of Virginia and a confidant of James Madison who helped write the Bill of Rights, employed the controversial analogy of a wall of separation between church and state. Roger Williams, who founded Rhode Island, had coined this analogy, which the U.S. Supreme Court continues to cite. Some scholars think this analogy helps explain the relationship between church and state in the United States and warn against support of the former by the latter. Others, including William Rehnquist, who served as Chief Justice of the United States from 1986 to 2005, believe this analogy has impeded clear thinking on the subject.

Rehnquist, whose views on church and state were accommodationistic, argued that the government violated the establishment clause only when it attempted to establish a national religion or when it favored one religion over another. He believed that government may favor religion over irreligion. Others believe that the clause mandates neutrality even in such cases. However they differ, neither side of the debate has advocated tying politics to the kinds of acute religious controversies that have plagued so many other countries and have sometimes led to intense warfare.

Application of the Establishment Clause

Relying on the establishment clause, the Supreme Court ruled in *Engel v. Vitale* (1962) that the states may not compose prayers for children to say in public schools. In *Abington School District v. Schempp* (1963) it prohibited such schools from having devotional exercises consisting of Bible reading and prayer. In *Lee v. Weisman* (1992), the Court further extended its ban on public prayer to primary and secondary school graduation exercises, and in *Santa Fe Independent School District v. Doe* (2000) it invalidated student-led prayers at public high school football games.

The Supreme Court has opposed religious instruction, not instruction *about* religion, on public school grounds during the school day. It has denied most forms of state aid to parochial schools, making some exceptions for bus transportation and the provision of secular textbooks under the "child-benefit theory," tax write-offs that apply to school expenses as long as such write-offs apply to parents of children of both public and parochial school (*Mueller v. Allen*, 1983), and (in *Mitchell v. Helms*, 2000) computers and other instructional materials. In *Witters v. Washington Dept. of Services for Blind* (1993), the Supreme Court allowed a blind student attending a religious college to use state vocational assistance monies, and in *Zobrest v. Catalina Foothills School District* (1993) the Court permitted a deaf student attending a Roman Catholic high school to use a publicly funded sign language interpreter. More recently, the Court reversed an earlier precedent and decided in *Agostini v. Felton* (1997) that public school teachers can deliver remedial education to disadvantaged students within a parochial school setting. In *Locke v. Davey* (2004), however, the Court ruled that the establishment clause did not obligate a state to extend scholarships to students pursuing degrees in "devotional theology."

In *Elk Grove Unified School District v. Newdow* (2004), the Supreme Court overturned a decision by the Ninth U.S. Circuit Court of Appeals that had invalidated the recitation of the pledge of allegiance in public schools because it contained the words "under God." Newdow had likened these words to a prayer, or religious affirmation. The majority of the U.S. Supreme Court rested its decision on the belief that Newdow, the noncustodial lawyer/doctor parent who had brought the suit, had not established standing, but some justices wanted to go further and affirm that the words "under God" did not violate the establishment clause.

Although the Lemon Test limited governmental ties to religion, the Supreme Court sometimes bypasses the test and sometimes uses it to uphold legislation. The Court has thus upheld Sunday closing laws, or blue laws, on the basis that they have a secular purpose and effect quite apart from any impact they have in encouraging church attendance. Moreover, in *Marsh v. Chambers* (1983), the Supreme Court allowed a state legislature to continue to hire a chaplain to say prayers at the beginning of its sessions on the basis that historical practice, including that of the first Congress, has validated the constitutionality of such prayers and that they are not as likely to embarrass nonparticipants as prayers in the more restrictive school environment.

The Supreme Court generally attempts to ascertain the legitimacy of state-sponsored religious symbols according to their contexts. In *Lynch v. Donnelly* (1984), the Supreme Court thus upheld the display of a religious creche on public property as part of a much larger Christmas display that included numerous secular symbols. By contrast, in *County of Allegheny v. American Civil Liberties Union, Greater Pittsburgh Chapter* (1989), the Court ruled that a religious creche standing alone on the courthouse steps was unconstitutional, while it simultaneously allowed a thirteen-foot Chanukah Menorah displayed next to a Christmas tree. In *Stone v. Graham* (1980), the Supreme Court invalidated a Kentucky law that required the display of the Ten Commandments in each school classroom, and the U.S. Supreme Court refused in 2003 to accept an appeal by Alabama Chief Justice Roy Moore who had been suspended from his post after he displayed a two-ton monument in the lobby of the Alabama Judicial Building. In *McCreary County v. ACLU* (2005), the Court struck down the framed display of the Ten Commandments in two Kentucky courtrooms while deciding in a companion case, *Van Orden v. Perry*, that a monument of the

Ten Commandments on the grounds of the Texas state capitol was acceptable. The Court thus continues to take a case by case approach.

On other occasions, free exercise rights have prevailed over establishment concerns. Thus, in *Westside Community Board of Education v. Mergens* (1990), the Supreme Court upheld a congressional "equal access" law that provides that public schools open to noncurricular clubs must allow religious organizations to participate on the same basis as others.

The Free Exercise Clause and the Belief/Practice Dichotomy

The First Amendment's "free exercise" guarantee is not absolute. At least since the Supreme Court upheld the conviction of a Mormon for bigamy in *Reynolds v. United States* (1879), the Court has distinguished between religious belief and religious practice. The Constitution protects both, but it permits the government to exercise far greater control over conduct that might affect others than over beliefs, which are internal.

Religious advocacy, or speech, occupies an intermediate category. Courts may restrict governments from controlling its content, but they permit them to adopt reasonable regulations relative to time and place considerations. Thus, an individual has the right to believe in polygamy. Similarly, an individual can advocate legislation to repeal current antipolygamy laws, albeit not in the middle of a busy highway or during a class devoted to calculus. However, a state may prosecute an individual who marries more than one spouse.

Application of the Free Exercise Clause

Litigants often link free exercise claims to other claims within the First Amendment. Two early cases that mixed religious and free speech issues involved saluting the American flag. Jehovah's Witnesses consider the pledge to be a form of idolatry. In *Minersville School District v. Gobitis* (1940), the Court rejected their plea that saluting the flag was an unconstitutional violation of their religious beliefs, and it upheld a compulsory flag salute as a way of promoting patriotism. It subsequently overturned this decision in *West Virginia State Board of Education v. Barnette* (1943), deciding, in an opinion it issued on Flag Day, that governments should not force students to affirm a belief against their principles.

In a more recent free exercise case, *Wisconsin v. Yoder* (1972), the Court upheld the right of Amish parents to withdraw their children from public schools after the eighth grade rather than risk the threat of worldliness. In an earlier case, *Sherbert v. Verner* (1963), the Supreme Court prohibited a state from denying unemployment benefits to a Seventh-day Adventist whose employer fired her from her job and who would not accept other available employment because such jobs required that she work on Saturday, contrary to her convictions. Similarly, the decision in *Lambs Chapel v. Center Moriches Union Free School District* (1993) prohibited a school from specifically excluding religious groups from using school property after hours, and *Zobrest v. Catalina Foothills School District* (1993) ruled that a state could not deny a sign language interpreter to a student simply because that student was enrolled in a Roman Catholic high school.

In 1988 and 1990, many observers expressed alarm over two decisions in which the Supreme Court extended less scrutiny to laws affecting religious exercise than it had previously. In *Lyng v. Northwest Indian Cemetery Protective Association* (1988), the Court allowed the forest service to build a road through an area of national forests that Native Americans regarded as sacred. Similarly, in *Employment Division, Department of Human Resources of Oregon v. Smith* (1990), the Court allowed Oregon to deny unemployment benefits to two Native Americans whose employer fired them for ingesting peyote in connection with longstanding religious rituals.

Even before the Religious Freedom Restoration Act directed courts to give greater scrutiny to laws restricting religious freedom, the Court had in *Church of the Lukami Babalu Aye v. City of Hialeah* (1993) struck down a Florida city ordinance restricting animal sacrifices as improperly motivated by a desire to restrict religious exercise. In *Rosenberger v. Rector and Visitors of the University of Virginia* (1995), the Court subsequently ruled that the University of Virginia, which was state-supported, could not deny funding to a religious publication simply because it advanced religious views. The Court rested this latter decision largely on the doctrine that any restriction of freedom of speech must be content-neutral. On a related issue, the Court in 2000 refused to exempt students at the University of Wisconsin from contributing to student activity funds that went to programs whose politics they opposed. The Court decided that funding such groups would further enhance university diversity.

However, in *City of Boerne v. Flores* (1997), the Supreme Court struck down the Religious Freedom Restoration Act. The Court decided that the powers that Section 5 of the Fourteenth Amendment granted to Congress to enforce the Fourteenth Amendment did not give Congress the power to change judicial interpretations of constitutional provisions, which this amendment applied to the states. In this case, it found no special cause to exempt the property of a Catholic Church in San Antonio, Texas, that wanted to expand the capacity of its sanctuary from normal zoning procedures, just because it was a church. Congress responded by passing the Religious Land Use and Institutionalized Persons Act of 2000, which required the government to extend religious accommodations (subject to the compelling state interest test) to individuals in state custody or to programs receiving federal funding. The U.S. Supreme Court upheld the application of this law, which Congress adopted under the commerce and spending clauses, to state prisoners in *Cutter v. Wilkinson* (2005).

Amendment I. [Congress shall make no law] abridging the freedom of speech,

---

JUSTIFICATIONS FOR FREEDOM OF SPEECH

After delineating the rights relative to religion, the First Amendment guarantees freedom of speech and press. These rights are inextricably linked both in legal theory and the popular mind. In *Palko v. Connecticut* (1937), Justice Benjamin Cardozo correctly identified freedom of speech as part of "the matrix, the indispensable condition, of nearly every other form of freedom." Freedom of speech acknowledges individual worth. Moreover, because the United States is a democratic-republic where the people select their own rulers, citizens need to be able to discuss and write about these potential rulers without fear of recrimination.

The nineteenth-century English philosopher John Stuart Mill argued in the essay *On Liberty* that speech not only served to ferret out the truth, but also helped individuals understand their own beliefs. He argued that people would not hold their beliefs with the same degree of understanding unless others could challenge them. Justice Oliver Wendell Holmes, Jr. further defended speech by using the analogy of the "marketplace of ideas." By this analogy, ideas that cannot survive public scrutiny are likely to be weak. Most Americans probably take a less philosophical view and simply regard the right to self-expression as a basic right that helps make their nation unique.

TESTS FOR SUBVERSIVE SPEECH

Freedom of speech is critical, but it is not unlimited. In an early case dealing with subversive speech known as *Schenck v. United States* (1919), Justice Oliver Wendell Holmes, Jr. offered a compelling example of such a limit. Confronted with a radical who had mailed pamphlets urging potential draftees during World War I to resist the draft, Holmes used "the clear and present danger test" to uphold Schenck's conviction under the Espionage Act of 1917. He argued that while Schenck would ordinarily be justified in communicating in the way he did, the government had the right to suppress his speech because Schenck's interference with the war effort and with national security created a clear and present danger that the government had the right to prevent.

Observing that "the character of every act depends upon the circumstances in which it is done," Holmes formulated an example to show that freedom of speech is not absolute. He observed that, "The most stringent protection of free speech would not protect a man in falsely shouting fire in a theater and causing a panic." Even scholars who contest both whether Schenck presented a clear and present danger and whether Holmes's test is adequate for all subversive speech cases generally believe that Holmes's example shows that free speech is not absolute.

The Supreme Court has applied many tests to subversive speech that were not as liberal as Holmes's. In *Gitlow v. New York* (1925), the Court reverted to the "bad tendency" test, or the "kill-the-serpent-in-the-egg approach." It thus upheld New York's conviction of a socialist under its criminal anarchy law for distributing a little-noticed pamphlet advocating the overthrow of the government even though it did not present the wartime danger that *Schenck* had. Noting that "A single revolutionary spark may kindle a fire that, smouldering for a time, may burst into a sweeping and destructive conflagration," the Court undermined protections for unpopular speech by focusing on the potential long-term negative effects of speech on public peace and safety.

Similarly, *Dennis v. United States* (1951) reformulated the clear and present danger test as a "gravity of the evil" test. Confronting a worldwide communist conspiracy to overthrow all capitalist governments, the Court upheld the conviction of leading American communists under the Smith Act. The law made it a crime to advocate the forceful overthrow of the government or organize a party for this purpose.

Over time, however, the Supreme Court has reasserted the priority position of the right of free speech except in cases that threaten direct or imminent harm. Thus, in *Brandenburg v. Ohio* (1969), the Court overturned Ohio's Criminal Syndicalism Act and the conviction of a Ku Klux Klansman who had uttered racial slurs at a Klan rally and spoken of "revengeance" against government officials. The Court ruled that advocacy would only be illegal when it was "directed to inviting or producing imminent lawless action and is likely to incite or produce such action." In concurring opinions, Justices Black and Douglas announced the death of the more restrictive clear and present danger test.

SUBSIDIARY PRINCIPLES

Courts have developed a number of doctrines to protect free speech and press. Under the "overbreadth doctrine," the Supreme Court routinely invalidates laws that are so broad that they threaten to sweep in protected as well as unprotected speech. Governments must not define obscenity so broadly as to also enjoin speech that is not obscene. Similarly, the Court often cites "the vice of vagueness" in voiding laws that do not clearly distinguish protected from unprotected speech, and it insists that the government use the "least means" necessary to regulate speech.

The Court looks suspiciously upon any content-based restrictions of free speech. It permits reasonable time, place, and manner restrictions but insists that they apply equally to all speeches and not be broader than necessary. Governments might thus prohibit a speaker from preaching in the middle of an interstate highway, or bar sound trucks from a public park in a residential neighborhood, but only if they apply and administer such regulations equally to all. Moreover, although states might reduce littering by barring individuals from distributing all handbills, they can use less embracive means to accomplish the same object without so broadly interfering with speech.

Some scholars of free speech have argued that the First Amendment primarily protects "political" speech and speech of a religious or philosophic nature. Increasingly, the Supreme Court has also protected commercial speech. Even such protection, however, does not give individuals the right to engage in libel, pander obscenity, or solicit individuals to criminal activities as in bribery or murder-for-hire cases. Thus, while expanding political and related forms of speech, the Supreme Court has carved out some areas that it does not believe are part of the legitimate "freedom" the First Amendment protects.

OBSCENITY

The Court has consistently ruled that obscenity is *not* a form of speech that the First Amendment protects. The Court has found it more difficult to get beyond Justice Potter Stewart's honest observation that "I know it when I see it" and devise a clearer test for what is obscene and what is not.

For many years American courts applied the Hicklin Test, which English courts had formulated in *Regina v. Hicklin* (1868). It judged works according to "whether the tendency of the matter charged as obscene is to deprave and corrupt those whose minds are open to such immoral influence and into whose hands a publication of this sort may fall." In such cases as *Roth v. United States* (1957) and *Alberts v. California* (1957), the Court liberalized this standard, but, after experimenting with several tests, some justices, most prominently, William Brennan, decided that the attempt to define obscenity was impossible and that the Court should abandon it.

Newly appointed Chief Justice Warren Burger was determined to not to do so. He successfully mustered his colleagues around a three-part test now known as the Miller Test because the Court first formulated it in *Miller v. California* (1973). In this case, the Court said that it would consider a work to be obscene: (1) if an average person, applying contemporary community standards, would find that the work taken as a whole appeals to a prurient (lustful) interest in sex; (2) if it depicts or describes in a patently offensive way sexual conduct specifically described by law; and (3) if the work lacks any serious literary, artistic, political, or scientific value. These standards have pushed much of the controversy over obscenity back to local communities, but the Supreme Court still occasionally intervenes to see that states do not apply these standards arbitrarily or in a fashion that would threaten legitimate speech rights.

In *New York v. Ferber* (1982), the Supreme Court unanimously voted to uphold laws prohibiting the distribution of materials showing children under the age of sixteen in sexual activities. The Court has further allowed states to regulate pornography through the use of zoning laws.

Still, the Court recognizes that even performances of a sexual nature have some expressive value. In *Barnes v. Glen Theatre, Inc.* (1991), it upheld a South Bend, Indiana, statute requiring dancers at the Kitty Kat Lounge and other establishments to wear at least pasties and G-strings during their performances. The Court reaffirmed this decision in 2000 when it upheld an Erie, Pennsylvania, ordinance banning public nudity and applying it to an establishment known as "Kandyland." The Court justified the law on the basis that its primary purpose was not to restrict erotic expression as such, but to prevent such unwholesome secondary consequences as prostitution and increased crime that often accompanied establishments featuring nude dancing.

Even before its *Miller* decision, the Court had distinguished between the obscene and the merely offensive. In *Cohen v. California* (1971) the Court ruled that a man's display of a provocative four-letter word with sexual connotations on his jacket in opposition to the military draft was not erotic and thus not obscene. Although Cohen had worn his jacket in a public place, the Court decided that passer-bys could avert their eyes and thus did not constitute a "captive audience."

By contrast, the Court ruled in *Federal Communications Commission v. Pacifica Foundation* (1978) that the Federal Communications Commission can consider a station's use of sexual language—in this case the playing of George Carlin's monologue about "seven dirty words"—when deciding whether to renew its license. The Court reasoned that the pervasiveness of the electronic media and their accessibility to children created special needs in this area. The Federal Communications Commission accordingly fined television networks for airing a performance in which entertainer Janet

Jackson exposed a breast during the 2004 Super Bowl halftime performance.

The World Wide Internet system has created a host of problems for would-be regulators who are concerned about indecency. Juveniles can often access the Internet, but the Supreme Court has been wary of reducing adults to the level of the conversation of children. In *Reno v. American Civil Liberties Union* (1997), the Court struck down provisions of the Communications Decency Act of 1996 for being overly broad, and courts are now struggling with provisions of the Child Online Protection Act of 1998. Courts are willing to restrict indecent materials going to youth if governments can enforce such laws without interfering with adult access to such materials. In *United States v. American Library Association, Inc.* (2003), the Court thus upheld the Children's Internet Protection Act (IPA) banning federal aid to libraries that did not install filters to block obscenity or child pornography.

The Court has also permitted schools to impose greater restrictions on both speech and press. In *Bethel School District No. 403 v. Fraser* (1986), the Court allowed a school to punish a student who presented a speech to a school assembly that was lewd but not obscene. Similarly, in *Hazelwood School District v. Kuhlmeier* (1988), the Court allowed a school principal to censor articles about teenage pregnancy in a student newspaper although government censorship would clearly have been impermissible in other settings.

SYMBOLIC SPEECH

Symbolic speech has inspired a great deal of controversy. American courts have increasingly included symbolism within the general ambit of freedom of speech. As indicated earlier, the Supreme Court in *West Virginia Board of Education v. Barrette* (1943) declared that freedom of speech meant that schools could not force Jehovah's Witnesses, who believed that saluting the flag was a form of idolatry, to salute or face expulsion. In *Tinker v. Des Moines* (1969), the Supreme Court further upheld the rights of high school students to wear black arm bands to school to protest the Vietnam War.

In an even more controversial set of decisions in *Texas v. Johnson* (1989) and *United States v. Eichman* (1990), a closely divided Court upheld the right of protestors to burn the American flag. While dissenting Supreme Court justices argued that the flag was a unique symbol that deserved special protection, the majority argued that freedom extended to the treatment of cherished symbols as well as to others. This decision led to immediate attempts, which continue and could ultimately prove to be successful, to reverse the decision via a constitutional amendment.

Sometimes the line between permissible symbolic speech and illegal action becomes quite blurred. Thus, in *United States v. O'Brien* (1968), the Court ruled that war protestors did not have the right to burn draft cards, which the Court classified as government property essential to the selective service system and hence the nation's defense. In *O'Brien*, the Court established a four-part test that it often applies to cases where governmental regulation of conduct has an incidental affect on freedom of speech. Under this test, "A government regulation is sufficiently justified if it is within the constitutional power of the Government; if it furthers an important or substantial governmental interest; if the government interest is unrelated to the suppression of free expression; and if the incidental restriction on alleged First Amendment freedoms is no greater than is essential to the furtherance of that interest."

In *R.A.V. v. St Paul* (1992), the Supreme Court struck down a city's application of the St. Paul Bias Motivated Crime Ordinance to a white teenager who burned a cross on the lawn of a black neighbor. The five-member majority decided that the act, which specifically singled out speech acts likely to arouse "anger or alarm" on the basis of "race, color, creed, religion, or gender," was not content-neutral, but identified certain types of speech considered particularly offensive. The four other members of the Court agreed with the decision but objected to the law on the basis that it was overbroad, potentially deterring speech protected by the First Amendment. While striking down this law, the Court left open state prosecutions under trespassing or related statutes. Moreover, *Wisconsin v. Mitchell* (1993), permitted states to impose stiffer sentences on individuals whose crimes were motivated by hate.

In *Virginia v. Black* (2003), the Supreme Court upheld a law criminalizing cross-burning for purposes of intimidation but rejected the idea that all cross-burning involved such a purpose. Justice Sandra Day O'Connor reasoned that a cross-burning designed as "a statement of ideology, [or] a symbol of group solidarity" would be permissible. Justice Clarence Thomas favored criminalizing all such cross-burnings on the basis that "a page of history is worth a volume of logic" and that the Klan, which had initiated the activity, was a "terrorist" organization.

FIGHTING WORDS

As in the case of symbolic speech, the Supreme Court has carved out special standards in the case of "fighting words." It has reasoned that certain derogatory words, which individuals speak directly in another person's face, are not the kind of rational discussion that the First Amendment protects, but are rather like force itself. *Chaplinsky v. New Hampshire* (1942) is the only decision in which the Court has upheld a conviction under this doctrine, and it has been reluctant to expand this exception. Attempts by some colleges to outlaw the use of certain derogatory terms directed against racial or other minorities has renewed interest in the doctrine. The aforementioned decision in *R.A.V. v. St. Paul* (1992) suggests that many such laws will run afoul of judicial standards that disallow regulations based on the specific content of speech.

LIBEL

Libel is another troublesome area in the realm of speech and press. Libel refers, of course, to the publication of false and damaging information about another. At the time the framers wrote the Constitution, English law did not allow defendants to use truth as a defense in libel suits. Indeed, some English judges regarded such libels as even more dangerous than those that were false. Laws both in England and in the colonies against so-called seditious libel had demonstrated that libel laws that are too strict, especially in regard to public figures, risk interfering with legitimate criticism of public officials. In the notorious trial of Peter Zenger, which took place in New York in 1735, attorney Andrew Hamilton successfully urged a jury to consider the truth of Zenger's criticisms of an unpopular governor in ex-onerating Zenger of seditious libel, and many scholars believe the framers incorporated this understanding into the First Amendment provision relative to freedom of the press.

In *New York Times Co. v. Sullivan* (1964), the Supreme Court invalidated a large libel judgment that an Alabama police commissioner initially won against the *New York Times* and a number of black ministers. They had run a full-page advertisement that contained some factual inaccuracies about activities in which he had participated but that did not mention the commissioner by name. The Court further established that public figures must establish "actual malice" in order to collect libel judgments. That is, they must show that those who published defamatory statements about them did so knowing that they were false or with "reckless disregard" as to whether they were true or false. This burden is so high that many public figures simply do not challenge most scandalous stories about them even when they are false.

COMMERCIAL SPEECH

Believing that the framers of the First Amendment primarily intended for freedom of speech to protect political and related forms of speech, the Supreme

Court did not until fairly recently extend similar protections to commercial speech, or advertising. After striking down a law that prohibited advertisements for abortion in *Bigelow v. Virginia* (1975), however, the Court issued increasingly expansive decisions in this area. In *Rubin v. Coors Brewing Co.* (1995), it overturned a federal law prohibiting advertisements from indicating how much alcohol their products contained, and in *44 Liquormart, Inc v. Rhode Island* (1996) it struck down a state law suppressing information about alcohol prices. Courts have permitted lawyers to advertise via the electronic media and public utilities to mail out promotional ads, but the Federal Communications Commission continues to curb false or misleading advertising.

CAMPAIGN CONTRIBUTIONS

Modern political campaigns are very expensive, and individuals and corporations attempt to advance their views, and gain special access to candidates, by contributing to such contests. U.S. courts have recognized that contributing to such campaigns and spending money on them are exercises of freedom of speech and association.

Fearful both that big contributors might attempt to buy undue influence and that such contributions can give the appearance of such influence, Congress has enacted a number of laws to limit contributions and provide for their reporting. In *Buckley v. Valeo*, 424 U.S. 1 (1976), the U.S. Supreme Court upheld most provisions of the Federal Election Campaign Act (FECA) of 1971, as amended in 1974, establishing a Federal Election Commission, limiting individual contributions, and requiring candidates to record and report contributions above a certain amount. Because it did not believe that individuals could unduly influence themselves by spending their own money, the Court ruled that Congress could not restrict the amount that individuals contributed to their own campaigns. This advantages wealthy candidates, like Ross Perot or Steve Forbes, who are willing to spend on their own behalf. Moreover, since the Court classified campaign expenditures as a form of speech, it also ruled that Congress could not limit a candidate's total expenditures, except when candidates accepted such limits in exchange for partial federal campaign financing.

In *McConnell v. Federal Election Commission* (2003), the Court further upheld most provisions of the Bipartisan Campaign Finance Reform Act of 2002, generally called the McCain-Feingold Act after two of its prominent sponsors. This law attempted to regulate "soft-money" contributions, which contributors spent on campaigns on their own rather than by contributing to them directly. Previous laws on the subject have had frequent unintended consequences, and it is likely that the full implications of this law will also take some time to reveal themselves.

> **Amendment I.** [Congress shall make no law . . . abridging the freedom of] the press . . .

FREEDOM OF THE PRESS AND PRIOR RESTRAINT

The law designates oral speech defaming another as slander and written speech doing the same as libel. Advocates of freedom of speech generally support freedom of the press. Historically, English judges defined freedom of the press as freedom from "prior restraint." Even in cases where a government might later punish publishers for what they printed, judges extended a strong presumption against any governmental attempts to censure publications before members of the public actually had a chance to see them and judge their contents. Largely as a result of Republican critiques of Federalist prosecutions under the Alien and Sedition Acts of 1798, freedom of the press has come to have an even more libertarian meaning in the United States.

Although the Supreme Court has not limited the meaning of the First Amendment to this presumption against prior restraint, the Court has highlighted this presumption as an essential element of such a free press. The Pentagon Papers Case, *New York Times Company v. United States* (1971), is a good example. The U.S. attorney general went to court to restrain publication of a series of papers that critically analyzed American participation in the Vietnam War. Absent a showing that these documents would result in identifiable harms to specific individuals, the Supreme Court denied the government's request for a continuing injunction and allowed newspapers to publish them. The justices indicated that once the newspapers published the Pentagon Papers, the government might still prosecute them if the materials they printed were libelous or if reporters had engaged in a crime to obtain them.

OTHER ISSUES

Two recurring issues that involve freedom of the press concern whether the press should have special access to certain stories and what, if any, other privileges members of the press should have. In *Houchins v. KQED, Inc.* (1978), the Court refused to extend access to a prison to members of the press that the government did not extend to others. Similarly, in *Branzburg v. Hayes, In re Pappas,* and *United States v. Caldwell* (1972), the Supreme Court refused to exempt members of the press from grand jury inquiries about information they had gathered about criminal activity during the course of their investigations. Many states have subsequently adopted "shield laws" to protect reporters who gain such information in their regular course of business, but, to date, Congress has not adopted a similar law. In 2005, the U.S. Supreme Court rejected an appeal from Matthew Cooper of *Time* magazine and Judith Miller of *The New York Times*, the latter of whom spent time in prison until she got permission from her source to tell federal prosecutors who had told her the name of an undercover CIA operative.

In *Zurcher v. The Stanford Daily* (1978), the Court permitted police to search newsrooms for photographs and other evidence of crimes. In response, Congress adopted the Privacy Protection Act of 1980, prohibiting police from making such unannounced searches except in unusual circumstances.

The Supreme Court has generally struck down "gag orders" limiting reporters' ability to report information about an ongoing investigation or trial. In *Nebraska Press Association v. Stuart* (1976), a case involving newspaper reports about the gruesome sexual assault and murder of family members in a small town, the Court noted that there were better means, like a change of venue and jury sequestration, to protect the integrity of a trial. It also observed that unchecked rumors might often do more to damage the integrity of a trial than unvarnished media reports.

Amendment I. [Congress shall make no law...abridging] the right of the people peaceably to assemble, and to petition the Government for a redress of grievances.

ASSEMBLY AND PETITION

Like the rights of freedom of speech and press, the rights of assembly and petition that round out the First Amendment are fundamental to the democratic-republican form of government. Without the right to assemble peaceably, individuals could not hold political rallies. Without the right to appeal to those in power, citizens would lack an effective way of influencing them. As Jefferson indicated in the Declaration of Independence, had George III responded positively to the petitions that the colonists had directed to him, they might never have had to resort to arms. John Quincy Adams cited the right of petition when, in the 1830s, he opposed southern attempts to reject petitions calling for the abolition of slavery.

Courts have recognized a wider right of association as an ancillary right to that of peaceable assembly. The Supreme Court in *NAACP v. Alabama* (1958) accordingly denied the right of the state of Alabama to get membership lists of the National Association for the Advancement of Colored People at a time when opponents often harassed known members.

Freedom of association and assembly do not, of course, apply to meetings that individuals hold for illegal purposes. Moreover, if individuals push such freedoms to an extreme, they may adversely affect other rights. The Civil Rights Act of 1964 thus allowed the national government to use its power over interstate commerce to limit the free association rights of those operating places of public accommodation who might otherwise discriminate against persons of other races. Similarly, in *Roberts v. U.S. Jaycees* (1984), the Court upheld Minnesota's application of its Human Rights Act to prohibit the U.S. Jaycees from excluding women from its meetings. The Court indicated, however, that it might have upheld such exclusion had the group been much smaller and more selective.

In *Hurley v. Irish American Gay, Lesbian and Bisexual Group of Boston, Inc.* (1995), the Court unanimously decided that organizers of a Boston St. Patrick's Day parade could exclude groups specifically participating in support of gay rights, since sponsors had the right to decide what messages they wanted to convey. Similarly, in *Boy Scouts of America v. Dale* (2000), a narrow margin of the Court upheld the right of the New Jersey Boy Scouts to oust James Dale, a former eagle scout, from a leadership position in the Scouts after a newspaper identified him as a leader in a gay student group. The Court decided that forcing the Scouts, who opposed homosexual conduct, to accept such a leader interfered with their rights to free expression and free association.

In another 2000 decision, the Supreme Court decided that California's "blanket primary" system allowing individuals to vote in one or both party contests regardless of party affiliation violated the parties' rights of free association. The Court has yet to decide whether this decision applies to so-called open primaries, in which voters can vote in a party (but only one such party each election) in which they are not officially enrolled.

Amendment II. A well regulated Militia, being necessary to the security of a free State, the right of the people to keep and bear Arms, shall not be infringed.

THE RIGHT TO BEAR ARMS

Few areas of the Constitution have generated more controversy than the Second Amendment. For many years, popular understandings and the weight of scholarly commentary diverged. Individual citizens often view gun ownership as a fundamental right, essential to self-protection in an increasingly violent society and to the sport of hunting. By contrast, many scholars, concerned about the increasing number of both intentional and accidental deaths from guns, have viewed the right to bear arms as an antiquated provision largely tied to the days when citizen militiamen defended the nation.

The very wording of the Second Amendment provides fuel for the controversy. Did the framers of the opening phrase of the amendment design it to limit the right to bear arms to members of the militia, or does it apply to everyone? There is currently an explosion of scholarly commentary on the subject. Much of it is increasingly more supportive of popular understandings of the amendment. Scholars note that the framers preferred a militia to a standing army and viewed the militia as a safeguard against governmental oppression. Almost all writers agree, however, that the right to bear arms is no more unlimited than other rights that the Constitution delineates.

To date, the Supreme Court has been relatively silent on the subject. Its decision in *United States v. Miller* (1939) has served as a fairly ambiguous precedent allowing for state and federal restrictions on gun ownership. These have included the five-day waiting period that Congress imposed in the Handgun Prevention Act of 1993 (the Brady Bill) and the ban on certain types of semiautomatic weapons.

In examining the background-check provisions of the Brady Bill in *Printz v. United States* (1997), Justice Clarence Thomas argued in concurrence that the right to bear arms was an individual, and not simply a collective, right. Some lower courts have affirmed this. When he served as Attorney General under George W. Bush, John Ashcroft expressed a similar view of the subject.

Amendment III. No Soldier shall, in time of peace be quartered in any house, without the consent of the Owner, nor in time of war, but in a manner to be prescribed by law.

THE PROHIBITION AGAINST QUARTERING TROOPS

The delegates to the Constitutional Convention of 1787 did not write the Constitution in a vacuum. In considering the rights that they hoped to protect, Americans kept a particularly keen eye on the abuses the British had inflicted on them. One such abuse, which was especially prominent in cities like Boston, the site of the so-called Boston Massacre, was the presence of English troops and their impositions upon private households. The Declaration of Independence had blamed the British for "quartering large bodies of armed troops among us." The Third Amendment accordingly provides that, in peacetime, the government cannot quarter troops in private homes without the owners' consent, and in wartime, when exigencies may require such housing, the government must do it lawfully. Fortunately, the government has rarely had to resort to such exigencies.

REFERENCES AND SUGGESTIONS FOR FURTHER STUDY

Cases

Abington School District v. Schempp, 374 U.S. 203 (1963).

Agostini v. Felton, 521 U.S. 203 (1997).

Alberts v. California, 354 U.S. 476 (1957).

Barnes v. Glen Theatre, Inc., 501 U.S. 560 (1991).

Barron v. Baltimore, 32 U.S. 243 (1833).

Bethel School District No. 403 v. Fraser, 478 U.S. 675 (1986).

Bigelow v. Virginia, 421 U.S. 809 (1975).

Board of Education of the Westside Community Schools v. Mergens, 496 U.S. 226 (1990).

Boy Scouts of America v. Dale, 530 U.S. 640 (2000).

Brandenburg v. Ohio, 395 U.S. 444 (1969).

Branzburg v. Hayes, In re Pappas, and United States v. Caldwell, 408 U.S. 665 (1972).

Buckley v. Valeo, 424 U.S. 1 (1976).

Chaplinsky v. New Hampshire, 315 U.S. 468 (1942).

Chicago, Burlington & Quincy Railroad Co. v. Chicago, 166 U.S. 226 (1897).

Church of the Lukumi Babalu Aye v. City of Hialeah, 508 U.S. 520 (1993).

Cohen v. California, 403 U.S. 15 (1971).

County of Allegheny v. American Civil Liberties Union Greater Pittsburgh Chapter, 492 U.S. 573 (1989).

Cutter v. Wilkinson, 125 S. Ct. 2113 (2005).

Dennis v. United States, 341 U.S. 494 (1951).

Elk Grove Unified School District v. Newdow, 542 U.S. 1 (2004).

Employment Division, Department of Human Resources of Oregon v. Smith, 494 U.S. 872 (1990).

Engel v. Vitale, 370 U.S. 421 (1962).

Federal Communications Commission v. Pacifica Foundation, 438 U.S. 726 (1978).

44 Liquormart, Inc. v. Rhode Island, 516 U.S. 484 (1996).

Gitlow v. New York, 268 U.S. 652 (1925).

Hazelwood School District v. Kuhlmeier, 482 U.S. 260 (1988).

Houchins v. KQED, Inc., 438 U.S. 1 (1978).

Hurley v. Irish-American Gay, Lesbian and Bisexual Group of Boston, 515 U.S. 557 (1995).

Hurtado v. California, 110 U.S. 516 (1884).

Lamb's Chapel v. Center Moriches Union Free School District, 508 U.S. 384 (1993).

Lee v. Weisman, 505 U.S. 577 (1992).

Lemon v. Kurtzman, 403 U.S. 602 (1971).

Locke v. Davey, 540 U.S. 712 (2004).

Lynch v. Donnelly, 465 U.S. 668 (1984).

Lyng v. Northwest Indian Cemetery Protective Association, 485 U.S. 439 (1988).

Marsh v. Chambers, 463 U.S. 783 (1983).

McConnell v. Federal Election Commission, 540 U.S. 93 (2003).

McCreary County v. ACLU, 125 S. Ct. 2722 (2005).

Miller v. California, 413 U.S. 15 (1973).

Minersville School District v. Gobitis, 310 U.S. 586 (1940).

Mitchell v. Helms, 530 U.S. 793 (2000).

Mueller v. Allen, 463 U.S. 388 (1983).

NAACP v. Alabama, 357 U.S. 449 (1958).

Nebraska Press Association v. Stuart, 427 U.S. 539 (1976).

New York v. Ferber, 458 U.S. 747 (1982).

New York Times Co. v. Sullivan, 376 U.S. 254 (1964).

New York Times Company v. United States, 403 U.S. 713 (1971).

Oregon v. Smith, 494 U.S. 872 (1990).

Palko v. Connecticut, 302 U.S. 319 (1937).

Printz v. United States, 521 U.S. 898 (1997).

R.A.V. v. St. Paul, 505 U.S. 377 (1992).

Regina v. Hicklin, L.R. 3 Q.B. 360 (1868).

Reno v. American Civil Liberties Union, 521 U.S. 844 (1977).

Reynolds v. United States, 98 U.S. 145 (1879).

Roberts v. U.S. Jaycees, 468 U.S. 609 (1984).

Rosenberger v. Rector and Visitors of the University of Virginia, 515 U.S. 819 (1995).

Roth v. United States, 354 U.S. 476 (1957).

Rubin v. Coors Brewing Co., 514 U.S. 476 (1995).

Santa Fe Independent School District v. Doe, 530 U.S. 290 (2000).

Schenck v. United States, 249 U.S. 47 (1919).

Sherbert v. Verner, 374 U.S. 398 (1963).

Stone v. Graham, 449 U.S. 39 (1980).

Texas v. Johnson, 491 U.S. 397 (1989).

Tinker v. Des Moines School District, 393 U.S. 503 (1969).

United States v. American Library Association, Inc., 539 U.S. 194 (2003).

United States v. Eichman, 496 U.S. 310 (1990).

United States v. Miller, 307 U.S. 174 (1939).

United States v. O'Brien, 391 U.S. 367 (1968).

Van Orden v. Perry, 125 S. Ct. 2854 (2005).

Virginia v. Black, 538 U.S. 343 (2003).

Wallace v. Jaffree, 472 U.S. 38 (1985).

Walz v. Tax Commission, 397 U.S. 664 (1970).

West Virginia State Board of Education v. Barrette, 319 U.S. 624 (1943).

Westside Community Board of Education v. Mergens, 496 U.S. 226 (1990).

Wisconsin v. Mitchell, 508 U.S. 476 (1993).

Wisconsin v. Yoder, 606 U.S. 205 (1972).

Witters v. Catalina Foothills School District, 509 U.S. 1 (1993).

Zobrest v. Catalina Foothills School District, 509 U.S. 1 (1993).

Zurcher v. The Stanford Daily, 436 U.S. 547 (1978)

Books

Henry J. Abraham and Barbara A. Perry, *Freedom and the Court: Civil Rights and Liberties in the United States*, 8th ed. (Lawrence: University Press of Kansas, 2003).

Arlin M. Adams and Charles J. Emmerich, *A Nation Dedicated to Religious Liberty: The Constitutional Heritage of the Religion Clauses* (Philadelphia: University of Pennsylvania Press, 1990).

Ellen Alderman and Caroline Kennedy, *In Our Defense: The Bill of Rights in Action* (New York: William Morrow & Company, 1991).

Akhil Reed Amar, *The Bill of Rights: Creation and Reconstruction* (New Haven, CT: Yale University Press, 1998).

Raymond Arsenault, ed., *Crucible of Liberty: 200 Years of the Bill of Rights* (New York: The Free Press, 1991).

David J. Bodenhamer and James W. Ely, Jr., eds., *The Bill of Rights in Modern America After 200 Years* (Bloomington: Indiana University Press, 1993).

Andrea L. Bonnicksen, *Civil Rights and Liberties* (Palo Alto, CA: Mayfield, 1982).

John Brigham, *Civil Liberties and American Democracy* (Washington, DC: Congressional Quarterly, Inc., 1984).

Irving Bryant, *The Bill of Rights: Its Origin and Meaning* (Indianapolis, IN: Bobbs-Merrill, 1965).

Stephen L. Carter, *The Culture of Disbelief* (New York: Basic Books, 1993).

Stephen L. Carter, *God's Name in Vain* (New York: Basic Books, 2000).

Zechariah Chafee, Jr., *Free Speech in the United States* (Cambridge, MA: Harvard University Press, 1964).

Neil H. Cogan, ed., *The Complete Bill of Rights: The Drafts, Debates, Sources, and Origins* (New York: Oxford University Press, 1997).

Richard C. Cortner, *The Supreme Court and the Second Bill of Rights: The Fourteenth Amendment and the Nationalization of Civil Liberties* (Madison: The University of Wisconsin Press, 1981).

Clayton E. Cramer, *For the Defense of Themselves and the State: The Original Intent and Judicial Interpretation of the Right to Keep and Bear Arms* (Westport, CT: Praeger, 1994).

Maurice Cranston, *What Are Human Rights?* (New York: Taplinger Publishing Co., Inc., 1973).

Derek Davis, *Original Intent: Chief Justice Rehnquist and the Course of American Church/State Relations* (Buffalo, NY: Prometheus Books, 1991).

Richard J. Ellis, *To the Flag: The Unlikely History of the Pledge of Allegiance* (Lawrence: University Press of Kansas, 2005).

Mary Ann Glendon, *Rights Talk* (New York: The Free Press, 1991).

Mark A. Graber, *Transforming Free Speech* (Berkeley: University of California Press, 1991).

Frank Guliuzza III, *Over the Wall: Protecting Religious Expression in the Public Square* (Albany: State University of New York Press, 2000).

Kermit L. Hall, ed., *By and For the People: Constitutional Rights in American History* (Arlington Heights, IL: Harlan Davidson, Inc., 1991).

Alexander Hamilton, James Madison, and John Jay, *The Federalist Papers*, Clinton Rossiter, ed. (New York: New American Library, 1961).

James Davison Hunter, *Culture Wars: The Struggle to Define America* (New York: Basic Books, 1991).

Leonard W. Levy, *The Establishment Clause and the First Amendment* (New York: Macmillan, 1986).

Anthony Lewis, *Make No Law: The Sullivan Case and the First Amendment* (New York: Random House, 1991).

Donald S. Lutz, *A Preface to American Political Theory* (Lawrence: University Press of Kansas, 1992).

David Lyons, *Rights* (Belmont, CA: Wadsworth Publishing Company, Inc., 1979).

John Stuart Mill, *On Liberty* (Indianapolis, IN: The Bobbs-Merrill Company, Inc., 1956).

Stephen V. Monsma, *Positive Neutrality: Letting Religious Freedom Ring* (Westport, CT: Greenwood Press, 1993).

Mark A. Noll, ed., *Religion and American Politics: From the Colonial Period to the 1980s* (New York: Oxford University Press, 1990).

David M. O'Brien, *Constitutional Law and Politics, Vol. 2, Civil Rights and Liberties*, 4th ed. (New York: W.W. Norton, 2000).

Robert S. Peck, *The Bill of Rights and the Politics of Interpretation* (St. Paul, MN: West Publishing Company, 1992).

Shawn F. Peters, *Judging Jehovah's Witnesses: Religious Persecution and the Dawn of the Rights Revolution* (Laurence: University Press of Kansas, 2000).

Lucas A. Powe, Jr., *The Fourth Estate and the Constitution: Freedom of the Press in America* (Berkeley: University of California Press, 1991).

C. Herman Pritchett, *Constitutional Civil Liberties* (Englewood Cliffs, NJ: Prentice-Hall, 1984).

A. James Reichley, *Religion in American Public Life* (Washington, DC: The Brookings Institution, 1985).

John Philip Reid, *Constitutional History of the American Revolution: The Authority of Rights* (Madison: University of Wisconsin Press, 1986).

Robert A. Rutland, *The Birth of the Bill of Rights, 1776–1791* (Chapel Hill: University of North Carolina Press, 1955).

Ellis Sandoz, *Conceived in Liberty: American Individual Rights Today* (North Scituate, MA: Duxberry Press, 1978).

David Schultz and John R. Vile, eds., *The Encyclopedia of Civil Liberties in America*, 3 vols. (Armonk, NY: M.E. Sharpe, 2005).

Bernard Schwartz, *A History of the American Bill of Rights* (New York: Oxford University Press, 1977).

Bernard Schwartz, ed., *The Roots of the Bill of Rights*, 5 vols. (New York: Chelsea House, 1980).

Steven H. Shiffrin and Jesse H. Choper, *The First Amendment: Cases—Comments—Questions* (St. Paul, MN: West Publishing Company, 1991).

Rodney A. Smolla, *Jerry Falwell v. Larry Flint: The First Amendment on Trial* (New York: St. Martin's Press, 1988).

Rodney A. Smolla, *Suing the Press: Libel, the Media and Power* (New York: Oxford University Press, 1986).

Frank J. Sorauf, *The Wall of Separation: The Constitutional Politics of Church and State* (Princeton, NJ: Princeton University Press, 1976).

Robert J. Spitzer, *The Politics of Gun Control* (Chatham, NJ: Chatham House Publishers, Inc., 1995).

Herbert J. Storing, *What the Anti-Federalists Were For: The Political Thought of the Opponents of the Constitution* (Chicago: The University of Chicago Press, 1981).

Wayne R. Swanson, *The Christ Child Goes to Court* (Philadelphia: Temple University Press, 1990).

Thomas L. Tedford, *Freedom of Speech in the United States* (New York: Random House, 1985).

Sanford J. Unger, *The Papers and the Papers* (New York: E.P. Dulton, 1972).

Melvin I. Urofsky, *The Continuity of Change: The Supreme Court and Individual Liberties, 1953–1986* (Belmont, CA: Wadsworth Publishing Company, 1991).

William W. Van Alstyne, *Interpretations of the First Amendment* (Durham, NC: Duke University Press, 1984).

Helen E. Veit, Kenneth R. Bowling, and Charles Bickford, *Creating the Bill of Rights* (Baltimore, MD: The Johns Hopkins University Press, 1991).

Chapter 8

The Bill of Rights and the Rights of the Accused—Amendments 4–7

The U.S. Supreme Court has ruled relatively rarely on the Second and Third Amendments. By contrast, it has frequently issued decisions on the four amendments that followed. They deal chiefly, albeit not exclusively, with the rights of individuals suspected of, or on trial for, wrongdoing.

> **Amendment IV.** The right of the people to be secure in their persons, houses, papers, and effects, against unreasonable searches and seizures, shall not be violated, and no Warrants shall issue, but upon probable cause, supported by Oath or affirmation, and particularly describing the place to be searched, and the persons or things to be seized.

UNREASONABLE SEARCHES AND SEIZURES

Like the Third Amendment, the Fourth rests implicitly on the hallowed principle of English common law (law developed and applied by judges) that one's home is one's castle. Although the Constitution refers to "private" property in the Fifth and Fourteenth Amendments, it does not explicitly use the term "privacy," but the Fourth Amendment arguably points toward this right. As in the case of the Third Amendment, the framers crafted the Fourth Amendment mindful of specific British abuses. In attempts to detect tax fraud and smuggling, British agents often swept down on suspects with general warrants, which remained valid throughout the life of the monarch who issued them. These gave agents practically unlimited authority to search and stimulated great colonial resentment. The Fourth Amendment thus protected the security of "persons, houses, papers, and effects, against unreasonable searches and seizures."

This language does not specifically define what "unreasonable" means. There is an obvious link to the second half of the amendment that provides for courts to issue search warrants since the framers designed such warrants to winnow out unreasonable searches. Courts have decided, however, that some warrantless searches are neither unreasonable nor unconstitutional. Thus, in *Terry v. Ohio* (1968), the Supreme Court allowed police officers to "stop and frisk" individuals they suspected might be carrying concealed weapons with which they might threaten the officers or the public. Similarly, the Court permits police to seize contraband in "plain view" or in "open fields" without warrants and to conduct searches when individuals consent to them. Judges also permit police to search vehicles whose drivers might depart before they return with a warrant, they allow governments to introduce evidence that police obtain in "hot pursuit" of a suspect, and they allow police to conduct searches where suspects consent to them.

Despite such exceptions, American courts generally expect police officers to obtain warrants to establish the reasonableness of their searches. The Supreme Court has even extended this requirement to electronic eavesdropping and wiretapping. In *Olmstead v. United States* (1928), the Court decided that words over a phone line were not physical things such as the Fourth Amendment described, and that police could therefore use such evidence obtained without warrants as long as they did not use force or physically penetrate the buildings in trespass actions. In subsequent cases like *Katz v. United States* (1967), however, the Supreme Court decided that the framers designed the Fourth Amendment to "protect people, not places," and that police had to obtain warrants for wiretaps even when they neither used force nor physically penetrated phone lines.

In a concurring opinion Justice John M. Harlan indicated that in privacy cases, the Court would ask whether a person exhibited an expectation of privacy and whether that privacy was reasonable. Applying such a test in *Kyllo v. United States* (2001), the Supreme Court invalidated the police use of a heat-seeking device to detect possible drug-growing in a private home without a search warrant. As in the case of electronic eavesdropping, the Court ruled that the Fourth Amendment intended to protect citizens in private residences even from equipment that did not invade the house's physical space.

With a view to past English abuses, the Fourth Amendment does not permit governments to issue general warrants, or so-called writs of assistance, which grant officers broad and unspecified powers to search wherever they please. Rather, warrants must particularly describe, "the place to be searched, and the persons or things to be seized." A police officer with a warrant to search for an illegal bazooka has no authority to lift the lid of an opaque cookie jar. By the same token, an officer who stumbles across a bazooka while executing a warrant for drugs—a case of "plain view"— could use this as the valid product of his search.

To get a warrant, an officer must appear before a neutral judge or magistrate—although, surprisingly, the Fourth Amendment does not precisely say so—and establish under "Oath or affirmation" what the Constitution calls "probable cause." As this phrase suggests, probable cause requires police to operate on more than mere suspicion. The amendment prohibits them from going on "fishing expeditions" that invade personal privacy every time they suspect that someone has violated the law.

Administrative Searches

The framers primarily intended for the Fourth Amendment to restrain police conduct. Increasingly, however, supervisors and employers also conduct searches at offices and places of employment, and administrative officials charged with maintaining public health and safety or accounting for governmental expenditures conduct searches of homes or businesses. In such cases, courts attempt to balance private and public interests, ascertaining the necessity of warrants by the nature of the search or establishment and whether the individual has a reasonable expectation of privacy in such locations. Thus, in *Wyman v. James* (1971), the Supreme Court decided that the state could deny benefits to a welfare recipient who refused to allow a social worker to search her home and check on her son without a warrant. Similarly, in *New Jersey v. T.L.O.* (1985), it ruled that a high school principal could search the purse of a student whom he reasonably suspected of possessing drugs.

A number of cases have upheld mandatory drug-testing programs. In *National Treasury Employees v. Von Raab* (1989), the Supreme Court upheld such a program for employees of the U.S. Customs Program, and in *Skinner v. Railway Labor Executives' Association* (1989), it sustained such provisions for railway employees who have been involved in accidents. In *Veronia School District 47J v. Acton* (1995), the Court supported random drug-testing of student athletes, and in *Board of Education of Earls* (2002), it approved a school district's decision to extend such tests to all students participating in extracurricular activities.

THE EXCLUSIONARY RULE

The Fourth Amendment does not specify what will happen when officers of the law violate the amendment and make unreasonable searches and seizures or conduct general searches without probable cause. One possible remedy is for victims to initiate civil actions against the officers involved in the illegal activity. Victims often find it difficult to win such cases, however, and monetary compensation may provide little relief for persons emotionally traumatized by an illegal search.

Recognizing such problems, courts have enforced the exclusionary rule. The Supreme Court applied this rule to the national government in *Weeks v. United States* (1914) and to the states in *Mapp v. Ohio* (1961). It prohibits prosecutors from introducing evidence at trials that officers have seized illegally. Although such exclusion does not void the original intrusion into privacy, judges have enforced this law both to deter future illegal conduct and to keep courts free of the taint of wrongdoing. More negatively, the exclusionary rule sometimes excludes probative evidence and allows guilty individuals to go free.

Critics have not succeeded in eliminating the rule, but courts have limited its application in a number of circumstances. In *Nix v. Williams* (1984), for example, the Supreme Court established an "inevitable discovery" exception. In this case the justices ruled that prosecutors could introduce the body of a ten-year-old murder victim. Although her murderer had taken officers to the scene as the result of what the courts later decided was an improperly obtained confession, search parties were in the vicinity, the victim's body was in plain view, and, since the weather was freezing, searchers would almost surely have discovered the body in pretty much the same condition as the officers found it. Similarly, in *United States v. Leon* (1984) and *Massachusetts v. Sheppard* (1984), the Court established a "good faith" exception to the exclusionary rule, which exempted officers from responsibility for flaws in warrants when they acted in "good faith."

Amendment V. No person shall be held to answer for a capital, or otherwise infamous crime, unless on a presentment or indictment of a Grand Jury, except in cases arising in the land or naval forces, or in the Militia, when in actual service in time of War or public danger;

INDICTMENT BY GRAND JURY

Scholars often describe the Fifth Amendment as protecting the rights of criminal defendants, but since governments can accuse anyone of crimes, the amendment actually extends to all citizens. The American legal system is accusatorial rather than inquisitorial. The framers based both the Fifth and Sixth Amendments on the presumption that an individual is legally innocent until proven guilty, and that it is better for many guilty individuals to go free than to convict an innocent person. More fundamentally, these amendments recognize that individuals do not cease to be persons who are entitled to humane treatment even when courts convict them of breaking the law.

The first part of the Fifth Amendment provides grand jury indictments in cases involving a possible death penalty ("capital cases") and in trials for other "infamous crimes," other than those arising in the military in cases of war or public danger, which fall under congressional regulatory power under Article I, Section 8. Whereas petit juries decide on guilt or innocence and on appropriate penalties, grand juries decide whether the government has presented sufficient evidence to proceed with a prosecution. The framers mandated such juries to shield individuals from venal or overzealous prosecutors.

Because laypersons often find it difficult to challenge a professional prosecutor's judgment, law professors and commentators sometimes quip that prosecutors can convince jurors to indict a ham sandwich! Perhaps as a consequence, the grand jury requirement remains one of the few provisions of the Bill of Rights that the Supreme Court has not applied to the states through the due process clause of the Fourteenth Amendment. Some states still use a system of "information" whereby prosecutors secure indictments simply by presenting formal written charges to a judge.

Amendment V. nor shall any person be subject for the same offence to be twice put in jeopardy of life or limb;

THE DOUBLE JEOPARDY PROVISION

The Fifth Amendment contains the double jeopardy clause. It prohibits the government from retrying individuals for crimes for which courts have already exonerated them. Without this provision, prosecutors could wear down defendants with legal costs and court appearances even after courts had declared them not guilty.

This provision does not bar separate state and federal prosecutions in cases where a crime violates laws in both. Similarly, courts permit retrials in cases of a hung (divided) jury, or in cases where judges voided an initial verdict because of it relied on illegally seized evidence or involved some other prosecutorial indiscretion. Thus, after the Supreme Court voided Gideon's conviction in *Gideon v. Wainwright* (1963), because Florida had denied him state-funded counsel, the state tried him in a second trial, which declared him not guilty. More recently, Mississippi retried, convicted, and jailed Byron de Le Beckwith on the basis of new evidence in the murder of civil rights leader Medgar Evers after two earlier juries had failed to reach a verdict. Similarly, in June of 2005, a Mississippi jury found Edgar Ray Killen guilty of manslaughter in the 1964 slaying of civil rights workers James Chaney, Andrew Goodman, and Michael Schwerner (depicted in the movie *Mississippi Burning*), even though a jury in 1967 had deadlocked on charges that he had violated their civil rights. In *Sattazahn v. Pennsylvania* (2003), the Supreme Court ruled that when a defendant appeals a murder conviction and gets a new trial, the second court may impose a death penalty even when the first imposed a lighter sentence.

Amendment V. nor shall be compelled in any criminal case to be a witness against himself,

---

PROTECTION AGAINST SELF-INCRIMINATION

Criminal defendants sometimes "take the Fifth," and refuse to testify against themselves. The Fifth Amendment applies this guarantee only to criminal cases. Thus, although O. J. Simpson did not take the stand in his criminal trial for murder, for which the court exonerated him, a court subsequently required him to testify in the civil action that the victims' families initiated, and that he lost.

The requirement that the government, rather than the accused, must establish its case is the essence of an accusatorial, rather than an inquisitorial, system. The Amendment also protects the rights of innocent individuals who may not come across as believable in court. Current laws prevent prosecutors from adversely commenting on individuals' decisions to exercise their rights. Defendants cannot exercise their Fifth Amendment rights on a selective basis. They may choose to testify or not, but once on the stand, they cannot individually select which questions they would decline to answer for fear of incriminating themselves. A defendant's decision whether or not to testify is critical to the outcome of many cases.

Courts have extended Fifth Amendment protections to congressional hearings where individuals are under oath. Thus when Oliver North testified in hearings about whether he had illegally arranged for an arms-for-hostages deal in the Reagan Administration by diverting money from Latin America to the Middle East, North demanded immunity for any incriminating testimony. Courts later invalidated his conviction on the basis that the special prosecutor had improperly gleaned information from the hearings.

Although its constitutional grounding is somewhat less certain (scholars frequently tie it to the next provision dealing with "due process"), courts will sometimes invalidate convictions when they believe that governments have "entrapped" individuals in crimes that they would not have committed without government encouragement. *Jacobson v. United States* (1992) illustrates such a situation. After finding that Jacobson had once ordered a publication, then legal, that depicted juvenile boys in various sexual poses, government agencies solicited Jacobson for more than two years before he finally ordered a pornographic publication that the Child Protection Act of 1984 made it illegal to possess. The Court majority concluded that although Jacobson had shown a previous disposition to view such pornography, he had not demonstrated a prior willingness to break the law in order to do so. The government could not both plant a disposition within an individual and then prosecute that individual for it. The government can, and does, sometimes engage in "sting" operations to catch those, including government officials, with prior dispositions to specific illegal activity, like accepting bribes.

Amendment V. nor [shall any person] be deprived of life, liberty, or property, without due process of law;

THE DUE PROCESS CLAUSE

The clause prohibiting the government from depriving anyone of "life, liberty, or property, without due process of law" is one of the most important in the entire Constitution. Ronald Dworkin argues in *Law's Empire* that the Constitution contains some very specific provisions, or conceptions, and other more general concepts, or principles. The due process clause falls in the latter category. Whereas judges can ascertain relatively easily whether a government has indicted an individual by a grand jury or subjected the individual to double jeopardy, they find it harder to decide whether a government has accorded that individual due process of law. This is because the clause points beyond specified procedures to more general notions of fairness.

When framers of the Fourteenth Amendment later sought to defend the rights of the newly freed slaves, they employed similar language. In an ironic development, the Court subsequently read an equal protection component into the due process clause. *Bolling v. Sharpe* (1954) thus applied the same requirements for racial desegregation to the District of Columbia, where the national government had jurisdiction, that *Brown v. Board of Education* (1954), had applied to the states.

Amendment V. nor shall private property be taken for public use, without just compensation.

THE TAKINGS CLAUSE

The last provision of the Fifth Amendment shifts its focus from criminal defendants to those who have property that the state desires to use for a public purpose. The United States has a capitalistic economy, or free enterprise system, in which private individuals own most property, but property rights are not absolute. The story in the Old Testament, or Hebrew Scriptures, of King Ahab and Queen Jezebel and their actions in taking Naboth's vineyard illustrates how rulers can commit injustice when they covet property that belongs to others. Most countries recognize a right of eminent domain in cases where governments need land to build roads, create public parks, or the like. Some communist governments have simply expropriated property without compensation, often branding its owners as enemies of the people for their wealth and/or class status. The last provision of the Fifth Amendment assures that the U.S. government must provide just compensation for such takings.

The Supreme Court interprets the "public use" provision relatively broadly as "public purpose." In *Berman v. Parker* (1954), the Court allowed the District of Columbia to condemn blighted slum property to sell to private developers for beautification. Similarly, confronting a situation tied to the state's feudal past in which a few individuals owned much of the land in the state, in *Hawaii Housing Authority v. Midkiff* (1984), the Court allowed the Hawaii legislature to condemn property owned by lessors and sell it to families who had been leasing such property and wanted to buy it. More recently, in *Kelo v. New London* (2005), the Court allowed a city to condemn houses that were not themselves blighted but that were part of a larger area that the city had slated for private industrial development.

As governments have enacted more environmental and land use regulations, property owners have looked increasingly to the takings clause to provide some limits. In *Nollan v. California Coastal Commission* (1987), California homeowners successfully fought a state attempt to force them to grant uncompensated public access to their beachfront property as a condition for building a new house on the property. Similarly, in *Lucas v. South Carolina Council* (1992), the Supreme Court ruled that if a South Carolina regulation prohibiting a property owner from building on an expensive beachfront lot had in fact made the land practically worthless for its intended purpose, it constituted a regulatory taking for which the government would have to provide compensation.

Amendment VI. In all criminal prosecutions, the accused shall enjoy the right to a speedy and public trial....

SPEEDY AND PUBLIC TRIALS

The Sixth Amendment focuses on the rights of such criminal defendants at trial. The amendment specifies that such trials will be both "speedy and public." In *Barker v. Wingo* (1972), the U.S. Supreme Court refused to set a precise time for governments to initiate trials but focused instead on four factors—the delay's length, the reason for it, when the defendant had begun asserting the right to a speedy trial, and whether the delay prejudiced the defendant's case. In *Barker*, the Court refused to strike a conviction that it took prosecutors five years to take to trial. Congress subsequently adopted the Speedy Trial Act of 1974. It requires the federal government to indict (charge) individuals within thirty days of their arrest, arraign them (that is, give them a chance to offer a plea) within ten days after indicting them, and try them within sixty days of the arraignment.

Courts have interpreted the right to a "public" trial as a right of the defendant to claim rather than for the public. In *Gannett Co. v. DePasquale* (1979), the Court thus permitted the court to close a pretrial hearing, when all parties agreed. Focusing on the First Amendment rights of the press and the public to information, however, in *Richmond Newspapers v. Virginia* (1980), the Court invalidated an attempt to close an entire criminal trial, and subsequent cases, for example *Press-Enterprise Co. v. Superior Court of California* (1986), have largely overturned the *Gannett* ruling on pretrial hearings on First Amendment grounds.

Amendment VI. [In all criminal prosecutions, the accused shall enjoy the right to a speedy and public trial,] by an impartial jury of the State and district wherein the crime shall have been committed; which district shall have been previously ascertained by law,

---

RIGHT TO A PETIT JURY

The most important provision of the Sixth Amendment guarantees individuals the right to a trial by an impartial jury. It further specifies that the government will draw the jury from the district where the crime was committed. This does not prohibit defendants from requesting a change of venue (location) in cases where they think a fair trial is impossible in their own districts.

The Sixth Amendment guarantees a petit jury, which determines guilt or innocence and/or recommends an appropriate penalty. The petit jury is deeply rooted in English common law. The English considered it to be a good way of pooling collective wisdom and deterring abuse by governmental officials. In *Democracy in America*, Alexis de Tocqueville, the astute French observer of nineteenth-century America, also argued that such juries serve an important educative function, familiarizing citizens with the laws and giving them input into their application.

Although a twelve-member jury was standard under English law, the Constitution neither explicitly requires a jury to have this precise number of individuals, nor specifically mandates juries to render unanimous verdicts. The Supreme Court has permitted states to innovate in both areas in recent years. Thus, in *Williams v. Florida* (1970), the Court upheld the use of six-person juries in noncapital cases—later rejecting juries of five in *Ballew v. Georgia* (1978) and verdicts of 5 to 1 in *Burch v. Louisiana* (1979). In earlier decisions in *Johnson v. Louisiana* (1972) and *Apodaca v. Oregon* (1972), the Court had already allowed for jury verdicts by margins of 9 to 3, 10 to 2, and 11 to 1.

Although this amendment entitles defendants to a petit jury, they may choose instead either to allow a judge to make the decision or to plea bargain, that is, to plead guilty in the hope of receiving a lesser penalty. In criminal cases, judges advise jurors that they should only convict if the prosecutor presents evidence "beyond a reasonable doubt"; in civil cases, by contrast, jurors decide for plaintiffs "by the preponderance of the evidence." Although these standards are fundamental and firmly fixed in American jurisprudence, the Constitution does not specifically state them.

Governments have designed a variety of mechanisms to assure fair juries. Typically, during the voir dire examination of potential jurors that takes place before either side presents evidence, judges allow lawyers for both sides to dismiss an unlimited number of jurors for cause, that is, for reasons such as relationship to, or obvious bias against, the defendant. Judges also give lawyers a number of so-called peremptory challenges that they can exercise without a stated cause. As the number of such challenges granted increases, so too does the possibility that one or the other side of a case will try to stack the jury with individuals that they believe for demographic or other reasons to be in sympathy with, or antagonistic to, the defendant. In *Batson v. Kentucky* (1986) and *Edmonson v. Leesville Concrete Co.* (1991), the Supreme Court limited the use of peremptory challenges to exclude individuals from juries on the basis of race and gender. In a related matter, in *A. L. Lockett v. McCree* (1986), the Supreme Court permitted governments to use so-called death qualified juries, excluding those who say they could not vote for the death penalty.

Amendment VI. [the accused shall enjoy the right] to be informed of the nature and cause of the accusation; to be confronted with the witnesses against him; to have compulsory process for obtaining witnesses in his favor,

THE RIGHTS OF NOTIFICATION, CONFRONTATION, AND COMPULSORY PROCESS

The Sixth Amendment requires governments to inform individuals of the charges, and confront them with the witnesses, against them. Without such a provision, defendants and their attorneys would be unable to contest the government's case or to examine hostile witnesses to see if they are telling the truth. While thus serving the truth, such confrontations can also sometimes deter honest witnesses from coming forward or pressing charges. This can be a special problem where victims are juveniles or where disclosure of the crimes against them (rape or sexual harassment, for example) could be embarrassing.

In *Coy v. Iowa* (1988), the Supreme Court invalidated the conviction of an individual for sexually assaulting two thirteen-year-old girls. It decided that the state's use of a translucent screen between the girls and the defendant denied his right to confrontation. Justice Antonin Scalia, who wrote the majority decision, especially insisted that the right to confrontation involved face-to-face meetings. By contrast, in *Maryland v. Craig* (1990), Justice Sandra Day O'Connor wrote an opinion upholding the use of a one-way, closed circuit television in examining a six-year-old girl in a child-abuse case. The state specifically determined that the girl would suffer "serious emotional distress" if the court required her to confront the defendant, and the state provided the defendant's attorneys with an opportunity to cross-examine her.

In addition to entitling defendants to cross-examine hostile witnesses, the Sixth Amendment also affords them the right to use "compulsory process." This permits them to subpoena witnesses who might be able to exonerate them.

Amendment VI. [the accused shall] have Assistance of Counsel for his defence.

THE RIGHT TO COUNSEL

The Sixth Amendment guarantees all criminal defendants the right to counsel. Courts now interpret this right not only to allow individuals who can afford to do so to hire attorneys but also to require that governments inform defendants that they have the right. Government must further provide attorneys to those who cannot afford them. Indeed, states now hire public defenders for this very purpose.

Early in the twentieth century, the Supreme Court ruled that states must provide attorneys only to those who, by reason of the seriousness of the crimes with which the state was charging them or other special circumstances surrounding their case, had special need for them. On this basis the Supreme Court voided the initial rape conviction against the Scottsboro Boys in *Powell v. Alabama* (1932). Alabama had failed to provide adequate counsel despite the fact that it was trying the defendants for a serious crime and that they were young, uneducated, away from home, and in a hostile environment.

Over time the Court recognized that even in noncapital felony cases where defendants were not especially ignorant or disadvantaged, few could adequately defend themselves. In *Gideon v. Wainwright* (1963), an indigent defendant successfully appealed his felony conviction to the U.S. Supreme Court, which mandated state-appointed counsel in all such cases. Gideon had filed his appeal to the Supreme Court's through a handwritten *in forma pauperis* (in the form of a pauper, or poor person) petition. The Supreme Court subsequently extended this right in all criminal cases involving possible imprisonment in *Argersinger v. Hamlin* (1972).

Appointed counsel may not always be the best counsel. Judges are generally reluctant to second-guess the strategies of fellow professionals, but from time to time they will set aside a verdict because legal assistance was inadequate. In *Strickland v. Washington* (1984), the Supreme Court set a relatively high standard for individuals arguing that their counsel was ineffective. They had to demonstrate both that counsel's performance was so defective that the counsel was not functioning as the type of counsel that the Sixth Amendment guaranteed and that there was a reasonable probability that the outcome of the trial would have been different, but for such errors. In *Williams v. Taylor* (2000), the Court granted habeas corpus relief to a death-row defendant whose attorney had inadequately prepared for trial and had failed to introduce a host of relevant mitigating factors in the sentencing phase of the case. Similarly in *Rompilla v. Beard* (2005), the Court overturned a death penalty conviction in a case where defense attorneys had interviewed family members but had not fully examined previous court records that the prosecution had introduced for possible mitigating factors.

The Supreme Court has recognized that defendants may need attorneys even before their trials begin. In *Escobedo v. Illinois* (1964), the Court accordingly overturned a conviction based on a confession that police obtained from a suspect they were holding in custody and whose request for an attorney they had denied. By the time of *Miranda v. Arizona* (1966), the Supreme Court had reviewed many cases of pretrial police misconduct. In an attempt to reduce such abuses, the Court decided that once the police had actually begun focusing on specific suspects, police needed to inform such suspects of their rights. These include the right to an attorney (state-appointed in the case of indigence), the right of defendants to remain silent, and a warning that the government can use all statements they make against them.

In 2000, the Supreme Court ruled that *Miranda* established a constitutional rule that remains in force, but the original decision continues to be controversial. Not only did the Court use the *Miranda* decision to reach far beyond the confines of the case, but its meticulous rules more closely resembled legislation than case-by-case decision-making. Predictions that suspects would refuse to confess to anything after police warned them of their rights proved to be exaggerated, but experts are still assessing Miranda's overall impact. Over the course of time, some police officers have preferred the specificity of the decision in that it leaves few areas for subsequent judicial decision-making.

As in the case of the Fourth Amendment, judges have enforced the Fifth and Sixth Amendments by excluding evidence in cases where police failed to give Miranda warnings. Again, too, courts have recognized certain limited exceptions, like the public safety exception. A police officer fearful that an unsuspecting child might pick up a loaded gun might not have time, for example, to warn a criminal of the incriminating consequences of giving an answer before inquiring as to where such a weapon was located. By and large, however, such cases are still exceptions, and the Miranda rules remain remarkably undisturbed.

Amendment VII. In Suits at common law, where the value in controversy shall exceed twenty dollars, the right of trial by jury shall be preserved, and no fact tried by a jury shall be otherwise reexamined in any Court of the United States, than according to the rules of the common law.

PETIT JURIES IN COMMON LAW CASES

Whereas the amendments immediately preceding deal with federal criminal trials, the Seventh Amendment deals with federal civil trials, such as diversity of citizenship cases and the like. The Seventh Amendment provides the right to a jury trial in all civil cases exceeding twenty dollars.

Despite this broad language, Supreme Court decisions have narrowed the amendment's reach. In the nineteenth century, the Court decided that the common law that the amendment applied was that of England at the time the amendment was adopted—the "historical test"—rather than that of individual states. Consistent with the Eleventh Amendment, courts have also limited the use of juries: in civil cases in which individuals attempt to sue the government—the so-called public rights exception; in cases involving maritime law or patent infringement; and in equity cases where individuals are seeking injunctions rather than monetary damages.

The provision for jury trials in civil cases remains one of the few provisions in the Bill of Rights that courts have not equally applied to the states, although some state constitutions protect this right. As it has done in criminal cases, in *Colgrove v. Battin* (1973), the Supreme Court upheld the constitutionality of six-person juries in civil cases. It decided that such juries performed the same functions as their larger counterparts.

REFERENCES AND SUGGESTIONS FOR FURTHER STUDY

Cases

A. L. Lockett v. McCree, 476 U.S. 836 (1986).
Apodoca v. Oregon, 406 U.S. 404 (1972).
Argersinger v. Hamlin, 407 U.S. 25 (1972).
Ballew v. Georgia, 435 U.S. 223 (1978).
Barker v. Wingo, 407 U.S. 514 (1972).
Batson v. Kentucky, 476 U.S. 79 (1986).
Berman v. Parker, 348 U.S. 26 (1954).
Board of Education v. Earls, 536 U.S. 822 (2002).
Bolling v. Sharpe, 347 U.S. 497 (1954).
Burch v. Louisiana, 441 U.S. 130 (1979).
Colgrove v. Battin, 413 U.S. 149 (1973).
Duckworth v. Eagen, 492 U.S. 195 (1989).
Edmonson v. Leesville Concrete Co., 500 U.S. 614 (1991).
Escobedo v. Illinois, 386 U.S. 478 (1964).
Gannett Co. v. DePasquale, 443 U.S. 368 (1979).
Gideon v. Wainwright, 372 U.S. 335 (1963).
Hawaii Housing Authority v. Midkiff, 467 U.S. 229 (1984).
Jacobson v. United States, 503 U.S. 540 (1992).
Johnson v. Louisiana, 406 U.S. 356 (1972).
Katz v. United States, 389 U.S. 347 (1967).
Kelo v. City of New London, 125 S. Ct. 2655 (2005).
Kyllo v. United States, 533 U.S. 27 (2001).
Lucas v. South Carolina Council, 505 U.S. 1003 (1992).
Mapp v. Ohio, 367 U.S. 643 (1961).
Maryland v. Craig, 497 U.S. 836 (1990).
Massachusetts v. Sheppard, 468 U.S. 981 (1984).
Miranda v. Arizona, 384 U.S. 436 (1966).
National Treasury Employees v. Von Raab, 489 U.S. 656 (1989).
New Jersey v. T.L.O., 469 U.S. 325 (1985).
Nix v. Williams, 467 U.S. 431 (1984).
Nollan v. California Coastal Commission, 483 U.S. 825 (1987).
Olmstead v. United States, 277 U.S. 438 (1928).

Powell v. Alabama, 287 U.S. 45 (1932).
Press-Enterprise Co. v. Superior Court of California, 477 U.S. 648 (1986).
Richmond Newspapers, Inc. v. Virginia, 488 U.S. 555 (1980).
Rompilla v. Beard, 125 S. Ct. 2456 (2005).
Sattazahn v. Pennsylvania, 537 U.S. 101 (2003).
Skinner v. Railway Labor Executives Association, 489 U.S. 609 (1989).
Strickland v. Washington, 446 U.S. 668 (1984).
Terry v. Ohio, 392 U.S. 1 (1968).
United States v. Leon, 468 U.S. 902 (1984).
Verona School District 47J v. Acton, 515 U.S. 646 (1995).
Weeks v. United States, 232 U.S. 383 (1914).
Williams v. Florida, 399 U.S. 78 (1970).
Williams v. Taylor, 529 U.S. 362 (2000).
Wyman v. James, 400 U.S. 309 (1971).

Books

Henry J. Abraham and Barbara A. Perry, *Freedom and The Court: Civil Rights and Liberties in the United States*, 8th ed. (Lawrence, KS: University Press of Kansas, 2003).

Liva Baker, *Miranda: Crime, Law and Politics* (New York: Atheneum, 1983).

David J. Bodenhamer, *Fair Trial: Rights of the Accused in American History* (New York: Oxford University Press, 1991).

Dan T. Carter, *Scottsboro: A Tragedy of the American South* (New York: Oxford University Press, 1969).

Ronald Dworkin, *Law's Empire* (Cambridge, MA: The Belknap Press of Harvard University Press, 1986).

James W. Ely, Jr., *The Guardian of Every Other Right: A Constitutional History of Property Rights* (New York: Oxford University Press, 1992).

Malcolm M. Feeley, *The Process Is the Punishment: Handling Cases in a Lower Criminal Court* (New York: Russell Sage Foundation, 1979).

David Fellman, *The Defendant's Rights Today* (Madison: University of Wisconsin Press, 1976).

Marvin F. Frankel, *Criminal Sentences: Law Without Order* (New York: Hill and Want, 1973).

Alfredo Garcia, *The Sixth Amendment in Modern American Jurisprudence: A Critical Perspective* (New York: Greenwood Press, 1992).

Kermit L. Hall, *The Magic Mirror: Law in American History* (New York: Oxford University Press, 1989).

James P. Levine, *Juries and Politics* (Pacific Grove, CA: Brooks/Cole Publishing Company, 1992).

Leonard W. Levy, *A License to Steal: The Forfeiture of Property* (Chapel Hill: The University of North Carolina Press, 1996).

Leonard W. Levy, *Origins of the Fifth Amendment* (New York: Oxford University Press, 1968).

Anthony Lewis, *Gideon's Trumpet* (New York: Vintage Books, 1964).

Peter W. Lewis and Kenneth D. Peoples, *Constitutional Rights of the Accused—Cases and Comments* (Philadelphia: W.B. Saunders Company, 1979).

Stuart S. Nagel, *The Rights of the Accused in Law and Action* (Beverly Hills, CA: Sage Publications, 1972).

David O'Brien, *Civil Rights and Liberties*, Vol. II of *Constitutional Law and Politics*, 6th ed. (New York: W.W. Norton, 2005).

Harold J. Rothwax, *Guilty: The Collapse of Criminal Justice* (New York: Random House, 1996).

David Schultz and John R. Vile, eds., *The Encyclopedia of Civil Liberties in America*, 3 vols. (Armonk, NY: M.E. Sharpe, 2005).

Alexis de Tocqueville, *Democracy in America*, J. P. Mayer, ed. (Garden City, NY: Anchor Books, 1969).

Jon M. Van Dyke, *Jury Selection Procedures: Our Uncertain Commitment to Representative Panels* (Cambridge, MA: Ballinger Publishing Company, 1977).

Alan F. Westin, *Privacy and Freedom* (New York: Atheneum, 1967).

Bruce Yandle, ed., *Land Rights: The 1990s' Property Tax Rebellion* (Lanham, MD: Rowman & Littlefield Publishers, Inc., 1995).

Chapter 9

The Bill of Rights
and Contemporaneous
Amendments—Amendments 8–12

The last three amendments in the Bill of Rights cover some fairly diverse subjects. This chapter discusses these three amendments, as well as the succeeding two amendments that the people adopted in the early years of the Republic. Because they followed so closely upon the Bill of Rights, these amendments also illume the views of the founding generation.

THE EIGHTH AMENDMENT

Although some constitutional provisions are highly specific, others leave matters of degree to future generations to decide. The provisions in the Eighth Amendment fit squarely within the latter category. The amendment respectively prohibits "excessive bail," "excessive fines," and "cruel and unusual punishments." Terms like "excessive" and "cruel and unusual" almost beg for some guidance, and both legislatures and courts have provided it.

> **Amendment VIII.** Excessive bail shall not be required, nor excessive fines imposed . . .

Bail and Fines

The Eighth Amendment prohibitions against excessive bail or fines are among the few that the Supreme Court has not yet applied to the states. A fine is a fee that courts impose to punish some crimes. The framers recognized that the amount of a reasonable fine would depend on the gravity of the offense that an individual committed. A fine for double parking should reasonably be less than one for stock manipulation.

Bail refers to refundable money that courts require defendants who want their freedom to advance in order to assure their appearance at trial. Consistent with guidelines that Congress established in the Bail Reform Act of 1984, judges set the amount of bail according to the nature of the crime with which the government is accusing a defendant, judgments about the defendant's character, the danger that a defendant poses to the community, and the defendant's ties to the community. It would typically be excessive to require a jaywalker to post any bail at all, but even a million dollars might not guarantee that a billionaire madman or wealthy drug dealer would appear at trial. Thus, courts have decided that the Eighth Amendment does not require the government to provide all defendants with bail, but that when governments set bail, it must be reasonable—see *United States v. Salerno*, 481 U.S. 739 (1987). In *Demore v. Kim* (2003), the Court thus upheld a provision of the Illegal Immigration Reform and Immigrant Responsibility Act of 1996 that permitted the detention without bail of certain deportable aliens who had been convicted of certain crimes.

Amendment VIII. . . . nor [shall] cruel and unusual punishments [be] inflicted.

Capital Punishment

The concept of cruel and unusual punishment is even more elusive. The notion of cruelty obviously varies from one age to another. Contemporary Americans would be horrified if modern governments engaged in drawing and quartering persons as they did in colonial England. Similarly, most Americans would be shocked at the public whippings that states still used at the time the framers wrote the Constitution.

The idea of progress led opponents of capital punishment to hope that judges would eventually abolish it. Clearly, the death penalty was in force at the time of the Constitution and long after, as both the references to governmental deprivations of life in the due process clauses of both the Fifth and Fourteenth Amendments and the Fifth Amendment's reference to "capital" crimes, indicate. Still, perhaps U.S. courts would follow European counterparts and declare that society had advanced to the point where they would regard all capital punishments as excessively cruel and/or unusual.

Opponents of the death penalty took hope when, in *Furman v. Georgia* (1972), the U.S. Supreme Court invalidated existing state death penalty laws as excessively arbitrary. Many states, however, adopted new capital punishment laws. These laws divided the trial and sentencing stages of judicial proceedings, required juries to weight aggravating and mitigating factors before deciding whether to impose the death penalty in individual cases, and mandated automatic appellate review of such sentences.

In *Gregg v. Georgia* (1976) and cases that followed, the Supreme Court subsequently accepted such laws in the face of intense arguments by Justices William Brennan and Thurgood Marshall (who Justice Harry Blackmun later joined) that all capital punishment was a cruel and unusual violation of basic human dignity. The Court did reject laws that automatically imposed the death penalty for certain crimes. Similarly, it prohibited governments from imposing the death penalty for crimes other than murder.

Recent years have witnessed the emergence of new issues relative to the death penalty. In *Penry v. Lynaugh* (1989), for example, the Supreme Court allowed for the execution of individuals who were mildly retarded, but in *Atkins v. Virginia* (2002), it reversed course and decided that the diminished intellectual capacity of retarded persons also lessened their moral culpability. In *McCleskey v. Kemp* (1987), the Supreme Court ruled that statistical evidence that seemed to show that states were applying the death penalty in a racially discriminatory fashion did not demonstrate that the state had discriminated against this specific defendant, an African American whom it had convicted of two counts of armed robbery and a murder.

After deciding in *Thompson v. Oklahoma* (1988) that the Eighth Amendment prohibited the execution of individuals who had committed murder at the age of fifteen, the Court ruled a year later in *Stanford v. Kentucky* that governments could impose the death penalty on individuals who were sixteen years old when they murdered. The Court overturned this decision in *Roper v. Simmons* (2005). It decided that the diminished capacity of juveniles to control their actions made it cruel and unusual to execute anyone who committed a murder before the age of eighteen.

In *Payne v. Tennessee* (1991), the Supreme Court also overturned an earlier decision and decided that consideration of victim-impact testimony in capital cases did not constitute "cruel and unusual" punishment. It thus allowed states to balance testimony of mitigating circumstances that defendants provided with consideration of aggravating considerations of the harm they had caused.

Recidivism Laws

In recent years, some states have adopted laws to combat recidivism. Proponents often designate these as "three-strikes-and-you're-out" laws, because they typically impose stiffer sentences after the third conviction. In *Ewing v. California* (2003), the Supreme Court upheld such a California law that imposed a life sentence for an individual who the state convicted of shoplifting about $1,200 worth of golf clubs but who had committed four prior felonies. The Court relied in part in this decision on *Harmelin v. Michigan* (1991), where the justices ruled that in noncapital cases the Court would apply only a "narrow proportionality principle." In short, if the nature of the punishment was not itself cruel or unusual, the Court would not second-guess its proportionality. In another controversial opinion in *Atwater v. City of Lago Vista*, 532 U.S. 318 (2001), the Supreme Court upheld the arrest and jailing of a woman for violating a seat-belt law that carried a $50 fine.

Amendment IX. The enumeration in the Constitution of certain rights shall not be construed to deny or disparage others retained by the people.

THE NINTH AMENDMENT AND THE RIGHT TO PRIVACY

In arguments with the Antifederalists, Federalist supporters of the new Constitution initially argued that a bill of rights was unnecessary because the national government was a government of enumerated powers that could only exercise powers that the Constitution specifically entrusted to it. Federalists argued that a bill of rights could even prove dangerous if those who enforced it regarded the rights listed there as exclusive. What if the government sentenced someone to prison for not tipping a hat to a government official simply because the Bill of Rights did not protect such a right?

The framers designed the Ninth Amendment to address this problem. The Ninth Amendment provides that the Constitution's enumeration of certain rights "shall not be construed to deny or disparage others retained by the people." This amendment leads to two immediate questions. First, specifically which unenumerated rights does the amendment cover? Second, which branch of government does it entrust with their protection? The bare text of the Ninth Amendment does not answer either question. Judge Robert Bork, an unsuccessful nominee for a Supreme Court appointment, once compared the elusiveness of the Ninth Amendment to an inkblot. While some scholars dismiss this analogy, individuals who rely on the Ninth Amendment do not always agree on which specific rights it protects.

Birth Control and Abortion

The most notable exception to the general disuse into which this amendment has fallen centers on the developing law of the right to privacy, which scholars often tie to the due process clause of the Fifth and Fourteenth Amendments or to other constitutional provisions. Even before Woodrow Wilson appointed him to the Supreme Court, Justice Louis Brandeis argued that the right to privacy, or "the right to be let alone," as he called it, was one of the most fundamental personal rights. Most privacy litigation, however, then revolved around interpretations of the Fourth and Fifth Amendments. Initially, the Court resisted applying the words of these amendments to innovations like wiretapping. The Court eventually overcame this hurdle, but other governmental intrusions that the Constitution did not otherwise specifically forbid still seemed clearly beyond its scope.

Matters of family life and sexuality, neither of which the U.S. Constitution specifically addressed, were among the most prominent of these areas. During the so-called Comstock Era, the Connecticut legislature passed a law prohibiting individuals from using any means of artificial birth control. Even more obtrusively, the act prohibited doctors from prescribing birth control devices, even in cases where pregnancy might jeopardize women's health. Many regarded such a law as clearly beyond the realm of either state or national authority, and because of the incorporation doctrine, most rights that courts applied to protect individuals against the national government also applied against the states. But which specific guarantees prohibited a law like Connecticut's?

After a number of delaying actions, the Supreme Court finally faced this issue in *Griswold v. Connecticut* (1965). Writing the majority decision, Justice William O. Douglas argued that the Constitution protected privacy even if it did not mention it. He believed that specific constitutional provisions cast penumbras, or shadows, that implicated the right to privacy. Douglas traced such an intention to the First Amendment's protection of assembly and association, the Third Amendment's protection for the home, the Fourth Amendment's provisions for search warrants, and the Fifth Amendment's provision against self-incrimination. Moreover, Justice Douglas continued, the Ninth Amendment further indicated the presence of penumbral rights connected with those that were enumerated but not specifically stated, and the Fourteenth Amendment applied such rights to protect against the states. Thus, the Court invalidated Connecticut's birth control law. In a concurring opinion, Justice Arthur Goldberg relied even more firmly on the argument from the Ninth Amendment. Even scholars who support the outcome continue to debate the validity of the Court's reasoning, and especially its reliance on the Ninth Amendment.

Disputes over *Griswold* paled beside the firestorm that the Supreme Court's decision in *Roe v. Wade* (1973) provoked. The plaintiff had challenged a Texas anti-abortion law as unduly infringing privacy rights related to sexuality and family matters. *Roe* pitted the rights of women against the rights of the unborn, whose defenders argued that they were "persons" whom the Fifth and Fourteenth Amendments protected against deprivation of "life" without due process of law.

Justice Harry Blackmun authored the Court's opinion. In the face of widespread disagreement on the subject, he said that the Court was no more capable than religious leaders or philosophers of deciding when human life, or personhood, began. Blackmun did observe that the Fourteenth Amendment's references to all persons "born or naturalized" in the U.S. applied to postnatal, as opposed to prenatal, life.

The Court proceeded to fashion its decision on its earlier privacy analysis in *Griswold*. In examining the origin of American abortion laws in the latter half of the nineteenth century, Blackmun argued that their primary purpose was to protect the health of the woman, although legislators also sometimes designed such laws to guard morality by leaving open the possibility of pregnancy (an objective that Texas did not argue in this case), and protect fetal life. Whereas all abortions could be dangerous prior to the discovery of antiseptics to prevent infections, modern abortions at certain stages of pregnancy could actually be less risky for a woman than carrying a child to term. Blackmun thus ruled that in the first trimester (three months) of pregnancy, when modern risks of abortion for a woman were so minimal, the state had no right to legislate against abortion at all.

Blackmun limited state interests during the second trimester to health concerns such as the licensing of doctors and facilities where abortions could take place. In the third trimester, the typical point of "viability" at which most fetuses could now survive outside their mothers' wombs (a point similar, but not identical, to the common-law point of "quickening," when a mother could feel a baby's movements), Blackmun ruled that states could restrict abortion on behalf of fetal life. Even then, states would have to make exceptions for cases where pregnancy threatened the life or health of women. Blackmun thus steered between those who had argued that abortion was an absolute right tied to a woman's unlimited right to control her own body and those who favored complete state control over abortions on behalf of fetal rights and other state interests.

Roe v. Wade initiated further controversies over a host of related issues. The more such cases have arisen, the clearer it has become how difficult courts find it to resolve such issues under an amendment as ambiguous as the Ninth. In *Harris v. McRae* (1980), the Court upheld the Hyde Amendment to the Medicaid Program, which allowed states to fund childbirth without funding elective abortions. Over protests by dissenting justices who believed this denied equal protection of the laws to poor women, the Court distinguished between the existence of a right and the state's obligation to finance it.

In *Planned Parenthood v. Casey* (1992), five justices reaffirmed a "liberty interest" in a woman's decision to choose abortion and sought to exempt such a choice from an "undue burden." In the same decision, the majority, led by Justices Sandra Day O'Connor, Anthony Kennedy, and David Souter, weakened *Roe*'s rigid trimester analysis and upheld state requirements for: a twenty-four-hour waiting period; counseling on the risks of, and alternatives to, abortion; and parental consent for minors, with the possibility of a judicial bypass. This same decision rejected laws requiring married women to obtain spousal consent.

In *Stenberg v. Carhart* (2000), the Supreme Court narrowly decided that a Nebraska law prohibiting late-pregnancy "partial-birth abortions," in which doctors extract part of the baby from the birth canal before draining the contents of its skull, was illegal. It based its ruling on the ground that the law, which the state designed to eliminate dilation and extraction (D&X), could also criminalize more common dilation and evacuation (D&E) procedures in which an arm or leg of a fetus is sometimes in the birth canal.

Other Privacy Issues

In *Bowers v. Hardwick* (1986), the Court, by a razor-thin 5 to 4 vote, refused to extend privacy protection to acts of consensual sodomy that states had outlawed. In *Lawrence v. Texas* (2003), however, Anthony Kennedy wrote a decision reversing course and deciding that considerations of both privacy and equal protection necessitated that the court overturn laws directed to noncommercial consensual sexual acts between adults. In dissent, Justice Antonin Scalia expressed fears that such reasoning could invalidate laws against bigamy or mandate gay marriages, but, to date courts in Vermont and Massachusetts that have invalidated laws against homosexual marriage have based their decisions on state constitutions rather than on the federal right to privacy.

The right to privacy has raised questions about the right to die. The Supreme Court has resisted expanding such a right into a constitutional principle. In *Cruzan v. Director, Missouri Department of Health* (1990), the Court thus ruled that a state could require "clear and convincing evidence" that a person on life-support would want to terminate it before authorizing this. A pair of 1997 cases, *Washington v. Glucksberg* and *Vacco v. Quill*, further upheld a state's right to allow patients to refuse heroic treatments without thereby mandating that it allow doctors to aid those seeking to terminate their own lives. In 2005, the U.S. Supreme Court declined to review the lower court decision allowing the husband of Terri Schiavo, who had experienced brain damage after a heart attack and was classified as being in a persistent vegetative state, to remove her feeding tube. The Court will be issuing a decision on Oregon's physician-assisted suicide law in its 2005–2006 term.

While not explicitly evoking the Ninth Amendment, the U.S. Supreme Court has, in a number of other decisions, endorsed the importance of rights for which it might have claimed Ninth Amendment warrant since the Constitution does not otherwise specifically address them. Thus, the Supreme Court ruled in *Shapiro v. Thompson* (1969) and in *Saenz v. Roe* (1999) that the right to travel is a fundamental right that the Constitution protects. So too, in *Pierce v. Society of Sisters of the Holy Name* (1925), the Court affirmed the right of parents to send their students to parochial schools, and in *Meyer v. Nebraska* (1923), it prohibited the state, which was reacting to fears of foreign influence during World War I, from outlawing the teaching of modern foreign languages in school. Similarly, in *Troxel v. Granville* (2000), the Supreme Court overturned a broad Washington State law, allowing grandparents to request visitation privileges with their grandchildren. The Court thought that parents, who were otherwise deemed to be "fit," could make the decision better than the state. The right to teach a foreign language, to travel, and to raise one's children are all unenumerated rights, which the people arguably never intended to vest in either the state or the national government.

Amendment X. The powers not delegated to the United States by the Constitution, nor prohibited by it to the States, are reserved to the States respectively, or to the people.

THE TENTH AMENDMENT AND STATES' RIGHTS

The authors of the Tenth Amendment sought to address Antifederalist fears that the new national government would simply swallow the rights of the states. In protecting the states, this amendment further indicated that the national government was a government of enumerated powers. As the last amendment in the Bill of Rights, it is especially fitting that the Tenth Amendment ends, like the preamble to the Constitution begins, by referring to "the people."

Article I, Section 10 lists the powers that the Constitution specifically denies to the states. It is more difficult to ascertain which powers the Constitution delegates to the national government, however, because such powers include not only those that Article 1, Section 8 and other sections list, but also those that the necessary and proper clause and other grants of powers reasonably imply. In upholding the constitutionality of the national bank in *McCulloch v. Maryland* (1819), Chief Justice Marshall addressed the argument that, because the Constitution did not mention it, the Constitution had reserved the power to create a bank to the states. Marshall noted that the Tenth Amendment did not refer to "the powers not specifically delegated," but simply to "the powers not delegated" to the United States, thus leaving open the possibility of implied powers. Justice Harlan Fiske Stone thus later observed in *United States v. Darby* (1941) that the Tenth Amendment "states but a truism that all is retained which has not been surrendered."

Such generality notwithstanding, the Tenth Amendment has played an important place in American history, especially during its first one hundred and fifty years. The Tenth Amendment affirms the idea of reserved powers, or state police powers. These labels signify that state powers remain paramount with respect to such functions as the health, welfare, education, land management, and the policing of their own citizens. The Supreme Court used this argument in *United States v. E. C. Knight* (1895) when it voided the application of the Sherman Anti-Trust Act to the sugar-refining industry by deciding that states had the responsibility of regulating monopolies.

Similarly, the Supreme Court once voided many other national economic regulations involving child labor, the hours of labor, and minimum wages, on the basis that the Tenth Amendment left such matters to the states. Eventually, recognitions of expanded national powers under the taxing power, interstate commerce clause, and war-powers eroded notions that the Constitution intended to leave large areas of the economy completely free of national control. By and large, the Supreme Court has expected states to protect their own interests through their representation in Congress, most notably those in the Senate where each state has two delegates.

In *New York v. United States* (1992), however, the Court majority struck down a provision of the Low-Level Radioactive Waste Policy Amendments Act of 1985 for commandeering states into a federal regulatory scheme. Morcover, in *United States v. Lopez* (1995), the Supreme Court invalidated a law regulating guns near schools on the basis that Congress had not adequately tied this power to its control over commerce and that it interfered with traditional state control over education and criminal law. In *United States v. Morrison* (2000), it further voided a provision of the Violence Against Women Act for exceeding congressional powers under the interstate commerce clause. Such cases appear to signal an increasing willingness on the Court's part to enforce some limits on federal power.

However, in *Gonzales v. Raisch* (2005), the Supreme Court invalidated provisions of California's Compassionate Use Act that attempted to provide for a medical exception for the use of marijuana. In a 6 to 3 vote, Justice John Paul Stevens found that even though the cultivation and use of marijuana at issue was local in nature, it was part of an economic class of activities that had a substantial effect on interstate commerce and that Congress could therefore regulate in contradiction to state law. Justices Sandra Day O'Connor, William Rehnquist, and Clarence Thomas worried in dissent that the case effectively obliterated the distinctions between activities that were commercial and noncommercial and local and national.

Amendment XI. [1798] The Judicial power of the United States shall not be construed to extend to any suit in law or equity, commenced or prosecuted against one of the United States by Citizens of another State, or by Citizens or Subjects of any Foreign State.

THE ELEVENTH AMENDMENT AND SUITS AGAINST THE STATE

The Eleventh Amendment, which Congress proposed in 1794 and the states ratified in 1798, was the first to overturn a Supreme Court decision. In *Chisholm v. Georgia* (1793), the Court accepted a case that a citizen of another state brought against Georgia for debts that it owed him from the Revolutionary War era. Some states were naturally sensitive about such suits, which subjected them to payments they hoped to avoid. Moreover, although the language of Article III appeared to include such suits, some Federalists had given assurances at state ratifying conventions that because states were sovereign entities, the Constitution would not permit individuals to sue them without their consent (the doctrine of sovereign immunity).

Despite adoption of the Eleventh Amendment, Chief Justice John Marshall ruled in *Osborn v. Bank of the United States* (1824) that the amendment did not bar suits against state officials and in *Cohens v. Virginia* (1821) that it did not bar appeals to federal courts when states instituted suits. The Court gave the Eleventh Amendment its biggest boost in the years following the Civil War and Reconstruction when it expanded interpretation of the amendment— most notably in *Hans v. Louisiana* (1890)—to bar unwanted suits by in-state as well as out-of-state citizens.

Subsequent cases involving the exercise of federal powers under the commerce clause and the enforcement of Fourteenth Amendment rights have somewhat narrowed state immunity. However, in *Seminole Tribe v. Florida* (1996) the Court reaffirmed the broad ruling in *Hans* by deciding that the Eleventh Amendment barred Indian tribes from suing a state over what they alleged to be its failure to negotiate in good faith over establishing casinos on Indian lands. Similarly, in *Kimel v. Florida Board of Regents* (2000), the Court ruled that the Age Discrimination in Employment Act of 1967, as amended, violated the Eleventh Amendment by improperly subjecting states to age-discrimination suits without their consent. As in other recent decisions, the Court majority decided that congressional power under Section 5 of the Fourteenth Amendment allowed Congress to enforce—but not to decree—the substance of that Amendment. In *Lapides v. Board of Regents of the University of Georgia* (2002), the Supreme Court ruled that a state cannot claim sovereign immunity when it was the one seeking remedy in a federal court, but in *Federal Maritime Commission v. South Carolina State Ports Authority* (2002), it affirmed that the Eleventh Amendment continued to protect states against suits brought by the national government, in this case questioning South Carolina's refusal to berth a cruise ship with gambling at its facilities.

Amendment XII. [1804] The Electors shall meet in their respective states, and vote by ballot for President and Vice-President, one of whom, at least, shall not be an inhabitant of the same state with themselves; they shall name in their ballots the person voted for as President, and in distinct ballots the person voted for as Vice-President, and they shall make distinct lists of all persons voted for as President, and of all persons voted for as Vice-President, and of the number of votes for each, which lists they shall sign and certify, and transmit sealed to the seat of the government of the United States, directed to the President of the Senate;—The President of the Senate shall, in the presence of the Senate and House of Representatives, open all the certificates and the votes shall then be counted;—The person having the greatest number of votes for President, shall be the President, if such number be a majority of the whole number of Electors appointed; and if no person have such majority, then from the persons having the highest numbers not exceeding three on the list of those voted for as President, the House of Representatives shall choose immediately, by ballot, the President. But in choosing the President, the votes shall be taken by states, the representation from each state having one vote; a quorum for this purpose shall consist of a member or members from two-thirds of the states, and a majority of all the states shall be necessary to a choice. *And if the House of Representatives shall not choose a President whenever the right of choice shall devolve upon them, before the fourth day of March next following, then the Vice-President shall act as President as in the case of the death or other constitutional disability of the President.*—The person having the greatest number of votes as Vice-President, shall be the Vice-President, if such number be a majority of the whole number of Electors appointed, and if no person have a majority, then from the two highest numbers on the list, the Senate shall choose the Vice-President; a quorum for the purpose shall consist of two-thirds

continued on next page

> of the whole number of Senators, and a majority of the whole number shall be
> necessary to a choice. But no person constitutionally ineligible to the office of
> President shall be eligible to that of Vice-President of the United States.

THE TWELFTH AMENDMENT AND THE
ELECTORAL COLLEGE

The Twelfth Amendment remedied a problem that developed along with the
rise of national political parties under the new Constitution. Because of this
development, candidates for president and vice president began running
together on a ticket. When, in the election of 1800, all electoral delegates
who voted for Jefferson as president also cast their second votes for fellow
Republican Aaron Burr, the election tied, throwing the selection to the U.S.
House of Representatives. If Federalists (including Alexander Hamilton,
whom Burr later killed in a duel) has not mistrusted Burr even more than
Jefferson, they could have frustrated the popular will even though they
belonged to the losing party.

To prevent this possibility, the Twelfth Amendment provided that electors would now designate separate votes for their choice of president and
vice president. If no one received a majority of the presidential votes, the
amendment further provided that the House of Representatives would
choose among the top three candidates—rather than, as Article II, Section 1
had specified, the top five. In choosing among them, each state delegation
has a single vote regardless of its population.

When the election of 1824, which featured four presidential candidates,
went to the House, it selected John Quincy Adams of Massachusetts as
president over Andrew Jackson of Tennessee (the other candidates were
Henry Clay of Kentucky and William Crawford of Georgia), who had garnered more popular votes. Similarly, in the elections of 1876 and 1888, as in
the election of 2000, the winners of the popular vote did not win the electoral
vote. These elections, as well as scenarios possible in cases with three or more
presidential candidates—for example, the election of 1968, which featured
George Wallace as a third-party candidate, and the election of 1992, which
featured Ross Perot in this capacity—have made the electoral college a source
of continuing controversy.

The most frequently proposed alternative to the electoral college is
popular election; many such plans envision a run-off if no candidate receives 40 percent or more of the vote. Other plans would award electoral
votes by districts or by an electoral proportion of each state, rather than by
the winner-take-all, or unit-rule, formula that most states currently use but
that the Constitution does not mandate. Still other plans propose eliminating

the possibility of so-called faithless electors, who vote for a candidate other than the one to whom they pledged. In cases where no candidate wins a majority of the electoral college, another proposal would allow the people to choose among the top two candidates, rather than allowing the members of the House of Representatives to make this choice. Some proponents of the electoral college system, however, believe that it helps support political parties and strengthens federalism by representing states as states.

POSTSCRIPT TO THE ELECTION OF 2000

The presidential election of 2000, which pitted Vice President Al Gore, Jr. against Texas Governor George W. Bush, highlighted many of the controversies surrounding the electoral college. After a tumultuous election night in which newscasters first called the state of Florida for Gore, next for Bush, and then decided that the state was too close to predict, Florida became the battleground whose twenty-five electoral votes would decide the contest. Although Bush initially led in the state by about 1,800 votes, Gore gained votes in a mandatory machine recount. His supporters went to court to get hand counts in other districts where they alleged that all votes had not been accurately counted. They noted that many of the computer cards that voters punched to indicate their preferences had "dimples" or "hanging chads," which machines could not accurately read. Although Gore gained additional votes, not all counties completed their recounts by the initial deadline, which the Florida Supreme Court established. It extended the deadline again and ordered an extensive hand recount but did not establish a uniform standard for ascertaining which ballots should be counted.

In *Bush v. Gore* (2000), the second of two unprecedented decisions that the U.S. Supreme Court issued on the subject, seven justices agreed that the variable counting procedures violated the equal protection clause of the Fourteenth Amendment. Although two of these justices thought that there was still time to establish such standards and to have a fair recount before looming electoral college deadlines, their five colleagues disagreed and stopped the process. Even though Gore led the national popular vote by just over 500,000 votes, Bush held to his narrow Florida lead and won the presidency with 271 electoral votes, one more than he needed. Bush thus became the first candidate to win the electoral college without winning the popular vote in more than a hundred years.

Newly elected New York Senator Hillary Rodham Clinton was among those who called for electoral college reform. Proponents tempered hope for such proposals with the realization that it would take three-fourths of the states, including many that the electoral college advantaged, to ratify such an amendment. In 2004, George W. Bush won both the electoral and the popular vote, but, although he won more than 3 million more votes than John Kerry, Kerry could have won the election had he carried 120,000 more votes in Ohio.

REFERENCES AND SUGGESTIONS FOR FURTHER STUDY

Cases

Atkins v. Virginia, 536 U.S. 304 (2002).

Atwater v. City of Lago Vista, 532 U.S. 318 (2001).

Bowers v. Hardwick, 478 U.S. 186 (1986).

Bush v. Gore, 531 U.S. (2000).

Chisholm v. Georgia, 2 U.S. 419 (1793).

Cohens v. Virginia, 19 U.S. 264 (1821).

Cruzan v. Director, Missouri Department of Health, 497 U.S. 261 (1990).

Demore v. Kim, 538 U.S. 510 (2003).

Ewing v. California, 538 U.S. 11 (2003).

Federal Maritime Commission v. South Carolina State Ports Authority, 535 U.S. 743 (2002).

Furman v. Georgia, 408 U.S. 238 (1972).

Garcia v. San Antonio Metropolitan Transit Authority, 469 U.S. 528 (1985).

Gonzales v. Raich, 125 S. Ct. 2195 (2005).

Gregg v. Georgia, 428 U.S. 153 (1976).

Griswold v. Connecticut, 381 U.S. 479 (1965).

Hans v. Louisiana, 134 U.S. 1 (1890).

Harmelin v. Michigan, 501 U.S. 957 (1991).

Harris v. McRae, 448 U.S. 297 (1980).

Kimel v. Florida Board of Regents, 528 U.S. 62 (2000).

Lapides v. Board of Regents of the University of Georgia, 535 U.S. 743 (2002).

Lawrence v. Texas, 539 U.S. 558 (2003).

McCleskey v. Kemp, 481 U.S. 279 (1987).

McCulloch v. Maryland, 17 U.S. 316 (1819).

Meyer v. Nebraska, 262 U.S. 390 (1923).

New York v. United States, 505 U.S. 144 (1992).

Osborn v. Bank of the United States, 9 Wheat (22 U.S.) 738 (1824).

Payne v. Tennessee, 501 U.S. 808 (1991).

Penry v. Lynaugh, 492 U.S. 302 (1989).

Pierce v. Society of Sisters of the Holy Name, 268 U.S. 510 (1925).

Planned Parenthood v. Casey, 505 U.S. 833 (1992).

Roe v. Wade, 410 U.S. 113 (1973).

Roper v. Simmons, 125 S. Ct. 1183 (2005).

Saenz v. Roe, 526 U.S. 489 (1999).

Seminole Tribe v. Florida, 517 U.S. 44 (1996).

Shapiro v. Thompson, 394 U.S. 618 (1969).
Stanford v. Kentucky, 429 U.S. 361 (1989).
Stenberg v. Carhart, 530 U.S. 914 (2000).
Thompson v. Oklahoma, 487 U.S. 815 (1988).
Troxil v. Granville, 530 U.S. 57 (2000).
United States v. Darby Lumber Company, 312 U.S. 100 (1941).
United States v. E. C. Knight Company, 156 U.S. 1 (1895).
United States v. Lopez, 514 U.S. 549 (1995).
United States v. Morrison, 514 U.S. 549 (2000).
United States v. Salerno, 481 U.S. 739 (1987).
Vacco v. Quill, 521 U.S. 793 (1997).
Washington v. Glucksberg, 521 U.S. 702 (1997).

Books

Bruce Ackerman, *The Failure of the Founding Fathers: Jefferson, Marshall, and the Rise of Presidential Democracy* (Cambridge, MA: Belknap Press, 2005).

Randy Barnette, ed., *The Rights Retained by the People: The History and Meaning of the Ninth Amendment* (Fairfax, VA: George Mason University Press, 1989).

Walter Berns, ed., *After the People Vote: A Guide to the Electoral College*, rev. ed. (Washington, DC: American Enterprise Institute, 1992).

Judith A. Best, *The Case against Direct Election of the President: A Defense of the Electoral College* (Ithaca, NY: Cornell University Press, 1975).

Judith A. Best, *The Choice of the People: Debating the Electoral College* (Lanham, MD: Rowman & Littlefield Publishers, Inc., 1996).

Barbara H. Craig and David M. O'Brien, *Abortion and American Politics* (Chatham, NJ: Chatham House Publishers, Inc., 1993).

Lee Epstein and Joseph F. Kobylka, *The Supreme Court & Legal Change: Abortion and the Death Penalty* (Chapel Hill: The University of North Carolina Press, 1992).

Lee Epstein and Thomas G. Walker, *Rights, Liberties, and Justice*, part of *Constitutional Law for a Changing America*, 5th ed. (Washington, DC: Congressional Quarterly Press, 2004).

David J. Garrow, *Liberty and Sexuality: The Right to Privacy and the Making of Roe v. Wade* (New York: Macmillan Publishing Company, 1994).

Alexander Hamilton, James Madison, and John Jay, *The Federalist Papers*, Clinton Rossiter, ed. (New York: New American Library, 1961).

Clyde E. Jacobs, *The Eleventh Amendment and Sovereign Immunity* (Westport, CT: Greenwood Press, 1972).

John W. Johnson, *Griswold v. Connecticut: Birth Control and the Constitutional Right of Privacy* (Lawrence: University Press of Kansas, 2005).

Tadahisa Kuroda, *The Origins of the Twelfth Amendment: The Electoral College in the Early Republic, 1787–1804* (Westport, CT: Greenwood Press, 1994).

Leonard W. Levy, *Original Intent and the Framers' Constitution* (New York: Macmillan Publishing Company, 1988).

Michael Meltsner, *Cruel and Unusual: The Supreme Court and Capital Punishment* (New York: William Morrow & Company, 1974).

James C. Mohr, *Abortion in America: The Origins and Evolution of National Policy, 1800–1900* (New York: Oxford University Press, 1978).

John V. Orth, *The Judicial Power of the United States: The Eleventh Amendment in American History* (New York: Oxford University Press, 1987).

Bennett B. Patterson, *The Forgotten Ninth Amendment* (Indianapolis, IN: Bobbs-Merrill, 1955).

Neal R. Pierce, *The Peoples' President: The Electoral College in American History and the Direct-Vote Alternative* (New York: Simon and Schuster, 1968).

Laurence H. Tribe, *Abortion: The Clash of Absolutes* (New York: W.W. Norton, 1990).

Chapter 10

The Post-Civil War Amendments—Amendments 13–15

The states of the North and South engaged in the Civil War from 1861 to 1865. Congress proposed, and the states ratified, three constitutional amendments in the years from 1865 to 1870. Over time, these amendments, and their subsequent interpretations, have initiated profound changes in American racial relations and in the relationship between the national government and the states.

BACKGROUND

The causes of the Civil War were complex, but differences between the North and South over slavery were among the most fundamental. Although Abraham Lincoln initially waged the war primarily to preserve the Union, in time he used it to justify emancipating and protecting the former slaves. During the war, Lincoln issued his pathbreaking Emancipation Proclamation, but both its scope and legal foundation were limited. Essentially a war measure that Lincoln took as commander in chief, the Emancipation Proclamation applied only behind enemy lines where the North initially had limited ability to enforce it. Moreover, as a presidential directive, the Proclamation lacked constitutional permanency. Lincoln joined those who favored amendments to guarantee that former slaves would remain free and would have the privileges of citizenship.

Between 1865 and 1870, Congress proposed, and the states ratified, the Thirteenth, Fourteenth, and Fifteenth Amendments amid intense political debate and acrid controversy. Each amendment had a different objective. The

Thirteenth Amendment ended slavery. The Fourteenth Amendment over-turned the notorious *Dred Scott* decision of 1857 by vesting blacks with citizenship and granting them constitutional rights. This amendment further reversed the restrictive black codes that some states had enacted in the wake of Emancipation as a way to regulate the movements and other freedoms of former slaves. The Fifteenth Amendment focused more explicitly on voting rights.

Amendment XIII. [1865] Section 1. Neither slavery nor involuntary servitude, except as punishment for crime whereof the party shall have been duly convicted, shall exist within the United States, or any places subject to their jurisdiction.

Section 2. Congress shall have power to enforce this article by appropriate legislation.

THE THIRTEENTH AMENDMENT AND THE END OF SLAVERY

The Thirteenth Amendment was the easiest to enforce. Although it did not eliminate the economic dependence that soon manifested itself in the system of sharecropping that developed in the South after the Civil War, the amendment once and for all eliminated the earlier system of chattel slavery.

Slavery involved much more than physical bondage. Interpreters have differed on how far the enforcement provision of the Thirteenth Amend-ment might extend to eliminate what Justice John Marshall Harlan I referred to in the *Civil Rights Cases* (1883) as "the badges of slavery and servitude." In *Jones v. Alfred H. Mayer Co.* (1968), the Supreme Court used the amendment to uphold an 1866 federal statute prohibiting discrimination in the private sale of housing, but the Court more frequently relies on the more explicit provisions of the Fourteenth Amendment.

Amendment XIV. [1868] Section 1. All persons born or naturalized in the United States and subject to the jurisdiction thereof, are citizens of the United States and of the State wherein they reside.

CITIZENSHIP PROVISIONS OF THE FOURTEENTH AMENDMENT

With five sections, the Fourteenth Amendment is the longest. Congress required rebel states to ratify this amendment before it recognized their government and seated their representatives. The first section of this amendment extended citizenship rights to "All persons born or naturalized in the United States and subject to the jurisdiction thereof."

This clause overturned the *Dred Scott* decision (1857), which had declared that blacks were not, and could not, become citizens of the United States under the Constitution of 1787. The elusive reference to persons born in the United States but not "subject to the jurisdiction thereof" exempted those, like children of foreign ambassadors, who are born in the nation but that the laws of diplomatic immunity do not subject to its laws. It might also apply if children were ever born in the United States to foreign occupiers or invaders.

For a time, judicial interpretations of this phrase excluded Native Americans from citizenship, but in the Indian Citizenship Act of 1924 Congress overturned this narrow reading and granted citizenship to all Native Americans who had been born in the United States. Congress has adopted further legislation clarifying the provision applied to persons born in the United States so that it includes not only those who are born on U.S. soil (legally called *jus soli*, law of the soil), but also those born to an American citizen or citizens abroad (*jus sanguinis*, law of the blood). In the latter case, if a person born of only one American parent wants to claim U.S. citizenship, that person's parent must meet a residency requirement and the person must live for ten years in the United States, including five continuous years from age fourteen to twenty-eight.

Amendment XIV. Section 1. No State shall make or enforce any law which shall abridge the privileges or immunities of citizens of the United States; nor shall any State deprive any person of life, liberty, or property, without due process of law; nor deny to any person within its jurisdiction the equal protection of the laws.

THREE IMPORTANT GUARANTEES

After defining citizenship, the Fourteenth Amendment listed three primary guarantees—the privileges and immunities clause, the due process clause, and the equal protection clause. Because the framers of the Bill of Rights sought to protect citizens against arbitrary actions by the national government, the First Amendment begins with the words, "*Congress* shall make no law . . ." By contrast, the framers of the Fourteenth Amendment designed it to protect citizens' rights against the states—hence the opening words, "No *state* shall . . ." In time the Supreme Court utilized the due process clause of the Fourteenth Amendment to extend the protections that the Bill of Rights previously applied only against federal action to the states as well.

Although the Fourteenth Amendment eventually had far-reaching consequences, its initial influence was much more limited. The central problem was that the goal of protecting newly freed slaves often conflicted with the continuing desire to preserve the federal system, which emphasized state decision-making. As Reconstruction ended and the United States withdrew federal troops from the South in 1877, the nation's wish to return to normalcy translated into less support nationally for the rights of blacks. Moreover, early Supreme Court decisions initially decimated many of the rights that the amendment appeared to provide to African Americans.

SUPREME COURT DECISIONS LIMITING THE IMPACT OF THE FOURTEENTH AMENDMENT

The Fourteenth Amendment guaranteed African Americans, like other persons, "the privileges and immunities of citizens of the United States." This phrase had appeared earlier in Article IV of the Constitution, and courts had primarily interpreted it to guarantee that states would extend the same treatment to out-of-state citizens as their own. A broader interpretation would have threatened traditional ideas of the respective rights of states in regard to their own citizens.

The *Slaughterhouse Cases* (1873) were the first to reach the U.S. Supreme Court under the Fourteenth Amendment. The Court's decision narrowly interpreted the privileges and immunities clause. The case involved a Louisiana law that required all butchers in New Orleans to work in specific abattoirs. The legislation bore the hallmarks both of legitimate health and sanitation concerns and political corruption. When butchers challenged the law as a threat to their livelihood, the Supreme Court had to decide whether the right to employment was a privilege and immunity of U.S. citizenship, or whether it remained a matter of state citizenship. The dissenters argued that the Fourteenth Amendment ended state control over fundamental liberties, but the majority argued that such an interpretation stood the Constitution on its head. The majority refused to accept such a revolutionary interpretation in the absence of more conclusive constitutional language. Accordingly, the majority defined the privileges and immunities of national (versus state) citizenship about as narrowly as possible, referring, for example, to the right of citizens to use seaports and to come to the seat of government. This left little of substance for the privileges and immunities clause to defend. Newly freed blacks would have to depend on other provisions of the new amendment.

The Supreme Court eventually used the due process clause to apply the chief guarantees of the Bill of Rights, which had previously bound only the national government, to the states through the process of "absorption" or "incorporation." Throughout the nineteenth and early twentieth centuries, however, the Supreme Court more frequently interpreted the due process clause to enable American businesses to stave off governmental regulations than as a means of protecting individuals against discriminatory state action. Corporate lawyers persuaded judges that corporations were "persons" under the law, and courts often struck down laws that interfered with natural economic laws of supply and demand as unconstitutional.

This development still left defenders of black rights with the potentially powerful equal protection clause, a clause that had finally incorporated Jefferson's noble assertion of equality in the Declaration of Independence into the fundamental law of the land. Initially, however, Supreme Court decisions in the *Civil Rights Cases* (1883) and in *Plessy v. Ferguson* practically decimated this amendment. In the *Civil Rights Cases*, the Court struck down the Civil Rights Act of 1875, a far-ranging law that prohibited discrimination in places of public accommodation. The Court focused on the words "no State shall" to distinguish illegal state action from permissible private discriminatory action. It classified discrimination in public accommodations as the latter.

Although today's Supreme Court is far more sympathetic to minority rights, it still applies the equal protection clause only to causes of state action. In *Moose Lodge No. 107 v. Irvis* (1972), for example, it held that discriminatory membership policies of a Moose Lodge did not translate into state action simply because the state had granted the lodge a liquor license. Because of this state action requirement, Congress relied on its powers under the commerce clause, rather than on the equal protection clause, when it prohibited discrimination in places of public accommodation in the Civil Rights Act of 1964.

Congress adopted no such expedient in the aftermath of the *Civil Rights Cases* of 1883, and the Court compounded the problem still further in 1896. By the 1890s, states had implemented a complex system of Jim Crow laws that not only allowed individuals to discriminate, but that also actually mandated racial segregation. The Supreme Court examined these laws in *Plessy v. Ferguson* (1896). Plessy, who was one-eighth black, challenged a law, which Louisiana euphemistically designated as "a law to promote the comfort of passengers," requiring blacks and whites to sit in different railroad passenger cars. Over the vigorous dissent of John Marshall Harlan I, a one-time Kentucky slaveholder, the Court ruled that state-mandated separate facilities for whites and blacks were not discriminatory as long as such facilities were equal. Harlan stated his belief that:

> In view of the constitution, in the eye of the law, there is in this
> country no superior dominant ruling class of citizens. There is no
> caste here. Our Constitution is color-blind, and neither knows nor
> tolerates classes among citizens. In respect of civil rights, all citizens
> are equal before the law.

The Court majority, however, ruled that states did not need to extend what it regarded as special protection to blacks. It further said that blacks should not assume that state mandates of separate facilities designated their inferiority. Harlan protested that it was no more reasonable for states to require racial segregation than to separate natural-born and naturalized citizens or Catholics and Protestants, and he predicted that the laws would further racial antagonism. By contrast, the majority viewed Jim Crow laws as reasonable exercises of state police powers that would promote peace. This interpretation of the equal protection clause remained in place until 1954.

BROWN AND THE REBIRTH OF THE FOURTEENTH AMENDMENT

In 1954, the treatment of African Americans remained far more separate than equal. In a number of prior cases, most relating to the field of higher education, the Supreme Court began enforcing the "equal" provision of the "separate but equal" doctrine. Thus, in *Sweatt v. Painter* (1950), the Court ruled that Texas had to admit an African American to the University of Texas law school in the absence of a comparable institution for blacks. Similarly, in *McLaurin v. Oklahoma* (1950), it required the University of Oklahoma to treat an African American doctoral student it had admitted equally with whites.

Still, legitimate questions remained as to whether a separate system could indeed be equal. The Supreme Court confronted this question in *Brown v. Board of Education* (1954), which the Court unanimously decided not long after Earl Warren became chief justice. Thurgood Marshall, whom President Lyndon Johnson later appointed as the first black Supreme Court justice, argued on behalf of the National Association for the Advancement of Colored People (NAACP) for desegregation, and John Davis, prominent attorney and one-time Democratic presidential candidate, supported the status quo.

The decision in *Brown* was among the Supreme Court's most important twentieth-century decisions. After arguments, and rearguments, the Supreme Court remained uncertain whether the framers of the Fourteenth Amendment originally intended to prohibit segregation, so it focused chiefly on the psychological effects of such segregation and on the role of education in modern life. Relying in part on psychological and sociological evidence, it decided that segregation generated feelings of inferiority that adversely affected the self-esteem and motivation of minority children to learn. It further established that education played a far more important role in the twentieth century than it had in the nineteenth and that the consequences of segregation were therefore more detrimental. The Supreme Court thus decided that "separate educational facilities are inherently unequal." In a companion case, *Bolling v. Sharpe* (1954), the Court used the due process clause of the Fifth Amendment to extend its ruling to schools in the District of Columbia, which was not a state to which the Fourteenth Amendment applied.

The Court realized the difficulty of implementing desegregation, and it ordered the parties in *Brown* to give it guidance. After hearing their arguments, in *Brown v. Board of Education II* (1955), it subsequently vested lower courts with primary responsibility for overseeing desegregation and encouraged them to use flexible equitable remedies. More ambiguously, it decided that states should desegregate "with all deliberate speed." Subsequent decades showed the difference between mandating and actually accomplishing change. Many southern politicians supported a policy of "massive resistance," while those in other areas of the country worried about the impact of the Court's rulings to their own regions.

SCHOOL BUSING AND AFFIRMATIVE ACTION PROGRAMS

The Court had to decide on the reach of permissible remedies to bring about racial desegregation. The emotional issue of school busing pitted advocates of community schools against those who thought racial balance was more important. In *Swann v. Charlotte-Mecklenburg Board of Education* (1971), the Court approved the use of busing to achieve racial balance and to remedy the effects of past de jure (legally mandated) segregation without mandating rigid quotas. In *Milliken v. Bradley* (1974), however, the Court subsequently confined remedies to counteracting de jure versus de facto segregation. It thus voided an ambitious interdistrict busing plan that a lower court had formulated for Detroit to remedy intradistrict de jure segregation.

Long after the states ratified the Fourteenth Amendment, governments used racial classifications invidiously to discriminate against African Americans and other minorities in the United States. More recently, advocates of minority rights have supported using racial classifications for the more benign purposes of compensating for past discrimination, providing role models in minority communities, bringing certain services to minority members (by, for example, minority graduates of law and medical schools), and promoting greater diversity. Opponents of such "affirmative action" programs have criticized such racial preferences as a form of "reverse discrimination."

The Supreme Court has tolerated some racial preferences while simultaneously limiting their scope. The best-known case in this area is still *Regents of the University of California v. Bakke* (1978). The Court reviewed a program that the medical school at the University of California at Davis, with no prior history of de jure segregation, had initiated. Under this program, the university allocated 16 of 100 entry-level slots to racial minorities. The university accordingly denied entry to Allan Bakke, a white, while accepting other less-qualified minority applicants.

Few decisions have been more complex. Four justices supported Davis's program. They viewed quotas as a legitimate means of overcoming the effects of past racial discrimination and assuring that minorities would achieve specified goals. Four justices opposed not only Davis's quota system, but all considerations of race. Justice Lewis Powell of Virginia took a middle position. He rejected Davis's quota program as too rigid and thus voted to admit Bakke to the medical school at Davis, but he also argued that the university could consider race as a plus when seeking the most diverse student body it could achieve. This decision thus upheld some use of race but struck down strict quotas.

The decision did little to stem the flow of cases that affirmative action programs generated. In *Fullilove v. Klutznich* (1980), for example, the Supreme Court upheld a congressional law setting aside 10 percent of its public-work contracts to minority-owned businesses, and in *Johnson v. Transportation Agency, Santa Clara, California* (1987), it permitted governments to consider gender when promoting a qualified female to a position where women had been traditionally underrepresented. However, in *City of Richmond v. J. A. Croson* (1989), the Court struck down a program, which the Richmond City Council created, requiring contractors on city projects to subcontract 30 percent of all work to Minority Business Enterprises. Just a year later, in *Metro Broadcasting v. Federal Communications Commission*, the Court permitted the Federal Communications Commission to consider race positively in deciding whom to award station licenses. The Court reversed this opinion, however, in a 5 to 4 decision in *Adarand Constructors, Inc., v. Pena* (1995). In that case, Justice Sandra Day O'Connor laid down three principles—"skepticism," "consistency," and "congruence." The first principle subjected any racial classification to searching scrutiny. The second applied such a standard, whether the group receiving unequal treatment was the majority or minority race. The third applied consistent standards to both state and federal considerations of race.

Two 2003 Supreme Court decisions largely reiterated *Bakke's* Solomonic formulation. Thus, a 6 to 3 majority that Chief Justice Rehnquist led in

Gratz v. Bollinger invalidated the undergraduate admission system at the University of Michigan, which automatically awarded African Americans 20 of the needed 100 points required for admission. That same day, Justice O'Connor led a 5 to 4 majority in *Grutter v. Bollinger*, upholding a less rigid admission plan at the University of Michigan Law School against charges that it, too, had crossed the line established by the equal protection clause in seeking a "critical [but numerically unspecified] mass" of minority students. Some justices did suggest that governments might realistically expect to end all affirmative action efforts after twenty-five additional years.

EQUAL PROTECTION AND GENDER-BASED CLASSIFICATIONS

The framers of the equal protection clause did not specifically limit its application to racial discrimination, and, in recent years, the Supreme Court has used this clause to extend heightened scrutiny to classifications based on sex and gender. Like race, one is born with one's sex. Moreover, like race, sex is a visible characteristic that governments have long used to discriminate against individuals. Accordingly, some justices of the U.S. Supreme Court have argued that they should regard all classifications based on gender as suspect, requiring the Court's highest level of scrutiny. A Court majority has not yet gone this far, but it has extended "heightened scrutiny" to gender classifications, requiring that governments go beyond a mere showing that such classifications have a "rational basis."

This approach reversed decades during which the Court refused to apply the equal protection clause to gender classifications. In *Bradwell v. Illinois* (1873), for example, the Supreme Court ruled that a law that banned women from practicing law was both reasonable and consistent with natural law. Although the majority based its decision on a restrictive reading of the privileges and immunities clause, Justice Joseph Bradley wrote a concurring opinion, which two other justices joined, saying that, "The paramount destiny and mission of woman are to fulfill the noble and benign offices of wife and mother. This is the law of the Creator."

In more recent years, a Court majority, while refusing to regard gender as a suspect category, has formulated an intermediate test. It requires governments to show that they have based gender classifications on, and substantially related them to, important interests, rather than on mere sexual stereotypes. Thus, in *Reed v. Reed* (1971), the Court struck down a law that automatically regarded males, rather than females, as better qualified to be executors of estates. In *Frontiero v. Richardson* (1973), it voided a federal statute that automatically granted a dependence allowance to married male servicemen but required married females to prove that their spouses depended on them. In *Craig v. Borden* (1976), the Court also struck down an Oklahoma law allowing eighteen-year-old females, but not eighteen-year-old males, to purchase beer that contained 3.2 percent alcohol.

In 1996, the Supreme Court announced in a 7 to 1 ruling that, as a public institution, the historic all-male Virginia Military Institute (VMI) had to admit women. Led by Justice Ruth Bader Ginsburg, who had once argued as a lawyer for women's rights, the Court rejected an alternative leadership program that the state of Virginia created for women at nearby Mary Baldwin College in Staunton as inadequate. Going somewhat beyond earlier formulations, Ginsburg insisted that states using gender classifications "must demonstrate an 'exceedingly persuasive justification' for that action."

Michael M. v. Superior Court of Sonoma County (1982) is one of the Supreme Court's more provocative decisions dealing with gender differences. Reviewing a California law that defined sexual intercourse by a male with an underage female, but not by a female with an underage male, as statutory rape, the Court upheld the state's conviction of the law to a seventeen-and-a half-year-old male who had intercourse with a sixteen-and-a half-year-old female. Writing for a 5 to 4 majority, Justice Rehnquist justified the law as a way of equalizing the burden of intercourse on the sexes by compensating for the fact that males could not get pregnant. The dissenting justices favored gender-neutral statutory rape laws, such as other states had adopted, based simply on age differences.

In *Meritor Savings Bank v. Vinson* (1986), the Supreme Court upheld provisions of the Civil Rights Act of 1964 that penalized sexual harassment. The law prohibits both direct *quid pro quo* sexual harassment, in which a superior asks for sexual favors in exchange for special consideration, and the creation of a hostile environment in the workplace.

Although it has struck down many sexual classifications as unreasonable, in *Rostker v. Goldberg* (1981), the Supreme Court upheld a congressional law requiring eighteen-year-old men, but not eighteen-year-old women, to register for the Selective Service System. Had the nation adopted the Equal Rights Amendment (ERA), the Court might have reconsidered the decision, but ERA fell three states short of the necessary number needed for ratification. Ironically, the Court's own liberal stance toward gender rights undercut arguments for the urgency and necessity of this proposed amendment.

EQUAL PROTECTION AND OTHER CLASSIFICATIONS

Increasingly, lawyers have applied the concept of equal protection to classifications based on such characteristics as age, wealth, legitimacy, mental or physical disability, and homosexuality. The Supreme Court has taken some halting steps in some of these areas, but, to date, it has not subjected any of these classifications to the intense scrutiny that it accords to racial and gender classifications.

In a number of cases, especially relating to rights of inheritance, the Court has struck down laws that discriminate arbitrarily against those born out of wedlock. However, in *Michael H. v. Gerald D.* (1989), the Court upheld the presumption that a child born to a married couple resulted from that union, thus making it difficult for a third party to establish paternity.

Recognizing that states sometimes use classifications based on mental or physical disabilities to protect or extend care to such individuals, the Court has allowed law-makers relative freedom to formulate protections in this area. Even applying its lowest level of scrutiny (the "rational basis" test), however, in *City of Cleburne, Texas v. Cleburne Living Center* (1985), the Court invalidated a city ordinance preventing mentally retarded persons from living in group homes.

In a number of cases, the Court has invalidated laws that deny benefits to poor persons, albeit not always on equal protection grounds. In *Gideon v. Wainwright* (1963), the Court extended the right to appointed counsel to indigents; similarly, in *Griffin v. Illinois* (1956), it prohibited states from denying transcripts to indigents who needed them to file appeals. Relying chiefly on what it perceived to be interference with the right to travel rather than on wealth per se, in *Shapiro v. Thompson* (1969), the Court invalidated a state's one-year residency requirement for recipients of Aid to Families with Dependent Children, and in *Plyler v. Doe* (1982), the Court ruled that schools could not punish children of illegal aliens by denying them education in the public schools. Ironically, almost a decade earlier, the Court had ruled in *San Antonio v. Rodriguez* (1973) that the equal protection clause did not mandate equal state funding of public schools. Although that decision left in place a Texas system that relied heavily on local property taxes, Texas courts, like courts in other states, later used its own state constitution to invalidate this system.

Congress has adopted some legislation on the subject of age discrimination, but the Court has refused to treat age classifications as inherently suspect, arguing that they are often rationally related to legitimate state interests. Thus, in *Massachusetts Board of Retirement v. Murgia* (1976), the Court upheld a state law requiring uniformed police officers to retire at fifty; in *Gregory v. Ashcroft* (1991), it upheld a Missouri law setting a retirement age of seventy for public employees; and in *Kimel v. Florida Board of Regents* (2000), it refused to subject state governments to the federal Age Discrimination in Employment Act of 1967.

In *Romer v. Evans* (1996), the Supreme Court invalidated a referendum through which Colorado adopted an amendment to the state's constitution striking down all local civil rights laws specifically designed to protect or promote the interests of homosexuals. Justice Anthony Kennedy said that the law raised "the inevitable inference that the disadvantage imposed is born of animosity toward the class of persons affected." Citing the Court's earlier decision in *Bowers v. Hardwick* (1986) upholding laws against homosexual sodomy, Justice Antonin Scalia argued in dissent that, if states could adopt such laws, they could also prohibit special benefits to those engaged in such activities. In *Lawrence v. Texas* (2003), however, the Supreme Court overturned *Bowers* and invalidated a state sodomy law as a denial of due process.

EQUAL PROTECTION AND LEGISLATIVE APPORTIONMENT

In the twentieth century, federal courts used the equal protection clause to supervise both congressional and state legislative apportionment. It eventually established the principle of "one person, one vote." As late as the 1940s, the Supreme Court declared that issues of state legislative apportionment were political questions that the Constitution entrusted to the elected branches of government. This led to a cruel dilemma since legislators from malapportioned legislatures had little incentive to reform the system that had put them there. Eventually, in *Baker v. Carr* (1962), the Supreme Court reversed its stance and declared that apportionment was justiciable. In *Gray v. Sanders* (1963), the Supreme Court articulated the "one person, one vote" standard in invalidating Georgia's county unit system of deciding primary elections. The Court applied this standard to congressional districts in *Wesberry v. Sanders* (1964) and to both houses of the state legislature in *Reynolds v. Sims* (1964) and subsequent cases. The Court has, however, recognized that some population variances are permissible. It generally allows greater deviations among state legislative districts, which often follow county lines and other historic divisions, than among congressional districts.

Some dissenting justices, as well as some historians who focused on the original intent of the framers of the Fourteenth Amendment, thought that the Court's rulings went beyond the Amendment's original aims. The Court majority was not about to give up a remedy for an evil that otherwise seemed insoluble. John Hart Ely, who authored *Democracy and Distrust*, has been among the legal commentators who have argued that democratic-reinforcing decisions demonstrate the operation of the courts at their best.

Recent cases have underscored the manner in which even simple principles like "one person, one vote" can become complicated. Legislatures have continued to gerrymander, or draw districts so as to favor one party or group, even while assigning relatively equal populations to districts. Moreover, states that once used gerrymandering to discriminate against minorities are now creating districts to favor them. In 1995 and 1996, the Supreme Court voided oddly shaped districts in Georgia, North Carolina, and Texas that legislatures configured to maximize representation for racial minorities. The Court stopped short, however, of saying that states could never use race in drawing district lines, and in *Easley v. Cromartie* (2001), it upheld North Carolina's creation of a majority-minority district as a permissible partisan, rather than an impermissible, racial gerrymander. Such controversies show how the brief words of Section 1 of the Fourteenth Amendment continue to revolutionize American constitutional law.

A REBIRTH OF THE DUE PROCESS CLAUSE?

From the late nineteenth century until 1937, the U.S. Supreme Court routinely used the due process clauses of the Fifth and Fourteenth Amendments to invalidate economic legislation. Recent cases have directed renewed attention to this area. In *BMW of North America, Inc. v. Gore* (1996), the Supreme Court thus voided a 2 million dollar punitive damage award against a company that had sold a repainted car without disclosing this to the buyer. The Court decided that the relationship between this punitive damage award and actual damages, estimated at $4,000, was too excessive. Similarly, in *State Farm Mutual Insurance Company v. Campbell* (2003), the Court invalidated a $145 million punitive damage award against an insurance company. The Court observed that "The Due Process Clause of the Fourteenth Amendment prohibits the imposition of grossly excessive or arbitrary punishment on a tortfeasor [wrongdoer]." Dissenters argued that the due process clause did not provide adequate standards for deciding when such awards were excessive and favored leaving such determinations to the states.

Amendment XIV. Section 2. Representatives shall be apportioned among the several States according to their respective numbers, counting the whole number of persons in each State, excluding Indians not taxed. But when the right to vote at any election for the choice of electors for President and Vice President of the United States, Representatives in Congress, the Executive and Judicial officers of a State, or the members of the Legislature thereof, is denied to any of the male inhabitants of such State, being twenty-one years of age, and citizens of the United States, or in any way abridged, except for participation in rebellion, or other crime, the basis of representation therein shall be reduced in the proportion which the number of such male citizens shall bear to the whole number of male citizens twenty-one years of age in such State.

REVERSING THE THREE-FIFTHS CLAUSE

Section 2 of the Fourteenth Amendment reversed the three-fifths clause by providing that blacks and whites would thereafter count equally toward state representation in the U.S. House of Representatives. This raised an immediate political problem. Republicans had supported the post-war amendments against solid Democratic opposition, mostly concentrated among southern whites. If the representation of southern states that formerly held slaves increased, this could weaken the Republican majorities that had supported the post-war amendments and work against the goals the Civil War had achieved. Southern states might even gain congressional representation while they were disenfranchising blacks. The authors of Section 2 of the Fourteenth Amendment accordingly provided that states restricting black voting would lose congressional representation, but this provision was never enforced.

This section further disappointed leaders of the women's suffrage movement, who hoped that the new amendments would also expand their rights. The text of 1787 did not actually deny women the right to vote, but it allowed states to set their own qualifications. By contrast, this section specifically recognized voting as a "*male*" prerogative. In *Minor v. Happersett* (1875), the Supreme Court accordingly ruled that the Fourteenth Amendment did not require states to give women the right to vote. This decision remained in effect until states ratified the Nineteenth Amendment in 1920.

Article XIV. Section 3. No person shall be a Senator or Representative in Congress, or elector of President and Vice President, or hold any office, civil or military, under the United States, or under any States, who, having previously taken an oath as a member of Congress, or as an officer of the United States, or as a member of any State legislature, or as an executive or judicial officer of any State, to support the Constitution of the United States, shall have engaged in insurrection or rebellion against the same, or given aid or comfort to the enemies thereof. But Congress may be a vote of two-thirds of each House, remove such disability.

RESTRICTIONS ON FORMER REBELS

Section 3 of the Fourteenth Amendment addressed the eligibility of former congressmen and other civil and military personnel who had joined the Confederacy to hold offices. Essentially linking such individuals to the crime of treason, this section barred them from office absent a two-thirds vote of each house. In 1872 Congress voted by the required two-thirds majority to remove the restrictions on most southerners.

> **Amendment XIV. Section 4.** The validity of the public debt of the United States, authorized by law, including debts incurred for payment of pensions and bounties for services in suppressing insurrection or rebellion, shall not be questioned. But neither the United States nor any State shall assume or pay any debt or obligation incurred in aid of insurrection or rebellion against the United States, or any claim for the loss or emancipation of any slave; but all such debts, obligations and claims shall be held illegal and void.

VALID AND INVALID PUBLIC DEBTS

Section 4 provided that the United States would take responsibility for debts it had incurred during the war but not for those of the Confederacy. This section further exempted the government from paying compensation for "the loss or emancipation of any slave." Some statesman had previously contemplated paying slaveholders to free their slaves, an idea that they sometimes coupled with the possibility of transporting blacks back to Africa. When Congress abolished slavery in the District of Columbia in 1862, prior to the ratification of the Thirteenth Amendment, it provided compensation for owners who were loyal to the Union.

> **Amendment XIV. Section 5.** The Congress shall have power to enforce, by Appropriate legislation, the provisions of this article.

ENFORCEMENT OF THE FOURTEENTH AMENDMENT

The fifth section of the Fourteenth Amendment grants Congress power—"by appropriate legislation"—to enforce its provisions. Congress has re-discovered this clause in recent years. On occasion, the courts have granted Congress wider latitude under this provision than if it were acting alone. Thus, in *Katzenbach v. Morgan* (1966), the Supreme Court upheld the provision of the Voting Rights Act of 1965 prohibiting state-mandated literacy tests, even though it had previously upheld their constitutionality against equal protection challenges. Justice William Brennan likened the powers of Congress under Section 5 of the Fourteenth Amendment to its broad powers under the necessary and proper clause.

In recent decisions, however, the Supreme Court has treated congressional powers over affirmative action programs similarly to, rather than more expansively than, state powers in this same area. Likewise, in striking down the Religious Freedom Restoration Act in *City of Boerne v. Flores*, the Supreme Court said that Congress's power to enforce the Fourteenth

Amendment did not give it a right to interpret and enforce that amendment differently than the Court. In invalidating a provision of the Violence Against Women Act in *United States v. Morrison* (2000), the Supreme Court reiterated that the provision limited Congress to restricting state, rather than private, action.

Amendment XV. [1870] Section 1. The right of citizens of the United States to vote shall not be denied or abridge by the United States or by any State on account of race, color, or previous condition of servitude.

    Section 2. The Congress shall have power to enforce this article by appropriate legislation.

THE FIFTEENTH AMENDMENT

The Fifteenth Amendment, which prohibited governments from denying the right to vote on the basis of race, lay largely dormant for nearly a century. It was the victim of grandfather clauses, literacy tests (which administrators often applied unevenly to whites and blacks or in conjunction with arbitrary "understanding clauses"), poll taxes, all-white primaries, and even physical intimidation by the Ku Klux Klan and other such organizations. Eventually, however, courts used the amendment to strike down some of these mechanisms, as in *Smith v. Allwright* (1944) in which the U.S. Supreme Court voided the all-white primary. The Voting Rights Act of 1965 and its various extensions further reinvigorated the amendment by outlawing mechanisms that had suppressed voting and by authorizing federal registrars to enroll voters. The amendment is no longer a hollow set of words but a living guarantee that has brought dignity and power to those who were once enslaved and disenfranchised.

THE LESSON OF THE POST-WAR AMENDMENTS

The Civil War Amendments illustrate the tremendous power inherent in the constitutional amending process. They overturned a notorious Supreme Court decision and extended rights to a whole new class of persons. In this respect, the Civil War Amendments were even more important than the Bill of Rights. Less positively, the nation took many years to implement many of the guarantees in the post-Civil War Amendments. These amendments demonstrate that interpretations of constitutional language can sometimes take strange twists and turns that the temper of the times affect as much as constitutional language.

REFERENCES AND SUGGESTIONS FOR FURTHER STUDY

Cases

Adarand Constructors Inc., v. Pena, 515 U.S. 200 (1995).
Baker v. Carr, 369 U.S. 186 (1962).
BMW of North America, Inc. v. Gore, 517 U.S. 559 (1996).
Bolling v. Sharpe, 347 U.S. 497 (1954).
Bowers v. Hardwick, 478 U.S. 186 (1986).
Bradwell v. Illinois, 83 U.S. 130 (1873).
Brown v. Board of Education, 347 U.S. 483 (1954).
Brown v. Board of Education II, 349 U.S. 294 (1955).
City of Cleburne, Texas v. Cleburne Living Center, 473 U.S. 432 (1985).
City of Richmond v. J. A. Croson, 488 U.S. 469 (1989).
The Civil Rights Cases, 109 U.S. 3 (1883).
Craig v. Borden, 429 U.S. 190 (1976).
Dred Scott v. Sandford, 60 U.S. 393 (1857).
Easley v. Cromartie, 532 U.S. 234 (2001).
Frontiero v. Richardson, 411 U.S. 677 (1973).
Fullilove v. Klutznick, 448 U.S. 448 (1980).
Gideon v. Wainwright, 372 U.S. 335 (1963).
Gratz v. Bollinger, 539 U.S. 244 (2003).
Gray v. Sanders, 372 U.S. 368 (1963).
Gregory v. Ashcroft, 501 U.S. 452 (1991).
Griffin v. Illinois, 351 U.S. 12 (1956).
Grutter v. Bollinger, 539 U.S. 306 (2003).
Johnson v. Transportation Agency, Santa Clara, California, 480 U.S. 616 (1987).
Jones v. Alfred H. Mayer Co., 392 U.S. 409 (1968).
Katzenbach v. Morgan, 384 U.S. 641 (1966).
Kimel v. Florida Board of Regents, 528 U.S. 62 (2000).
Lawrence v. Texas, 539 U.S. 558 (2003).
McLaurin v. Oklahoma State Regents, 339 U.S. 637 (1950).
Massachusetts Board of Retirement v. Murgia, 427 U.S. 307 (1976).
Meritor Savings Bank v. Vinson, 477 U.S. 57 (1986).
Metro Broadcasting v. Federal Communications Commission, 497 U.S. 547 (1990).
Michael H. v. Gerald D., 491 U.S. 116 (1989).
Michael M. v. Superior Court of Sonoma County, 450 U.S. 464 (1981).
Milliken v. Bradley, 418 U.S. 717 (1974).
Minor v. Happersett, 88 U.S. 161 (1875).
Moose Lodge No. 107 v. Irvis, 407 U.S. 163 (1972).
Plessy v. Ferguson, 163 U.S. 537 (1896).
Plyler v. Doe, 474 U.S. 202 (1982).
Reed v. Reed, 404 U.S. 71 (1971).
Regents of the University of California v. Bakke, 438 U.S. 265 (1978).

Reynolds v. Sims, 377 U.S. 533 (1964).
Romer v. Evans, 517 U.S. 620 (1996).
Rostker v. Goldberg, 453 U.S. 57 (1981).
San Antonio v. Rodriguez, 411 U.S. 1 (1973).
Shapiro v. Thompson, 394 U.S. 618 (1969).
The Slaughterhouse Cases, 83 U.S. 36 (1873).
Smith v. Allwright, 321 U.S. 649 (1944).
State Farm Mutual Insurance Company v. Campbell, 538 U.S. 408 (2003).
Swann v. Charlotte-Mecklenburg Board of Education, 402 U.S. 1 (1971).
Sweatt v. Painter, 339 U.S. 629 (1950).
United States v. Morrison, 529 U.S. 598 (2000).
Wesberry v. Sanders, 376 U.S. 1 (1964).

Books

Henry J. Abraham and Barbara A. Perry, *Freedom and the Court: Civil Rights and Liberties in the United States*, 8th ed. (Lawrence: University Press of Kansas, 2003).

Roaul Berger, *Government by Judiciary: The Transformation of the Fourteenth Amendment* (Cambridge, MA: Harvard University Press, 1977).

Daniel M. Berman, *It Is So Ordered: The Supreme Court Rules on School Segregation* (New York: W.W. Norton, 1966).

Margorie A. Bingham, *Women and the Constitution: Student Textbook* (Atlanta, GA: The Carter Center of Emory University, 1990).

Taylor Branch, *Parting the Waters: America in the King Years, 1954–63* (New York: Simon and Schuster, 1988).

Richard C. Cortner, *The Supreme Court and the Second Bill of Rights: The Fourteenth Amendment and the Nationalization of Civil Liberties* (Madison: University of Wisconsin Press, 1981).

Ward E. Y. Elliott, *The Rise of Guardian Democracy: The Supreme Court's Role in Voting Rights Disputes, 1845–1969* (Cambridge, MA: Harvard University Press, 1974).

John Hart Ely, *Democracy and Distrust: A Theory of Judicial Review* (Cambridge, MA: Harvard University Press, 1980).

Don E. Fehrenbacher, *The Dred Scott Case: Its Significance in American Law and Politics* (New York: Oxford University Press, 1978).

Eric Foner, *Reconstruction: America's Unfinished Revolution, 1863–1877* (New York: Harper & Row, 1988).

John Hope Franklin and Alfred A. Moss, Jr., *From Slavery to Freedom*, 6th ed. (New York: Alfred A. Knopf, 1988).

Alan P. Grimes, *Democracy and the Amendments to the Constitution* (Lexington, MA: Lexington Books, 1978).

Robert J. Harris, *The Quest for Equality* (Baton Rouge: Louisiana University Press, 1960).

Harold M. Hyman, *A More Perfect Union: The Impact of the Civil War and Reconstruction on the Constitution* (Boston: Houghton Mifflin Company, 1975).

Donald W. Jackson, *Even the Children of Strangers: Equality Under the U.S. Constitution* (Lawrence: University Press of Kansas, 1992).

Harry V. Jaffa, *Crisis of the House Divided: An Interpretation of the Issues in the Lincoln-Douglas Debates* (Chicago: University of Chicago Press, 1982).

Joseph B. James, *The Ratification of the Fourteenth Amendment* (Macon, GA: Mercer University Press, 1984).

Woody Klein, ed., *Toward Humanity and Justice: The Writings of Kenneth B. Clark, Scholar of the 1954* Brown v. Board of Education *Decision* (Westport, CT: Praeger, 2004).

Richard Kluger, *Simple Justice*, 2 vols. (New York: Alfred A. Knopf, 1975).

Peter F. Lau, *From the Grassroots to the Supreme Court:* Brown v. Board of Education *and American Democracy* (Durham, NC: Duke University Press, 2004).

Earl M. Malz, *Civil Rights, The Constitution, and Congress, 1863–1869* (Lawrence: University Press of Kansas, 1990).

James M. McPherson, *Abraham Lincoln and the Second American Revolution* (New York: Oxford University Press, 1991).

William L. Nelson, *The Fourteenth Amendment: From Political Principle to Judicial Doctrine* (Cambridge, MA: Harvard University Press, 1988).

David A. J. Richards, *Conscience and the Constitution: History, Theory, and Law of the Reconstruction Amendments* (Princeton, NJ: Princeton University Press, 1993).

Allan P. Sindler, *Bakke, DeFunis and Minority Admissions: The Quest for Equal Opportunity* (New York: Longman, 1978).

Girardeau A. Spann, *The Law of Affirmative Action: Twenty Five Years of Supreme Court Decisions on Race and Remedies* (New York: New York University Press, 2000).

Dorothy M. Stetson, *Women's Rights in the U.S.A.: Policy Debates and Gender Roles* (Pacific Grove, CA: Brooks/Cole Publishing Company, 1991).

Bernard Taper, *Gomillion v. Lightfoot* (New York: McGraw Hill Book Company, Inc., 1962).

Melvin I. Urofksy, *A March of Liberty: A Constitutional History of the United States* (New York: Alfred A. Knopf, 1988).

J. Harvie Wilkinson III, *From Brown to Bakke* (New York: Oxford University Press, 1979).

Juan Williams, *Eyes on the Prize: America's Civil Rights Years, 1954–1965* (New York: Viking, 1967).

Chapter 11

The Progressive Era Amendments—Amendments 16–19

The supermajorities that the Constitution requires to propose and ratify one amendment often reflect sentiments strong enough to initiate others. Thus, states ratified the first ten amendments in 1791, two years after Congress proposed them. Similarly, states ratified the Thirteenth through Fifteenth Amendments from 1865 to 1870. After a forty-three-year hiatus during which some scholars criticized the amending process for being overly rigid, the nation adopted Amendments 16 through 19 within the seven-year span from 1913 to 1920.

This period roughly corresponds to the Progressive Era in American politics. Reformers who sought to root out corruption, refine American politics, and make it more democratic dominated this era and influenced the amendments. At the state level, this era witnessed the introduction of the initiative (whereby voters could introduce legislation), the referendum (by which voters could affirm or reject legislation), and the recall (by which voters could call for new elections), as well as far greater reliance on the primary election as a way for rank and file members rather than bosses to select party nominees.

Amendment XVI. [1913] The Congress shall have power to lay and collect taxes on incomes, from whatever source derived, without apportionment among the several States, and without regard to any census or enumeration.

THE SIXTEENTH AMENDMENT AND THE NATIONAL INCOME TAX

The Sixteenth Amendment grants Congress power to levy a national income tax. Article I, Section 9 had provided that "No Capitation, or other direct, Tax shall be laid, unless in Proportion to the Census or Enumeration herein before directed to be taken." This elusive language did not specifically define a "direct tax," but the Supreme Court decided in *Pollock v. Farmer's Loan and Trust Company* (1895) that a tax on income was a direct tax and that because Congress levied it on income rather than on state population, it was therefore void. The Sixteenth Amendment reversed this judgment.

There are at least two ties between this amendment and the Progressive Era. First, a stable and adequate revenue base enables Congress to enact social welfare programs that it might not otherwise be able to afford, especially during times of war, when hostilities often disrupt revenue from duties and tariffs. Second, the income tax permits Congress to shift tax burdens to those best able to pay them. Attorneys who opposed the income tax before the U.S. Supreme Court portrayed it as a socialistic measure through which the government would redistribute income. Although their fears were not realized, an income tax does allow Congress to tax those who earn more income at higher rates (supporters call this a progressive tax). By contrast, many states rely chiefly on more regressive taxes, like those on sales and property, which fall disproportionately on those who are less able to pay.

Amendment XVII. [1913] The Senate of the United States shall be composed of two Senators from each State, elected by the people thereof, for six years; and each Senator shall have one vote. The electors in each State shall have the qualifications requisite for electors of the most numerous branch of the State legislatures.

When vacancies happen in the representation of any State in the Senate, the executive authority of such State shall issue writs of election to fill such vacancies: Provided, That the legislature of any State may empower the executive thereof to make temporary appointments until the people fill the vacancies by election as the legislature may direct.

This amendment shall not be so construed as to affect the election or term of any Senator chosen before it becomes valid as part of the Constitution.

THE SEVENTEENTH AMENDMENT AND THE ELECTION OF U.S. SENATORS

Of all the institutions the U.S. Constitution established, the U.S. Senate probably best reflected the federal nature of government. The founders granted each state an equal number of two senators in that body, and Article I, Section 2 further provided that state legislatures would select senators who states could expect to protect their interests. Over time, this arrangement provoked charges that the Senate had become a "millionaires' club" composed of wealthy people with inordinate influence in the states. Moreover, the system of indirect election was obviously not as democratic as direct election. George Haynes has observed that over time the senatorial selection system resulted in deadlocks, bribery, stampeded elections, unfilled vacancies, interference with regular state legislative business, and corruption.

Advocates of direct election had to persuade sitting senators, who were already profiting from the existing arrangement, to support such a change. Some reformers persuaded state legislatures to agree to choose whoever won state popular elections. Others pursued the alternate route under Article V, which obligated Congress to call a convention to proposed amendments if two-thirds of the states petitioned it to do so. These pressures propelled Congress to act. Once it proposed the amendment, the states quickly ratified. Whereas Article I, Section 2 had allowed the state executive to make temporary appointments that legislatures would then fill in cases of senatorial vacancies, the Seventeenth Amendment provided that state legislatures could empower governors to make temporary appointments until the legislatures could provide for elections to fill such vacancies.

The Seventeenth Amendment further democratized the Constitution and tied the legislative branch closer to the people, but it may also have undermined the link between the Senate and the federal system. Both for better and for worse, Senators are now more likely to view themselves as representatives of the people of their states rather than of their states as political entities. Given this structural change, some commentators have argued that the judiciary has greater responsibility for preserving federalism than in the past.

Amendment XVIII. [1919] Section 1. *After one year from the ratification of this article the manufacture, sale, or transportation of intoxicating liquors within, the importation thereof into, or the exportation thereof from the United States and all territory subject to the jurisdiction thereof for beverage purposes is hereby prohibited.*

Section 2. *The Congress and the several States shall have concurrent power to enforce this article by appropriate legislation.*

Section 3. *This article shall be inoperative unless it shall have been ratified as an amendment to the Constitution by the legislatures of the several States; as provided in the Constitution, within seven years from the date of the submission hereof to the States by the Congress.*

THE EIGHTEENTH AMENDMENT AND THE NATIONAL PROHIBITION OF ALCOHOL

The Eighteenth Amendment provided for national alcoholic prohibition. The amendment vested Congress and the states with concurrent enforcement powers. It did not provide for those who already owned or operated businesses devoted to such sales other than specifying a one-year phase-in.

Although these restrictions are quite intrusive, many proponents of reform in the Progressive Era obviously viewed the situation differently. Not unlike those who oppose illegal drugs today, reformers, encouraged by the sacrifices that citizens had already made to win World War I, dreamed of the further benefits that the nation could reap by eliminating alcohol and the saloons that dispensed it. Many reformers probably also reflected their own class bias. Drawn disproportionately from white Anglo-Saxon Protestants with a pietistic moralistic heritage that regarded the consumption of alcohol as inherently sinful, many progressives further associated drinking with newly arrived Catholic immigrants from Ireland and southern European nations for whom they had little sympathy or understanding.

The dream of morally reforming the nation through national alcoholic prohibition proved illusory. Fairly ordinary and otherwise law-abiding citizens who regarded the right to consume alcohol as a personal decision often violated the law and provided revenues for organized crime rings and gangsters in the process. The Twenty-first Amendment, which the states ratified through special conventions at the outset of Franklin Roosevelt's first administration in 1933, finally repealed the amendment although it permitted individual states to regulate alcohol within their own jurisdictions, which many do by allowing for local options.

The Constitution does not specify how long states have to ratify amendments. The Eighteenth Amendment was the first of several amendments that attempted to remedy this silence by requiring states to ratify the amendment within seven years after receiving it. This time has become standard for the amendments that have included such limits, but those proposing amendments could set a different time period.

Amendment XIX. [1920] The right of citizens of the United States to vote shall not be denied or abridged by the United States or by any State on account of sex.

Congress shall have power to enforce this article by appropriate legislation.

THE NINETEENTH AMENDMENT AND WOMEN'S SUFFRAGE

The Nineteenth Amendment further points to the link between the Progressive Era and direct democracy. Scholars often designate this as the Susan B. Anthony Amendment after one of its earliest and most dedicated supporters who lived from 1820 to 1906. From the time of the Seneca Falls Convention in New York in 1848, women had petitioned, in language that they modeled on that of the Declaration of Independence, for the right to vote. The authors of the Fourteenth and Fifteenth Amendments had ignored such pleas; indeed, Section 2 of the Fourteenth Amendment permitted Congress only to penalize states that denied the right to vote to *males* over the age of twenty-one. Few could have been surprised when in *Minor v. Happersett* (1875), the U.S. Supreme Court unanimously upheld a refusal by a voting registrar in Missouri to allow Virginia Minor to vote in the presidential election of 1872. Acknowledging that women were U.S. citizens, the Court ruled that the privileges and immunities clause of the Fourteenth Amendment did not protect the right to vote against state infringement.

Such diverse women as Carrie Chapman Catt, Julia Ward Howe, Lucretia Mott, Alice Paul, Elizabeth Cady Stanton, and Lucy Stone worked over a seventy-five-year period to get Congress to propose and the states to ratify the Nineteenth Amendment. Conservative women who had accepted the Fourteenth and Fifteenth Amendments as written, and more liberal women who thought that the rights of women and African Americans should advance together, had split after the Civil War into the American Woman Suffrage Association and the National Woman Suffrage Association. In 1890, the two groups finally merged into the National American Woman Suffrage Association and pushed for the Nineteenth Amendment.

Prior to 1920, the U.S. Constitution did not specifically prohibit women from voting in national elections (indeed New Jersey permitted some women to vote at the time it ratified the Constitution), but it allowed states to set voting qualifications. Most limited such suffrage to males. In the late nineteenth century, a number of western states beginning with Wyoming, which did so as a territory in 1869, extended this right to citizens regardless of gender. Such half-steps did not satisfy those who believed that voting was a necessary concomitant to effective citizenship and representation throughout the nation.

Opponents derided and feared women's suffrage. Responding to arguments that voting was a privilege of citizenship, opponents argued that their husbands and fathers already represented women in public councils and that God had created women for domestic concerns rather than for the rough and tumble of the political arena. Partly in response to such arguments, many progressive reformers accepted the assumption that women would vote differently from men. They argued that women would refine the political process, freeing it from much of its corruption and bringing ethical issues to the fore.

As an increasing number of states extended the vote to women, proponents of women's suffrage eventually prevailed in Congress as well. Some attribute this success partly to the adoption of the Eighteenth Amendment. Consistent with the view that women might vote differently, some who opposed prohibition had tried to keep women from voting, but once prohibition was adopted, they had less to lose.

Congress proposed the amendment in May 1919. Tennessee was the thirty-sixth state to ratify and push the amendment over the top in 1920. At his mother's request, a twenty-four-year-old state representative by the name of Harry Burn switched his vote to provide the winning margin of victory.

Political scientists continue to examine individual elections for evidence of a "gender gap," but, for better or worse, women typically do not vote much differently than men. At a time when some nations of the world still deny women the right to vote and treat them as second-class citizens, most Americans rightfully take pride in the amendment that keeps governments from denying individuals the right to vote simply because they are women.

REFERENCES AND SUGGESTIONS FOR FURTHER STUDY

Cases

Minor v. Happersett, 88 U.S. 162 (1875).
Pollock v. Farmers' Loan & Trust Company, 157 U.S. 429 (1895).

Books

Alan P. Grimes, *Democracy and the Amendments to the Constitution* (Lexington, MA: Lexington Books, 1978).

Richard H. Hamm, *Shaping the 18th Amendment: Temperance Reform, Legal Culture, and the Polity, 1880–1920* (Chapel Hill: The University of North Carolina Press, 1995).

George H. Haynes, *The Senate of the United States: Its History and Practice* (New York: Russell and Russell, 1960).

C. H. Hoebeke, *The Road to Mass Democracy: Original Intent and the Seventeenth Amendment* (New Brunswick: Transaction Publishers, 1995).

Richard Hofstadter, *The Age of Reform: From Bryan to F.D.R.* (New York: Vintage Books, 1955).

Aileen S. Kraditor, *The Ideas of the Women's Suffrage Movement, 1890–1920* (New York: Columbia University Press, 1965).

David E. Kyvig, *Alcohol and Order: Perspectives on National Prohibition* (Westport, CT: Greenwood Press, 1985).

Charles Leedham, *Our Changing Constitution* (New York: Dodd, Mead Company, 1964).

Arthur S. Link and Richard L. McCormick, *Progressivism* (Arlington Heights, IL: Harlan Davidson, Inc., 1983).

John R. Vile, *The Constitutional Amending Process in American Political Thought* (New York: Praeger, 1992).

Majorie S. Wheeler, ed., *One Woman, One Vote: Rediscovering the Woman Suffrage Movement* (Troutdale, OR: New Sage Press, 1995).

Majorie S. Wheeler, ed., *Votes for Women: The Woman Suffrage Movement in Tennessee, the South, and the Nation* (Knoxville: The University of Tennessee Press, 1995).

Robert Wiebe, *The Search for Order, 1877–1920* (New York: Hill and Wang, 1967).

Chapter 12

The Recent Amendments— Amendments 20–27

As of the publication of this book, it has been almost fifteen years since Congress has proposed, and states have ratified, a constitutional amendment. The Constitution continues to vest this power in "We the People," operating according to specified forms. This chapter outlines the amendments that the people have adopted since the Progressive Era.

Amendment XX. [1933] Section 1. The terms of the President and Vice President shall end at noon on the 20th day of January, and the terms of Senators and Representatives at noon on the 3d day of January, of the years in which such terms would have ended if this article had not been ratified; and the terms of their successors shall then begin.

Section 2. The Congress shall assemble at least once in every year, and such meeting shall begin at noon on the 3d day of January, unless they shall by law appoint a different day.

THE LAME-DUCK AMENDMENT

Republican Senator George W. Norris of Nebraska was most responsible for the Twentieth Amendment, which scholars often call the "lame-duck" amendment. It shortened the time that so-called lame-duck presidents, vice presidents, and legislators remain in office. Lame-duck office-holders are those who serve out the remaining time of their terms in office after voters have defeated them for reelection. They thus lack the element of electoral accountability that guides other office-holders.

Under a law that the Articles of Confederation enacted, the first Congress met on March 4; prior to the adoption of the Seventeenth Amendment, this enabled state legislatures, many of which met in January, to choose their senators. Because Article I, Section 4 of the Constitution specified that the annual meeting of Congress should begin on the first Monday in December, a new Congress did not come into session until thirteen months after the November election. In the meantime, the old Congress could meet (and out-going presidents continued to serve) from the December after the election until the following March, thus undermining responsibility to the people.

Such lame-duck representatives created the judicial seats, one of which led to the case of *Marbury v. Madison* (1803), where John Marshall an-nounced the principle of judicial review of national legislation. Similarly, in 1873, an outgoing Congress approved the so-called Salary Grab Act, boosting salaries from $5,000 to $7,500 per year and applying the law retroactively to the beginning of the session. In 1922 another outgoing Congress adopted a ship subsidy bill, despite the fact that voters had de-feated many of the bill's sponsors.

By moving the date that members of Congress take office to the third day of January rather than March, this amendment shortened lame-duck ses-sions. Similarly, it provided for presidential inaugurations on the twentieth of January.

Amendment XX. Section 3. If, at the time fixed for the beginning of the term of the President, the President elect shall have died, the Vice President elect shall become President. If a President shall not have been chosen before the time fixed for the beginning of his term, or if the President elect shall have failed to qualify, then the Vice President elect shall act as President until a President shall have qualified; and the Congress may by law provide for the case wherein neither a President elect nor a Vice President elect shall have qualified, declaring who shall then act as President, or the manner in which one who is to act shall be selected, and such person shall act accordingly until a President or Vice President shall have qualified.

Section 4. The Congress may by law provide for the case of the death of any of the persons from whom the House of Representatives may choose a President whenever the right of choice shall have devolved upon them, and for the case of the death of any of the persons from whom the Senate may choose a Vice President whenever the right of choice shall have devolved upon them.

continued on next page

Section 5. Sections 1 and 2 shall take effect on the 15th day of October following the ratification of this article.

Section 6. This article shall be inoperative unless it shall have been ratified as an amendment to the Constitution by the legislatures of three-fourths of the several States within seven years from the date of its submission.

PRESIDENTIAL VACANCIES

Section 3 of the Twentieth Amendment deals with cases in which a president–elect dies before inauguration, or in which the nation does not choose the president before the newly set inauguration date. The death in November 1872 of Democrat Horace Greenley prior to the time that the electoral college had to choose between him and Republican candidate Ulysses S. Grant highlighted the need for this amendment. This amendment specifies that the newly elected vice president will serve in cases where the nation has yet to choose a new president or the president-elect dies prior to being selected. Section 4 further authorizes Congress to adopt legislation to deal with cases where one of the presidential or vice presidential nominees dies before Congress breaks an electoral deadlock. Perhaps because Congress has rarely faced such deadlocks, it has not yet exercised its legislative powers under this provision.

Amendment XXI. [1933] Section 1. The eighteenth article of amendment to the Constitution of the United States is hereby repealed.

Section 2. The transportation or importation into any State, Territory, or possession of the United States for delivery or use therein of intoxicating liquors, in violation of the laws thereof, is hereby prohibited.

Section 3. This article shall be inoperative unless it shall have been ratified as an amendment to the Constitution by conventions in the several States, as provided in the Constitution, within seven years from the date of the submission hereof to the States by the Congress.

THE REPEAL OF NATIONAL ALCOHOL PROHIBITION

The Twenty-first Amendment is the only amendment that has ever directly repealed another. It demonstrates that public opinion can change substantially. When the Eighteenth Amendment instituted national alcoholic prohibition, many reformers anticipated the elimination of a serious social vice. Although the amendment reduced the consumption of alcohol, it also stimulated widespread resistance. Prosecutions of bootleggers clogged the courts, and organized criminals gained substantial toeholds in supplying what legal businesspersons could not. Moreover, the alcohol industry was a potential source of both employment and tax monies at a time when the nation confronted the Great Depression. After incoming President Franklin D. Roosevelt and the Democratic Party endorsed the Twenty-first amendment in the 1932 presidential election, the outgoing Congress proposed it in early 1933. Fearing that conservative legislatures would never ratify the amendment, and perhaps influenced by the U.S. Supreme Court decision in *Hawke v. Smith* (1920), which invalidated an Ohio law permitting voters to ratify the Eighteenth Amendment through referendum, Congress vested ratification in special state-ratifying conventions. The necessary majority of such conventions ratified the amendment by the end of the year. Most such conventions met relatively briefly and took a straight up-or-down vote.

Section 2 of the Twenty-first Amendment continued to allow states to regulate alcohol if they so chose. Many states have, in turn, allowed localities to decide policy in regard to this matter. In *44 Liquormart v. Rhode Island* (1996), however, the Supreme Court decided that the First Amendment freedoms trumped the Twenty-first Amendment when it struck down state laws prohibiting stores from advertising liquor prices in newspapers or on billboards. Similarly, in a 5 to 4 decision in *Granholm v. Heald* (2005), the U.S. Supreme Court decided that Section 2 did not allow states to prohibit out-of-state wineries from shipping directly to consumers within them if they did not prohibit in-state wineries from doing the same. The Court ruled that such discrimination violated the commerce clause.

Amendment XXII. [1951] Section 1. No person shall be elected to the office of the President more than twice, and no person who has held the office of President, or acted as President, for more than two years of a term to which some other person was elected President shall be elected to the office of the President more than once. But this Article shall not apply to any person holding the office of President when this Article was proposed by the Congress, and shall not prevent any person who may be holding the office of President, or acting as President, during the term within which this Article becomes operative from holding the office of President or acting as President during the remainder of such term.

Section 2. This Article shall be inoperative unless it shall have been ratified as an amendment to the Constitution by the legislatures of three-fourths of the several States within seven years from the date of its submission to the States by the Congress.

A LIMIT ON PRESIDENTIAL TERMS OF OFFICE

The Twenty-second Amendment limits a president to serving two full terms, or, in the case of a vice president who comes to office during another's term, no more than ten years. Genuine fears of increased presidential powers and partisan Republican frustrations over the repeated election of the Democrat Franklin D. Roosevelt both contributed to state ratification of this amendment in 1951. Prior to Roosevelt, presidents had followed the example of George Washington, which Thomas Jefferson later confirmed, who left office after two terms. This rule was so well established that, by the 1920s, scholars rightly cited it as an example of America's unwritten constitution. Roosevelt's terms called the continuing validity of such a custom into question.

Some scholars think that the nation should have left the two-term limit as an unwritten practice, subject to change in cases of national emergency like World War II, instead of embodying it into the written Constitution. In addition to limiting who the people can elect to represent them, the Amendment probably works in an unintended and unanticipated fashion. It does so by undercutting a president's powers in the chief executive's second term, during which time the president is a lame duck.

Amendment XXIII. [1961] Section 1. The District constituting the seat of Government of the United States shall appoint in such manner as the Congress may direct:

A number of electors of President and Vice President equal to the whole number of Senators and Representatives in Congress to which the District would be entitled if it were a State, but in no event more than the least populous State; they shall be in addition to those appointed by the States, but they shall be considered, for the purposes of the election of President and Vice President, to be electors appointed by a State; and they shall meet in the District and perform such duties as provided by the twelfth article of amendment.

Section 2. The Congress shall have power to enforce this article by appropriate legislation.

ELECTORAL VOTES FOR THE DISTRICT OF COLUMBIA

Few constitutional mechanisms are more complex than the electoral college, which the framers invented to select presidents and vice presidents. In the aftermath of the unexpected tie between the presidential and vice presidential nominees in the election of 1800, the Twelfth Amendment amended the original system by providing that electors would cast separate votes for president and vice president. The Twenty-third Amendment provides for an additional, albeit not nearly as far-reaching, change.

Prior to 1961, residents of the nation's capital, the District of Columbia, lacked any voice in the electoral college, which apportioned votes only to states and determined each state's vote by adding the number of its representatives and senators. Because the District had neither, its inhabitants had no electoral votes. The situation seemed unfair in a democratic nation where the president represented everyone. The Twenty-third Amendment remedied this defect by giving the District a number of electoral votes no greater than that of the smallest state. Since every state is entitled to a minimum of one representative and two senators, the District of Columbia has three electoral votes. Currently, there are 538 electoral votes, resulting from the 435 representatives in the House of Representatives, 100 senators, and the District of Columbia's three votes. To win the presidency without going through the House of Representatives, a candidate needs a majority, or 270 or more votes.

The District still does not have voting representation in Congress. States rejected an amendment that Congress proposed in 1978 to grant the District representation equivalent to what it would have if it were a state.

Amendment XXIV. [1964] Section 1. The right of citizens of the United States to vote in any primary or other election for President or Vice President, for electors for President or Vice President, or for Senator or Representative in Congress, shall not be denied or abridged by the United States or by any State by reason of failure to pay any poll tax or other tax.

Section 2. The Congress shall have power to enforce this article by appropriate legislation.

THE PROHIBITION OF POLL TAXES

The Fifteenth, Seventeenth, Nineteenth, Twenty-third, Twenty-fourth, and Twenty-sixth Amendments have all prohibited infringements of the right to vote. The Twenty-fourth Amendment is the only amendment specifically to extend both to primary and general elections for national offices—although the Supreme Court had already declared in *United States v. Classic* (1941) that primaries were so integral to the electoral process that constitutional restrictions applied to them.

The Twenty-fourth Amendment invalidated the poll tax in federal elections. States had largely employed the tax to discourage the poor, which included a disproportionate number of African Americans, from voting.

Some states had heightened its impact by cumulating such taxes on those who had not voted in several elections. Although the Twenty-fourth Amendment applied only to national elections, in *Harper v. Virginia Board of Elections* (1966), the Supreme Court subsequently voided the use of such poll taxes in state elections on the authority of the equal protection clause of the Fourteenth Amendment. The right to vote no longer rests on one's ability to pay such a fee.

Amendment XXV. [1967] Section 1. In case of the removal of the President from office or of his death or resignation, the Vice President shall become President.

Section 2. Whenever there is a vacancy in the office of the Vice President, the President shall nominate a Vice President who shall take office upon confirmation by a majority vote of both Houses of Congress.

Section 3. Whenever the President transmits to the President pro tempore of the Senate and the Speaker of the House of Representatives his written declaration that he is unable to discharge the powers and duties of his office, and until he transmits to them a written declaration to the contrary, such powers and duties shall be discharged by the Vice President as Acting President.

Section 4. Whenever the Vice President and a majority of either the principal officers of the executive departments or of such other body as Congress may by law provide, transmit to the President pro tempore of the Senate and the Speaker of the House of Representatives their written declaration that the President is unable to discharge the powers and duties of his office, the Vice President shall immediately assume the powers and duties of the office as Acting President.

Thereafter, when the President transmits to the President pro tempore of the Senate and the Speaker of the House of Representatives his written declaration that no inability exists, he shall resume the powers and duties of his office unless the Vice President and a majority of either the principal officers of the executive department or of such other body as Congress may by law provide, transmit within four days to the President pro tempore of the Senate and the Speaker of the House of Representatives their written declaration that the President is unable to discharge the powers and duties of his office. Thereupon Congress shall decide the issue, assembling within forty-eight hours for that purpose if not in session. If the Congress, within twenty-one days after receipt of the latter written declaration, or, if Congress is not in session, within twenty-one days after Congress is required to assemble, determines by two-thirds vote of both Houses that the President is unable to discharge the powers and duties of his office, the Vice President shall continue to discharge the same as Acting President; otherwise, the President shall resume the powers and duties of his office.

VACANCIES AND DISABILITIES

The Twenty-fifth Amendment, like the Twentieth, deals with the presidency and vice presidency and the possibility of a death or disability in these offices. Several events in the twentieth century highlighted the urgency of such concerns. President Woodrow Wilson suffered a paralyzing stroke while in office, Franklin D. Roosevelt died, several presidents survived unsuccessful attempts on their lives, Dwight D. Eisenhower had a heart attack while in office, Lyndon B. Johnson had had one previously, and a gunman assassinated John F. Kennedy. When a vice president assumed the office of president, the vice president's office became vacant; had he died, the office would have gone by law to the Speaker of the House, who was not always fitted, and who voters had certainly not specifically chosen, for such a responsibility. America's important role in the modern world and its possession of nuclear weapons heightened the problem.

Vacancies in the Vice Presidency

Section 2 of the Twenty-fifth Amendment enables a president to fill a vice presidential vacancy subject to a majority vote of both Houses of Congress. This process differs from the confirmation process for most other presidential appointments, which requires a majority vote of the Senate. Under provisions of the Twenty-fifth Amendment, President Richard Nixon selected Gerald Ford to replace Vice President Spiro Agnew, who resigned in the wake of charges that he had, as a state official, accepted bribes. When Nixon later resigned, Ford thus became the nation's first unelected president. President Ford in turn nominated Nelson Rockefeller to be his vice president. Congress again confirmed this choice, although Ford ran unsuccessfully for reelection with Kansas Senator Bob Dole as his vice presidential candidate.

Cases of Presidential Disability

Although presidents have been able to fill vice presidential vacancies relatively easily, questions persist about cases of presidential disability. Section 3 deals with the easiest scenario by providing that when the president submits a written statement to the president pro tempore of the Senate and the speaker of the House of Representatives informing them that "he is unable to discharge the powers and duties of his office," the vice president shall serve as "Acting President" until the president informs them that he or she can resume his or her duties.

Presidents facing temporary incapacity may fear that evoking the Twenty-fifth Amendment will further contribute to the sense of crisis. Thus, Ronald

Reagan did not officially turn over his responsibilities to George H. W. Bush when Reagan remained in an emergency room after John Hinckley tried to assassinate him in 1981. Similarly, when he underwent surgery in 1985, Reagan wrote a letter indicating that he would entrust Bush with responsibilities while Reagan was under anesthesia without formally evoking the amendment, which he believed was designed to address longer disabilities.

Section 4 addresses the really difficult issue of what to do when a disabled president refuses to acknowledge the situation. The section provides that a vice president shall assume presidential duties when, acting in conjunction with a majority of the president's cabinet or "of such other body as Congress may by law provide," the vice president and this designated body transmit to the congressional leaders "their written declaration that the President is unable to discharge the powers and duties of his office."

What happens if the president contests this finding? The Twenty-fifth Amendment has probably done about as well as words can do in providing for the unpredictable, but the mechanism it establishes is hardly fail-safe. It provides that the president can resume powers when the president informs congressional officers that he or she is no longer disabled. If the vice president and a majority of cabinet or other officers contest this assertion in writing within four days, however, Congress has to decide whether the president is able to serve. It must do so by assembling within forty-eight hours for this purpose and voting within twenty-one days. Absent a two-thirds vote by both houses that the president is unable to discharge his duties, the president resumes such powers. The amendment is not altogether clear about who would be president in the interim.

Amendment XXVI. [1971] Section 1. The right of citizens of the United States, who are eighteen years of age or older, to vote shall not be denied or abridged by the United States or by any State on account of age.

Section 2. The Congress shall have power to enforce this article by appropriate legislation.

EIGHTEEN-YEAR-OLDS AND THE RIGHT TO VOTE

Prior to 1971, most states set the minimum voting age at twenty-one. In *Oregon v. Mitchell* (1970), the Supreme Court struck down the portion of a congressional law lowering this age to eighteen in both state and national elections by ruling that Congress could only set such qualifications in federal elections. Fearing that different standards could lead to an election nightmare, Congress proposed, and the states quickly ratified, the Twenty-sixth Amendment to eliminate this disparity.

Many factors motivated Americans to extend the franchise to eighteen-year-olds. Eighteen-year-olds were certainly better educated and thus better able to participate in the political process than ever before. Moreover, when the states ratified the amendment, many young people were risking their lives in Vietnam—as they had done in previous wars—on behalf of their country. Advocates of the amendment argued that if eighteen-year-olds were old enough to die for their country, they were old enough to vote.

Ironically, eighteen- to twenty-one-year-olds are among the least likely to vote. Like those who search for the elusive Loch Ness Monster, enthusiastic campaigners often make optimistic prophesies about a new wave of young voters in forthcoming elections, only to find that most—many of whom have not registered, are away from home, and have yet to assume full adult responsibilities in other areas—stay home. Such low turnout hardly means that the Twenty-sixth Amendment was unwise, but it again demonstrates that the authors of amendments are not always as successful as they hoped to be.

Amendment XXVII [1992]. No law, varying the compensation for the services of the Senators and Representatives, shall take effect, until an election of Representatives shall have intervened.

A TWENTY-SEVENTH AMENDMENT?

One of the more unexpected developments in American constitutional history occurred in 1992, when the states putatively ratified an amendment, which this author once dubbed "the stealth amendment," preventing a sitting Congress from raising its salaries. The amendment addressed a problem that has surfaced periodically ever since the Founding Fathers entrusted Congress with the power to set its own salaries. More problematically, the amendment that the states ratified in 1992 was one of twelve amendments that James Madison had introduced in 1789, ten of which the states ratified as the Bill of Rights in 1791.

Only six states initially ratified the congressional pay raise amendment, but the problem it addressed did not go away. In 1818, voters pressured Congress to repeal a law it had adopted the previous year that had established yearly, as opposed to per diem, pay. The "Salary Grab" Act of 1873 led to similar controversy, prompting Ohio to add its ratification to the earlier six. Wyoming added another vote after a 1978 pay hike. In 1982, Gregory Watson rediscovered the "Madison Amendment" when writing a term paper for a class at the University of Texas at Austin. Watson, an aide to a Texas legislator, subsequently led a movement, which he largely financed out of his own pocket, to muster the requisite state ratifications.

Watson's timing was nearly perfect. Not only had recent congressional pay raises generated opposition, but Congress's reputation was suffering from a number of other scandals that raised questions about whether its members were adequately representing their constituents' wishes. The result was that on May 8, 1992, the last state necessary for a three-fourths majority ratified the amendment, which the National Archivist subsequently certified.

Is the amendment valid? At this point, it is difficult to say with certainty. On the negative side, ratifications spread out over a two-hundred-year period stretch to the limit, if not the breaking point, the idea, which the Supreme Court articulated in *Dillon v. Gloss* (1921), that an amendment should reflect a contemporary consensus. On the positive side, in *Coleman v. Miller* (1939), the Supreme Court vested Congress with the authority to assess such contemporaneousness, and it accepted the amendment by an overwhelming vote on May 20, 1992. Whatever its status, the amendment has sent an unmistakable message to Congress, which is unlikely to try again to vote a raise for itself (albeit not necessarily for future congresses) whether the amendment remains on the books or not.

AUTHOR'S POSTSCRIPT ON THE AMERICAN FUTURE

I have spent many delightful hours studying and writing about the U.S. Constitution. This time has enhanced my great admiration and empathy for those who have written, ratified, and interpreted it. I have predicated this book on my conviction that we can best understand the Constitution by employing both our heads and our hearts.

James Madison observed in *Federalist* No. 51 that "if men were angels, no government would be necessary." By contrast, he did not expect that governments that are "administered by men over men" will ever be perfect. With some notable exceptions, the system that the U.S. Constitution ordained and established has protected the rights that the Declaration of Independence articulated and secured the goals that the Preamble to the Constitution stated.

The U.S. Constitution treats members of the polity as citizens rather than subjects. Its authors had enough faith in posterity to vest them with representative mechanisms for public participation and even for constitutional amendment. The American Constitution thus challenges detractors not to tear down but to join in bettering the government and even the document itself. While articulating essential purposes and establishing central structures, the Founding Fathers thus initiated a colloquy about the purposes and structures of government that has continued for the last two-hundred years. The Constitution offers the hope that if "We the People" continue to understand our system, participate in its government, and respect the rule of law, we may not only enjoy "the blessings of liberty" for ourselves, but also pass them to our own posterity.

REFERENCES AND SUGGESTIONS FOR FURTHER STUDY

Cases

44 Liquormart v. Rhode Island, 517 U.S. 484 (1996).
Coleman v. Miller, 307 U.S. 433 (1939).
Dillon v. Gloss, 256 U.S. 368 (1921).
Granholm v. Heald, 125 S. Ct. 1885 (2005).
Harper v. Virginia State Board of Elections, 383 U.S. 663 (1966).
Hawke v. Smith (I), 253 U.S. 221 (1920).
Marbury v. Madison, 5 U.S. 137 (1803).
Oregon v. Mitchell, 400 U.S. 112 (1970).
United States v. Classic, 313 U.S. 299 (1941).

Books

Herbert Abrams, *The President Has Been Shot: Confusion, Disability and the 25th Amendment in the Aftermath of the Attempted Assassination of Ronald Reagan* (New York: W.W. Norton, 1992).

John D. Feerick, *The Twenty-Fifth Amendment: Its Complete History and Earliest Applications* (New York: Fordham University Press, 1976).

Alan P. Grimes, *Democracy and the Amendments to the Constitution* (Lexington, MA: Lexington Books, 1978).

David E. Kyvig, *Repealing National Prohibition* (Chicago: University of Chicago Press, 1979).

Steven F. Lawson, *Black Ballots: Voting Rights in the South, 1944–1969* (New York: Columbia University Press, 1976).

Frederic Ogden, *The Poll Tax in the South* (Tuscaloosa: University of Alabama Press, 1958).

Kris E. Palmer, *Constitutional Amendments: 1789 to the Present* (Detroit, MI: Gale Group, 2000).

Ratification of the Twenty-First Amendment to the Constitution of the United States: State Convention Records and Laws, compiled by Everett Somerville Brown (Ann Arbor: University of Michigan Press, 1938).

Ronald Reagan et al., *Restoring the Presidency: Reconsidering the Twenty-Second Amendment* (Washington, DC: National Legal Center for the Public Interest, 1990).

Earl Spangler, *Presidential Tenure and Constitutional Limitation* (Washington, DC: University Press of America, Inc., 1979).

The Twenty-Fifth Amendment: Preparing for Presidential Disability. Special issue of the *Wake Forest Law Review*, Fall 1995.

Fifty Leading Cases

The U.S. Supreme Court has emerged as the most frequent interpreter of the Constitution. As a consequence, even a book like this, which aims at introductory students and general readers, can cite literally hundreds of case names. After explaining how to locate, cite, and brief cases, the author has listed and described the verdicts in fifty Supreme Court decisions—all of which he has cited in this text—that he thinks are the most important for students to learn.

LOCATING CASES AND UNDERSTANDING CITATIONS

Official Supreme Court decisions are published in the official *U.S. Reports* and in other sources, many of which are now available online. Students without access to West Law or Lexis/Nexis research services, to which may colleges and universities now subscribe, may find cases from 1990 forward at The Legal Information Institute and Project Hermes through Cornell University at http://supct.law.cornell.edu/supct/ or prior to 1990 at http://supct.law.cornell.edu/supct/cases/historic.htm. Students might also consult the Supreme Court's own Web site at http://www.supremecourtus.gov/index.html.

Legal citations use a standard format in which the number preceding the abbreviation of the case collection designates the volume number in which it is found and the number that follows the collection name designates the page number on which it begins. A student encountering a citation to *Brown v. Board of Education* at 347 U.S. 483; 74 S. Ct. 686; 98 L. Ed. 873 (1954), the case that overturned racial segregation in public education, would thus know that it is found in volume 347 of the *U.S. Reports* beginning on page 483, in volume 74 of the *Supreme Court Reporter* beginning on page 686, and on page 98 of the *United States Supreme Court Reports, Lawyer's Edition* beginning on page 873. The *Lawyer's Edition* does not cover early U.S. Supreme Court cases, but some such case citations will have a notation in parentheses designating the reporter who compiled the decision. The reference to *Marbury v. Madison*, 5 U.S. (1 Cranch) 137, 2 L. Ed. 60 (1803) thus indicates that *Marbury* is in the fifth volume of the *U.S. Reports*, and the first such volume compiled by William Cranch.

Other courts use similar systems. U.S. district court decisions are found in the *Federal Supplement*, designated as F. Supp. or F. Supp. 2d. Similarly, U.S. circuit court opinions are found in the *Federal Reporter*, designated as F., F.2d. or F. 3d. Recent U.S. Supreme decisions are often cited from *United States Law Week*, U.S.L.W., which prints and analyzes cases shortly after the Court decides them. The U.S. Supreme Court also issues "slip opinions," which identify cases by docket numbers, prior to official publication of opinions in the *U.S. Reports*.

Briefing Cases

Teachers typically encourage students to "brief" cases. Although the format will vary somewhat from one teacher to another, a student will list the **name, date, and/or citation** at the top of the page and follow with a brief description of the **facts**, a statement of the central **question** or questions that the case poses, the **decision** in the case and who wrote it, and the **reasons** that the justice gives for the decision. Such outlines should also briefly describe any **concurring or dissenting opinions**. Briefs should be long enough to include important details but short enough to use for study purposes. The reasoning sections will typically be the longest. Students seeking examples may want to consult Joseph F. Menez and John R. Vile, *Summaries of Leading Cases on the Constitution*, 14th ed. (Lanham, MD: Rowman & Littlefield Publishers, Inc., 2004).

Fifty Case Names and Decisions

Abington v. Schempp (1963): Extended *Engel v. Vitale* (1962), which had invalidated public prayer in public schools, by deciding that the establishment clause of the First Amendment outlawed public readings from the Bible and recitations of the Lord's Prayer in such schools.

Baker v. Carr (1962): Established that courts would no longer consider the issue of legislative apportionment to be a "political question" but that they would take cognizance of such cases.

Barron v. Baltimore (1833): Ruled that the Bill of Rights applied only to the national government and not to the states. Courts have subsequently applied most provisions of the Bill of Rights to the states via the due process clause of the Fourteenth Amendment.

Brown v. Board of Education (1954): Overturned the doctrine of "separate but equal" that the Supreme Court had established in *Plessy v. Ferguson* (1896) and decided that such racial discrimination would now be considered inherently unequal. In a companion case, *Bolling v. Sharpe* (1954), the Court applied the same ruling to the District of Columbia via the due process clause of the Fifth Amendment. In *Brown v. Board of Education II* (1955), the Court decided that desegregation should take place "with all deliberate speed."

Chisholm v. Georgia (1793): Decided that a state could be sued by citizens of other states. The Eleventh Amendment overturned this decision.

Civil Rights Cases (1883): In overturning the Civil Rights Act of 1875, the Court ruled that the Fourteenth Amendment outlawed only discriminatory state action and not discriminatory private action.

Cooley v. Board of Wardens (1851): Established the doctrine of "selective exclusiveness" according to which the Court recognized that some areas of commerce require a single uniform national rule and others permit state and local variations.

Dred Scott v. Sandford (1857): Declared that African Americans were not, and could not be, American citizens. This case, which also invalidated the Missouri Compromise of 1820, helped serve as a catalyst to the Civil War and was overturned by the Fourteenth Amendment.

Engel v. Vitale (1962): On the basis of the establishment clause of the First Amendment, this decision outlawed the public recitation of a nonsectarian prayer composed by the New York State Board of Regents for public schools.

Frontiero v. Richardson (1973): Struck down a military regulation whereby the government assumed that families of male members of the military depended upon them (thus making the serviceman eligible for an extra allowance) but required females to prove dependency by their family members.

Furman v. Georgia (1972): Struck down state capital punishment laws on the basis that, as then administered, such laws violated the cruel and unusual punishment provision of the Eighth Amendment as applied to the states by the Fourteenth Amendment.

Gibbons v. Ogden (1824): Overturned a monopoly that New York granted to steamboats on the basis that this monopoly interfered with piloting licenses that the national government had issued to other pilots under the interstate commerce clause.

Gideon v. Wainwright (1963): Extended the Sixth Amendment's right to appointed counsel to indigents in all felony cases.

Gitlow v. New York (1925): In upholding a conviction of a Socialist who had distributed incendiary literature, the Supreme Court used the "dangerous tendency" test rather than Holmes's "clear and present danger" standard. However, Justice Edward Sanford acknowledged that the Fourteenth Amendment applied First Amendment protections of speech and press to the states, thus helping to launch the movement for incorporation of other such guarantees in the Bill of Rights into the Fourteenth Amendment where they would restrain the states.

Gregg v. Georgia (1976): Upheld, as constitutional, new state capital punishment laws. Such laws provided for separate trials to determine guilt or innocence and settle on a penalty as well as for jury consideration of aggravating and mitigating circumstances.

Griswold v. Connecticut (1965): In striking down a Connecticut law prohibiting the use or prescription of birth control devices, the Court formulated a broad right to privacy that subsequently served as a basis for the rulings on abortion in *Roe v. Wade* (1973) and subsequent cases.

Home Building and Loan Association v. Blaisdell (1934): In upholding the Minnesota Mortgage Moratorium Law, the Court indicated that it would give a much more liberal reading to the contract clause than the Court had given in the nineteenth century.

Immigration and Naturalization Service v. Chadha (1983): Ruled that the "legislative veto" violated both the Constitution's presentment clause and its bicameralism requirement.

Katz v. United States (1967): Effectively overturned *Olmstead v. United States* (1928) by requiring police to get search warrants before engaging in electronic surveillance.

Korematsu v. United States (1944): Sanctioned the exclusion of Japanese Americans from areas in California where the government thought they posed a military threat. In this case, however, Justice Hugo Black said that any classifications based on race were "immediately suspect" and would be subject to increased scrutiny.

Lawrence v. Texas (2003): Overturned an earlier decision in *Bowers v. Hardwick* (1986) and decided that states laws prohibiting private consensual sodomy were unconstitutional.

Lemon v. Kurtzman (1971): Established a three-part test, known as the Lemon Test, by which courts can ascertain whether laws infringe on the establishment clause of the First Amendment. The test requires: that legislation have a secular legislative purpose; that its primary effect neither advances nor inhibits religion; and that it avoids excessive entanglement with religion.

Lochner v. New York (1905): Often cited as the epitome of the kind of laissez-faire jurisprudence typical of the Court before 1937, the Court struck down a New York law designed to regulate the working hours of bakers.

Marbury v. Madison (1803): In turning away a request by an individual who had been appointed as a justice of the peace but had never received his commission, the Court ruled that a section of the Judiciary Act of 1789 that seemed to grant the Court original jurisdiction was unconstitutional and therefore void, therefore asserting the Court's power of judicial review.

McCulloch v. Maryland (1819): Ruled that Congress had the implied power to establish a national bank and that the state of Maryland had no authority to tax it.

Miller v. California (1973): Established a three-part test for identifying obscenity that, with minor modifications, is still in effect today. The standard is based on local community standards.

Miranda v. Arizona (1966): In invalidating Miranda's conviction for kidnapping and rape, the Court established a set of guidelines that police officers must follow and a set of warnings they should give when interrogating criminal suspects.

Myers v. United States (1926): Established the president's sole right to fire executive officers that he had appointed with the advice and consent of the Senate.

New York Times Co. v. Sullivan (1964): Established "actual malice" as the standard that the Court would apply in adjudicating cases in which public figures allege that they are victims of libel.

New York Times Company v. United States (1971): The so-called Pentagon Papers Case in which the Court reaffirmed the strong presumption against prior restraint and permitted publication of papers relative to the history of United States involvement in Vietnam.

Palko v. Connecticut (1937): In deciding that the double jeopardy provision did not apply to the states—a decision that *Benton v. Maryland* later overturned (1969)—Justice Benjamin Cardozo forcefully articulated the doctrine of selective incorporation whereby the Court would apply only those rights within the Bill of Rights that it considered to be fundamental to the states via the due process clause of the Fourteenth Amendment.

Plessy v. Ferguson (1896): Upheld state Jim Crow laws by establishing the doctrine of "separate but equal," a doctrine not overturned until the decision in *Brown v. Board of Education* (1954).

Pollock v. Farmers' Loan & Trust Co. (1895): Invalidated the income tax as unconstitutional. The Sixteenth Amendment later overturned the decision.

Reed v. Reed (1971): Used the equal protection clause of the Fourteenth Amendment to overturn a state law that automatically preferred males to females as administrators of an estate.

Reynolds v. Sims (1964): Applied the principle of "one person, one vote" to both houses of state legislatures.

Roe v. Wade (1973): Held that the right to privacy encompassed a woman's right to procure an abortion in the first and second trimester of pregnancy and in cases in the third trimester where her life or health was at stake.

Schenck v. United States (1919): In upholding the conviction of a Socialist who had mailed pamphlets to potential draftees encouraging them to avoid the draft, Justice Holmes articulated the "clear and present danger" test designed to give broad protection to speech while indicating that it was not unlimited.

Slaughterhouse Cases (Butchers' Benevolent Association v. Crescent City Live-Stock Landing & Slaughter-House Co.), (1873): In rejecting the pleas of New Orleans' butchers who were required under state law to pursue their calling in specified abattoirs, the Court gave a very narrow reading to the privileges and immunities clause of the Fourteenth Amendment.

Swann v. Charlotte-Mecklenburg Board of Education (1971): Upheld the limited use of mandatory school busing as a means of dealing with prior de jure segregation.

Texas v. Johnson (1989): In a decision later reaffirmed in *United States v. Eichman* (1990), the Court ruled that a Texas law prohibiting flag desecration was an unconstitutional infringement of the First Amendment freedom of speech.

Tinker v. Des Moines Independent County School District (1969): Established the right of public school students to engage in nonviolent symbolic speech, in this case, the wearing of black arm bands in protest of the war in Vietnam.

United States v. Carolene Products Company (1938): The occasion for Justice Harlan Fiske Stone's famous footnote number four where he suggested that the Court would subject certain matters within the Constitution—most notably the first ten amendments, provisions providing for keeping the democratic processes open, and those involving the rights of minorities—to more exacting judicial scrutiny than others.

United States v. Curtiss-Wright Export Corp. (1936): In upholding a presidentially declared boycott of goods to a warring area of South

America, the Supreme Court said that the president has especially broad powers in the area of foreign affairs.

United States v. Lopez (1995): Overturned a federal law prohibiting guns near school grounds on the basis that such power was not directly related to congressional powers under the commerce clause.

United States v. Nixon (1974): Established that a president's executive privilege was limited and that President Nixon would have to turn over select Washington tapes to the Watergate Special Prosecutor.

U.S. Term Limits v. Thornton (1995): Decided that the qualifications listed for members in the Constitution were exclusive and that states could not add to this requirement by imposing their own term limits.

Wesberry v. Sanders (1964): Formulated the "one person, one vote" standard in invalidating Georgia's apportionment of its congressional districts.

West Coast Hotel v. Parrish (1937): In upholding a Washington State minimum wage law, the Court overturned an earlier decision in *Adkins v. Childrens' Hospital* (1923) and instituted the "switch in time that saved nine" by deflecting criticism that had led to Franklin D. Roosevelt's court-packing plan. From this case forward, the Court has generally given less attention to governmental regulations of economic matters than to other issues.

West Virginia State Board of Education v. Barnette (1943): Overturned the earlier decision in *Minersville School District v. Gobitis* (1940) and said that public school students with religious objections could not be disciplined for refusing to salute the American flag.

Youngstown Sheet & Tube Co. v. Sawyer (1952): A case, often simply called the Steel Seizure Case, in which the court ruled that President Truman did not have inherent authority as commander in chief to seize the American steel industry in order to avert a strike that threatened supplies needed to pursue the conflict then being waged in Korea.

Glossary

Actual Malice: A standard that courts apply in cases where public officials are suing for libel. This standard specifies that they must show either that such statements were published with knowledge that they were false or with reckless disregard of their truth or falsity.

Actual Representation: The position that the American colonists advocated in their dispute with Britain whereby they argued that the British Parliament could not tax them unless they actually had representatives sitting in that body.

Advice and Consent: The power of the Senate to approve or disapprove treaties signed by the president and/or nominees that he has nominated for office.

Advisory Opinions: Nonbinding court decisions that, by long-standing practice, U.S. courts will not issue.

Affirmative Action Programs: The name given to a variety of programs designed to increase minority representation that may or may not include racial preferences or quotas.

Alien and Sedition Acts: Laws that the Federalist Congress adopted in 1798. The former made it more difficult for aliens to establish citizenship, and the latter made it a criminal offense to criticize the government or its officials. Federalist lawmakers directed the law toward Democratic-Republicans, who strongly opposed them.

All-White Primary: A primary, or nominating election, that a political party opened only to white voters. The Supreme Court outlawed such primaries in *Smith v. Allwright* (1944).

Amicus Curiae Briefs: "Friend of the court" briefs that groups or individuals who are not party to a suit file to call their legal views to the court's attention.

Annapolis Convention: The meeting attended by representatives of five states that preceded the Constitutional Convention of 1787. Originally called to discuss the problems of commerce and navigation under the Articles, the Annapolis Convention served as a springboard for the Constitutional Convention that followed.

Antifederalists: Those who opposed ratification of the Constitution of 1787. Antifederalist opposition to the document is generally credited with exerting pressure on Federalist supporters of the Constitution to agree to the adoption of a bill of rights.

Appellate Jurisdiction: Refers to cases heard "on appeal," usually over issues of law rather than fact.

Articles of Confederation: The loose confederation of states, or league of friendship, in effect from 1781 to 1789. Under the Articles, the primary powers of government rested with individual states, which were equally represented in a unicameral Congress.

Bad Tendency Test: A test for freedom of speech that courts utilized both before and after development of the clear and present danger test. It allows governments to suppress speech that has a dangerous tendency.

Bail: Money that defendants in a criminal trial put up as a condition for release from custody while awaiting a trial. The Eighth Amendment prohibits such bail from being "excessive."

Beyond a Reasonable Doubt: The standard of proof that the law requires in criminal cases.

Bicameralism: Provides for the division of the legislative branch into two houses or chambers.

Bill of Rights: The first ten amendments to the U.S. Constitution that protect basic civil rights and liberties.

Bills of Attainder: Legislative punishments inflicted without the benefit of a trial. Article I, Section 9 of the Constitution outlaws such bills.

Blue Laws: Laws requiring the closure of certain businesses or forbidding the sale of certain items on Sundays. Courts have upheld these on a secular basis.

Cabinet: The heads of the executive agencies and other individuals the president may choose to consult about governmental policies.

Checks and Balances: A governmental system, like that which the U.S. Constitution creates, in which differing individuals and institutions exercise different powers, thus preventing any single individual or institution from abusing its powers.

Chief Justice: The head of the U.S. Supreme Court. Regarded as *primus inter pares*, or first among equals, the Constitution designates the Chief to preside over Senate impeachment trials of the president.

Circuit Courts of Appeal: The name of the thirteen courts in the federal system that are midway between the District Courts and the U.S. Supreme Court. Such circuit courts deal mostly with cases on appeal.

Citizenship: An acknowledgment of membership in a nation. The Fourteenth Amendment provides that persons born in the United States or naturalized are citizens. Article I, Section 8 grants Congress the power of naturalization.

Clear and Present Danger Test: A test that Justices Oliver Wendell Holmes, Jr. developed and applied to laws regulating freedom of speech in *Schenck v. United States* (1919). The test indicates that speech is highly protected but not absolute. Under this test governments can legitimately suppress speech that poses a "clear and present danger" that such governments have a right to prevent.

Commander in Chief: The title designating the president's power over the U.S. armed forces. Vesting this power in the presidency assures civilian control over the military.

Commerce Clause: The provision in Article I, Section 8 granting Congress power to regulate commerce "with foreign Nations, and among the several States, and with the Indian tribes." This has proved to be one of Congress' most expansive powers. The Congress under the Articles of Confederation did not have this authority.

***Common Sense*:** A work that Thomas Paine published in January 1776, in which he argued against monarchy and hereditary succession and urged the colonists to declare their independence.

Concurrent Jurisdiction: Authority over an area or subject more than one court or law enforcement agency share.

Concurrent Powers: Powers, like taxation and spending, that both state and national governments jointly exercise.

Concurring Opinion: A judicial decision in which one or more justices agree with the decision but write separately to give their own explanations and/or express their reservations.

Confederal Government: A government, like that under Confederation or the Confederate States of America, under which the constituent state governments hold primary power.

Connecticut Compromise: The Compromise, which delegates to the Constitution Convention of 1787 adopted, making Congress a bicameral body where states were represented according to population in the House of Representatives and equally in the Senate.

Constitutional Convention of 1787: The meeting held in Philadelphia from May through September. Ostensibly called to revise the Articles of Confederation, the Convention decided instead to redraw the government.

Constitutional Conventions: Article V of the Constitution specifies that Congress is obligated to call a convention to propose amendments when two-thirds of the state legislatures request it to do so. To date, the states have not yet called such Article V conventions, and questions remain as to how they would operate.

Constitutional Courts: American courts created under the authority of Article III and subject to various protections specified therein.

Continental Congresses: Meetings of American colonial representatives that were called to discuss grievances and formulate strategy against the British. The First Continental Congress met in 1774. The Second Continental Congress, which began meeting in 1775, approved the Declaration of Independence.

Contract Clause: The name of provision in Article I, Section 10 that prohibits states from passing laws "impairing the obligations of Contracts."

Council of Revision: A prominent provision of the Virginia Plan, which the Constitutional Convention did not adopt, that would have allowed the executive and members of the judiciary to veto acts of state and national legislation.

Court-Packing Plan: After the Supreme Court voided many of his New Deal programs, Franklin Roosevelt proposed adding one justice (up to fifteen) for every justice over age seventy. Congress rejected this plan which, while not illegal, appeared to threaten the independence of the judiciary.

Cruel and Unusual Punishments: Unspecified penalties, which the Eighth Amendment prohibits.

Death-Qualified Jury: A jury from which judges have dismissed opponents to the death penalty.

Declaration of Independence: The document, which Thomas Jefferson largely authored and the Second Continental Congress adopted in 1776, declaring the reasons the colonists were declaring their independence from Great Britain. The document appeals to natural rights.

de Facto: Caused by forces other than the law.

de Jure: Mandated by law.

Dickinson, John: The Pennsylvania delegate who drew up the initial Articles of Confederation, a document the Congress subsequently modified to vest greater power in the states.

Direct Taxes: Unidentified taxes, which Article I, Section 9 prohibited Congress from laying unless they apportioned them according to a state's population. The Sixteenth Amendment has modified this prohibition against direct taxes.

Dissenting Opinion: An opinion written by a justice who does not agree with the majority opinion of the court.

District Courts: The lowest rung of the U.S. federal court system, of which there are currently 94. Such courts are largely courts of original jurisdiction, hearing cases in the first instance.

District of Columbia: The area called Washington, D.C., that is designated as the nation's capital. Under the Constitution, Congress legislates for this area, which the Twenty-third Amendment has granted votes in the electoral college but whose citizens still have no voting members in the Congress.

Double Jeopardy: Trying an individual for a crime for which that individual has already been declared not guilty. The Fifth Amendment disallows such double jeopardy.

Dual Federalism: A view of governmental relations, prevalent prior to the New Deal, emphasizing that state and federal authorities have distinct spheres of authority.

Due Process Clauses: Provisions found in the Fifth and Fourteenth Amendments prohibiting the government from taking a person's life, liberty, or property without due process of law. The later provision has been the primary vehicle by which courts have applied the guarantees in the Bill of Rights to the states.

During Good Behaviour: A constitutional phrase indicating that federal judges serve until they die or resign, or until they are impeached, convicted, and removed from office.

Elastic Clause: The last sentence of Article I, Section 8, granting Congress all powers "necessary and proper" for carrying out its delegated powers. The clause has become the primary basis for the doctrine of implied powers.

Electoral College: The indirect system used in the United States to select the president and vice president. The Twelfth Amendment modified the original system so that electors now cast distinct votes for president and vice president.

Emancipation Proclamation: A presidential order that Abraham Lincoln issued on January 1, 1863, declaring freedom for slaves held behind Confederate lines. The Thirteenth Amendment later completely abolished slavery.

Eminent Domain: The power of governments to demand the sale of private property needed for public use. The Fifth Amendment requires that the government provide just compensation in the case of such takings.

Emoluments: A constitutional term used to refer to salaries or other monetary rewards.

Entrenchment Clauses: Two provisions listed in Article V of the Constitution limit the scope of amendments. One such provision, dealing with slave importation, has expired; the other provides that no state may be deprived of its equal representation in the Senate without its consent.

Enumerated Powers: Powers listed in the Constitution. The powers of Congress are chiefly granted, or enumerated, in Article I, Section 8.

Equal Protection Clause: A provision found within the Fourteenth Amendment requiring that state governments extend equal treatment to all persons.

Equal Rights Amendment: An amendment that Congress proposed in 1972 to eliminate discrimination based on sex; the amendment fell three states shy of ratification, even after Congress extended the period for ratification.

Establishment Clause: The provision in the First Amendment prohibiting government from making laws "respecting an establishment of religion."

Exclusionary Rule: A rule, which the U.S. Supreme Court first applied to the national government and subsequently to the states, prohibiting the introduction in court of illegally obtained evidence. Supporters defend the rule both as a means of deterring illegal police conduct and as a mechanism to keep governmental hands clean of wrongdoing; critics point to the criminals that it sometimes allow to go free.

Executive Agreements: Agreements made between the president and foreign governments that are not, like treaties, submitted to the Senate for approval. Most such agreements cover relatively minor matters.

Executive Branch: The branch of government that the president heads and that is responsible for executing, that is, enforcing, the laws. The American president is a single individual who serves as both head of government and head of state.

Executive Privilege: The right that presidents have asserted to withhold documents relating to national security or to refuse to testify about matters considered to be confidential. In *United States v. Nixon* (1974), the Supreme Court recognized that such a claim was subject to limits.

Ex Post Facto Laws: Retroactive criminal laws, which Article I, Section 9 of the Constitution forbids.

Extradition: The process by which states return a fugitive back to the state from which such a fugitive fled in order that the state may try such an individual for crimes committed or alleged to have been committed there. Article IV, Section 2 of the Constitution outlines this provision.

Federal Government: A governmental system that divides power between state and national authorities. In such systems, powers are almost always delineated by a written constitution, and both state and national governments have powers—as, for example, through taxation—to operate directly upon individual citizens.

***Federalist Papers*:** A series of eighty-five articles published in New York newspapers in defense of the Constitution. Written under the pen name of Publius, its authors were Alexander Hamilton, James Madison, and John Jay. The most famous of the *Federalist Papers* is No. 10 in which James Madison praised republican government as a cure for the mischief of factions.

Federalists: The name of those who supported ratification of the U.S. Constitution. Alexander Hamilton later founded a political party whose members called themselves Federalists.

Fighting Words: Highly emotional and inflammatory words expressed in a face-to-face setting that states may prohibit as having the effect of force. In *Chaplinsky v. New Hampshire* (1942), the Supreme Court said that the First Amendment did not protect such expressions.

Filibuster: A Senate practice, not specifically mentioned in the Constitution, whereby Senators can literally talk a bill or a nomination to death. Under current rules sixty Senators are required to vote cloture, and stop a filibuster.

Franchise: The right to vote.

Free Exercise Clause: The provision in the First Amendment barring the government from "prohibiting the free exercise of" religion.

Fugitive Slave Clause: A provision found in Article IV, Section 2 of the Constitution requiring that states shall deliver persons "held to Service or labor in one State, under the Laws thereof, escaping into another." Friction over this clause was particularly intense in the period leading up to the Civil War.

Full Faith and Credit Clause: The provision in Article IV, Section 1 of the Constitution obligating states to recognize civil acts of other states.

Gag Orders: Orders, which courts now severely limit, designed to squelch reports of ongoing hearings or trials in order to guarantee the fairness of trials.

Gerrymandering: The term for the process of configuring districts so as to advantage a particular party or group.

Good Faith: A recognized exception to the exclusionary rule designed to apply where police officers acted in good faith and without knowledge that a warrant was flawed.

Grand Jury: A body of citizens convened to determine whether there is sufficient evidence to bring an individual to trial.

Grandfather Clauses: Laws that states directed against racial minorities and that courts eventually overturned, which restricted voting to those who could prove that their grandfathers had voted prior to 1867, that is, prior to the time that African Americans achieved this right.

Granted Powers: Another name for enumerated, or constitutionally listed, powers.

Gravity of the Evil Test: A weaker reformulation of the clear and present danger test, which the Court applied in *Dennis v. United States* (1951), permitting judges to determine whether the gravity of the evil, discounted by its improbability, allows for legislative action.

Guarantee Clause: The provision in Article IV, Section 4 of the Constitution providing that the United States shall guarantee each state a republican, or representative, form of government.

Head of Government: The nation's chief elected official—in parliamentary systems, usually the prime minister; in the United States, the president.

Head of State: The individual—in the United States, the president; in parliamentary democracies, sometimes the monarch—who meets with diplomats and serves as the nation's overarching symbol.

Heightened Scrutiny: The intermediate level of review that the Supreme Court generally applies to classifications based on gender.

Hereditary Succession: The principle by which some nations pass monarchy from one generation to another on the basis of noble birth.

Hicklin Test: A standard, which U.S. courts have abandoned, according to which courts judged a work to be obscene if its tendency was such as to deprave and corrupt those whose minds were open to such influence and into whose hands such a work might fall.

High Crimes and Misdemeanors: The grounds the Constitution lists, along with bribery and treason, as grounds for impeachment. Although the parameters of high crimes and misdemeanors are vague, most scholars agree that the authors of this phrase designed it to prohibit impeachment and conviction of officers simply because of disagreements over policy.

House of Commons: The lower and most powerful house of the British Parliament.

House of Lords: The upper and less powerful house of the British Parliament, filled largely through heredity.

House of Representatives: The lower house of the U.S. Congress, currently with 435 voting members elected by members of their districts for two-year terms.

Impeachment: The process, instituted by the House of Representatives, of bringing charges against an executive or judicial official. Charges are tried by the U.S. Senate where a two-thirds vote is required for a conviction. The

Constitution lists treason, bribery, and other "high crimes and misde-meanors" as the only grounds for impeachment. Conviction results in re-moval from office.

Implied Powers: Unspecified constitutional powers that the necessary and proper clause of Article I, Section 8 recognizes as appropriate to carrying out the enumerated powers of Congress.

Impoundment: An executive practice, which Congress has limited, of refusing to spend all the monies that Congress has appropriated.

In Forma Pauperis Petition: A petition, like that which Gideon filed in *Gideon v. Wainwright* (1963), that defendants, unable to afford attorneys, file on their own behalf.

Incompatibility Clause: The provision in Article I, Section 6 of the U.S. Constitution that prevents members of Congress from holding other si-multaneous governmental offices.

Incorporation: The process by which courts have applied most of the guarantees found in the Bill of Rights to the state governments via the due process clause of the Fourteenth Amendment.

Inferior Officers: Offices other than cabinet heads, judges, ambassadors, and other constitutionally specified offices appointed by the president. The Constitution allows the president, courts of law, or heads of the departments to appoint such officers.

Information: An alternative to grand jury indictments whereby a prose-cutor presents information to a judge to establish that the state has sufficient evidence to proceed with a trial.

Inherent Powers: Powers, especially in the area of foreign affairs, that the president can exercise simply by virtue of his office.

Initiative: A mechanism, often associated with the Progressive Era and still confined to the state and local level, by which voters can through petitions introduce legislation or constitutional amendments.

Interposition: The doctrine, which Madison and Jefferson advanced in the Virginia and Kentucky Resolutions of 1798, whereby states had the right to interpose themselves against federal laws that they believed to be uncon-stitutional.

Interpretivists: Scholars and judges who emphasize adherence to the words of the Constitution and the intentions of its framers and ratifiers.

Item Veto: A veto that many states allow but the U.S. Constitution does not provide whereby an executive may void individual items of a bill, especially those related to appropriations.

Jim Crow Laws: Laws, now illegal, that mandated racial segregation.

Judicial Activism: The view that the judicial branch should take a leading role in government.

Judicial Branch: The branch of government, which the Supreme Court heads, that is responsible for interpreting the laws and ascertaining whether they are constitutional.

Judicial Restraint: The view that members of the judicial branch should be deferential to decisions that the two elected branches of government have made.

Judicial Review: The power American courts exercise of reviewing executive and administrative actions, as well as state and federal laws, that come before them in the course of judicial decision-making, and of deciding whether or not they are constitutional.

Jurisdiction: Areas in which courts or other bodies have authority to render decisions. U.S. courts exercise authority either based on the subject matter of the case or the parties to the suit. Jurisdiction of the courts may be further divided into original and appellate, the former dealing with cases courts hear for the first time, and the latter referring to cases they hear on appeal.

Jus Sanguinis: A term meaning "law of the blood" that recognizes that persons born abroad to citizens of a nation may still themselves acquire such citizenship rights.

Jus Soli: A term meaning "law of the soil" that recognizes that those born within a nation are citizens thereof.

Justiciable: Considered capable of judicial resolution.

Lame Ducks: Elected officials who are finishing out their terms but already know that they will not be returning to office. The Twentieth Amendment shortened the period during which lame-duck presidents and members of Congress serve.

Legislative Branch: The lawmaking branch of government. The U.S. Constitution vests this authority in Congress; Great Britain vests the power in Parliament.

Legislative Courts: American courts created apart from the provisions of Article III and thus not subject to the same constitutional protections.

Legislative Veto: An extra-constitutional mechanism, which the U.S. Supreme Court invalidated in the *Chadha* case, in which Congress delegates powers to the president, with the proviso that one or both houses can subsequently invalidate his actions.

Lemon Test: A three-part test, which the Court first fully formulated in *Lemon v. Kurtzman* (1971), to assess whether the establishment clause has been violated. The test, which the Supreme Court does not apply on a consistent basis, requires that legislation must have a secular legislative purpose, neither advance nor inhibit religion, and avoid excessive entanglement with religion.

Letters of Marque and Reprisal: Authorizations used in colonial times and in early American history providing for free lance shipmen to attack the ships of enemy nations and share in the spoils.

Libel: The publication of false and damaging information about another. Although U.S. courts have ruled that the First Amendment does not protect such libel, they have also made it difficult, especially for public figures, to prove accusations of libel.

Literacy Tests: Tests, now suspended by law, that were once a prerequisite for exercising the right to vote; states often administered such tests, combined with "understanding clauses," in a racially discriminatory fashion.

Madison, James: The Virginia delegate to the Constitutional Convention often designated both the "Father of the Constitution" and the "Father of the Bill of Rights." Madison was a major figure in the creation of the Virginia Plan and took the most extensive notes at the Constitutional Convention of 1787. He was one of three authors of *The Federalist Papers*, the leader of Congress who shepherded the Bill of Rights through the House of Representatives, and a leader, with Thomas Jefferson, of the Democratic-Republican Party.

Magna Carta: A Latin term meaning "great charter." This was a document that noblemen wrested from King John of England and that he signed at Runneymead in 1215. Often regarded as the fountainhead of English liberties, the document contained the principle of "no taxation without representation," which the American colonists cited in the dispute with Great Britain that led to the Revolutionary War, and contained the forerunner of today's idea of "due process of law."

Marshall, John: The fourth, and arguably the greatest, chief justice of the United States. Marshall established the power of judicial review in *Marbury* *v. Madison* (1803), the doctrine of implied powers in *McCulloch v. Maryland* (1819), and federal control over interstate commerce in *Gibbons v. Ogden* (1824). In his last major decision, *Barron v. Baltimore* (1833), Marshall decided that the Bill of Rights did not apply to the states.

Mayflower Compact: A charter of government, which New England pilgrims drew up before embarking from their ship, the *Mayflower*. This charter served as a prototype for later constitutions and as a symbol of the colorists' commitment to self-government.

Miller Test: A three-part test, which the U.S. Supreme Court formulated in *Miller v. California* (1973), for assessing whether works are obscene. Under this test, the Court considers a work to be obscene: if an average person, applying contemporary community standards, would find that the work, taken as a whole, appeals to a prurient (lustful) interest in sex; if it depicts or describes in a patently offensive way, sexual conduct specifically defined by law; and if the work lacks any serious literary, artistic, political, or scientific value.

Miranda Warnings: Statements that police officers must issue when arresting or cross-examining suspects. Such warnings, which the Supreme Court established in *Miranda v. Arizona* (1966), detail individual rights including the right to counsel and to remain silent.

Missouri Compromise: A law, which Congress adopted in 1820, admitting Maine as a free state and Missouri as a slave state and drawing a line in the territories north of which slavery would be excluded. The Supreme Court invalidated this compromise in the *Dred Scott* decision (1857).

Monarchy: Government by a single individual, usually a king or queen. In most modern democracies, this position is a largely symbolic one.

Natural Rights: Rights that individuals have by virtue of being human. The Declaration of Independence stated that such rights included "life, liberty, and the pursuit of happiness."

Naturalization: The process by which a person not born within a nation can become a citizen thereof. Article I, Section 8 vests this power in Congress.

New Jersey Plan: The plan that William Paterson of New Jersey introduced at the Constitutional Convention of 1787. In contrast to the previously introduced Virginia Plan, the New Jersey plan called for equal state representation in a unicameral Congress.

Noninterpretivists: Scholars and judges who emphasize sources other than the language of the Constitution and the intent of the framers and ratifiers in interpreting the Constitution.

Northwest Ordinance of 1787: The law, which Congress adopted during the Articles of Confederation, specifying how the territory in the American West would be governed and outlawing slavery in this region.

Nullification: The doctrine, which South Carolina Senator John C. Calhoun advocated, according to which states had the right to nullify, or void, federal laws that they believed were unconstitutional.

One Person, One Vote: The principle, which the Supreme Court first articulated in *Gray v. Sanders* (1963), according to which legislative and congressional districts must have approximately equal numbers of constituents.

Original Jurisdiction: Refers to the first time a case is heard before any court. Article III of the Constitution spells out the fairly limited original jurisdiction of the Supreme Court.

Overbreadth Doctrine: A doctrine, which courts apply to free speech cases, striking down laws so overly broad that they sweep both protected and unprotected speech within their ambit.

Pardon and Reprieve Power: A power to mitigate punishment that Article II, Section 2 of the Constitution gives to the president. This power includes that of granting general amnesties.

Parliament: The English legislature, composed of two houses, the House of Commons and the House of Lords. Under the theory of the British government, its parliament is sovereign.

Parliamentary Sovereignty: The doctrine, supported by the British in the dispute with the colonists, according to which the British Parliament had authority to make laws not only for Great Britain but also for the colonies. More generally, parliamentary sovereignty refers to the doctrine that there are no legal limits on what Parliament can do.

Per Curiam Opinion: An unsigned opinion issued on behalf of a court.

Peremptory Challenges: Dismissals of jurors during a voir dire examination for which they need provide no reason. Supreme Court decisions forbid lawyers from basing such dismissals on the basis of race or gender.

Petit Jury: A trial jury, typically consisting of twelve members of the community, which decides on a defendant's guilt or innocence and, in some cases, on an appropriate penalty.

Plea Bargains: Agreements in criminal cases in which prosecutors agree to seek a lesser charge in exchange for defendants' acknowledgment of guilt.

Pocket Veto: A veto exercised at the end of a congressional session, whereby a bill fails to become a law simply because the president pockets it and does not sign or veto it.

Political Questions: Issues that the courts refuse to hear, often in foreign policy realms, because they believe the Constitution has entrusted the resolution of such issues to other branches of government.

Poll Taxes: Taxes levied as a condition to voting. The Twenty-fourth Amendment prohibited the payment of such poll taxes as a condition for voting in federal elections.

Power of Judgment: The only power Alexander Hamilton said that the judiciary would have.

Power of the Purse: The powers over taxing, borrowing, and spending, which Article I, Section 8 of the U.S. Constitution allocates to Congress.

Power of the Sword: The power over the military that the Constitution allocates to the president.

Preamble to the Constitution: The opening paragraph that outlines the central purposes of the document.

Preponderance of the Evidence: The standard of proof that the law generally requires in civil cases.

Presentment Clause: The provision in Article I, Section 7 of the U.S. Constitution specifying that Congress must present all laws to the president for approval or veto.

President of the Senate: An office held by the U.S. vice president allowing him to preside and to cast tie-breaking votes.

Prior Restraint: The heart of freedom of the press in the United States is understood to rest in the strong presumption against any prior restraint of publication. Governments may, however, punish individuals for works that later proved to be obscene or libelous.

Privacy Rights: Although not specifically mentioned in the Constitution, the Supreme Court has ruled in *Griswold v. Connecticut* (1965) and subsequent cases that the Constitution protects such rights.

Privileges and Immunities Clause: The provisions in Article IV, Section 1 and in Section 1 of the Fourteenth Amendment, which provide that states must treat citizens of other states as they would their own.

Probable Cause: The standard of proof that the Fourth Amendment requires before police officers can secure search warrants.

Progressive Era: The time period early in the twentieth century during which there was a strong push for reform and democratization. Amendments 16 through 19 were proposed and ratified during this period.

Publius: The Roman pen name used by Alexander Hamilton, James Madison, and John Jay when they authored *The Federalist Papers*, defending the proposed Constitution.

Pure Democracy: A government that operates like those of ancient Greece where citizens meet together in person to debate and resolve matters of public policy.

Ratification: Formal approval. The Constitution requires a two-thirds majority of the U.S. Senate to ratify treaties and three-fourths of the states to ratify constitutional amendments.

Reasonable Basis Test (Rational Basis Test): The standard courts use to evaluate classifications that are not tied to a suspect class, a fundamental right, or to gender. This is the Court's most deferential level of review.

Recall: A mechanism by which some states and localities permit voters to remove elected officials from office before the end of their term.

Referendum: A mechanism, currently limited to the state and local level, whereby voters can veto laws or constitutional provisions.

Republican Government: A form of indirect, or representative, democracy, which James Madison and other American founders defended as superior to pure democracy.

Rescission: The process of withdrawing approval. The Constitution is silent as to whether states can rescind proposed amendments that the necessary three-fourths majority of the states have not yet approved.

Reserved Powers: Under the U.S. system, powers which the Constitution do not expressly or implicitly delegate to the national government are reserved to the states. The Tenth Amendment is the clearest statement of this principle.

Resulting Powers: The sum of both the enumerated and implied powers of Congress.

Revolution: The act of changing government through violent means. In the Declaration of Independence, the Americans argued that such revolution were justified when government did not secure individual rights and was unresponsive to the petitions of the people.

Riders: Amendments, not always germane, that legislators attach to bills in Congress.

Rights: Legitimate claims. Rights are historically divided into human rights, which apply to all persons, and civil rights, which extend only to citizens.

Rights of Men: Privileges, sometimes referred to as natural rights, to which human beings are entitled simply because they are human. The idea that governments had an obligation to protect such rights was prominent in the American struggle against the British.

Roll-Call Vote: A recorded vote in Congress.

Rule of Four: An informal rule that the Supreme Court utilizes, whereby it denies review to cases unless four or more justices agree that they want to hear them.

Salutary Neglect: The policy, which Great Britain pursued prior to the French and Indian War, that allowed the American colonies to exercise a good deal of self government.

Search Warrant: A document specifying a place to be searched and a person or place to be seized. Under the Fourth Amendment, courts cannot issue warrants unless police first establish probable cause.

Secession: The doctrine that argued that states had the right to withdraw from the Union without the consent of other states. The Civil War discredited this idea.

Selective Incorporation: The view, which Justice Benjamin Cardozo advanced in *Palko v. Connecticut* (1937), that the due process clause of the Fourteenth Amendment applied only the most fundamental provisions of the Bill of Rights to the states.

Selective Incorporation Plus: The view that the due process clause of the Fourteenth Amendment applies the most fundamental provisions of the Bill of Rights and other important unenumerated rights to the states.

Self-Incrimination: The act of testifying to crimes against one's self. The Fifth Amendment forbids compulsion against self-incrimination in criminal cases.

Senate: The upper house of the U.S. congress, currently consisting of one hundred members, two from each state. Since adoption of the Seventeenth Amendment, the people elect such members, who serve, as before, for six-year terms.

Senatorial Courtesy: The practice whereby the Senate allows a member of a president's party to block the nomination of a judge from the senator's state to whom the senator objects.

Seneca Falls Convention: A convention that met in New York in 1848 and issued a call for women's suffrage that eventually resulted in adoption of the Nineteenth Amendment (1920).

Separate but Equal: The principle, legitimating racial segregation, that the Supreme Court upheld in *Plessy v. Ferguson* (1896) but that *Brown v. Board of Education* (1954) subsequently repudiated.

Separation of Church and State: A principle emphasizing that the United States has a secular state. Although the Constitution does not use this specific language, some scholars believe that it expresses the meaning of the establishment clause of the First Amendment.

Separation of Powers: The principle of dividing government authority among different branches of government, in the United States, the legislative, executive, and judicial.

Shay's Rebellion: The revolt of debtors and taxpayers in Massachusetts in the winter of 1787 that convinced wavering states that they needed to strengthen the Articles of Confederation.

Shield Laws: Laws designed to shield reporters from grand jury inquiries about matters that they have discovered in their news-gathering capacities.

Slander: Defamatory speech. The oral equivalent of libel.

Social Contract Theorists: A group of philosophers, most notable of whom was the Englishman John Locke, who argued that people formed governments by consent in order to secure basic human rights. This idea is also embodied in the Declaration of Independence and the U.S. Constitution.

Sovereign: A word meaning supreme. The term sovereign designates the person or agency of government with final ultimate authority. In the U.S. system, such sovereignty is difficult to locate.

Sovereign Immunity: The doctrine, which the Eleventh Amendment affirms, that prohibits individuals from suing governments without their consent.

Speech and Debate Clause: The provision in Article I, Section 6, protecting members of Congress against prosecution for what they say within Congress.

Standing: The principle that requires that parties who bring cases to court must have a genuine stake in their outcome.

Stare Decisis: The doctrine, grounded in British common law, by which judges generally adhere to past precedents as a way of preserving legal stability and continuity.

State Action: The legal principle, which the Supreme Court forcefully articulated in the Civil Rights Cases of 1883, according to which discriminatory action is only illegal if engaged in by the state. Accordingly, purely private action is beyond the state's purview.

State of the Union Address: The president's annual message to Congress in January which, by modern practice, presidents deliver in person.

Statutory Construction: The powers courts exercise of construing the meaning of laws and administrative rulings.

Stop and Frisk: Brief on-the-street searches, usually for weapons or contraband, that the Supreme Court approved in *Terry v. Ohio* (1968) without requiring warrants.

Substantive Due Process: The idea that the due process clauses of the Fifth and Fourteenth Amendments do not simply limit the procedures governments may follow (procedural due process) but also the substance of such decisions.

Suffrage: The right to vote, which constitutional amendments have progressively expanded.

Supremacy Clause: The provision in Article VI of the Constitution (originating in the New Jersey Plan) that provides that the Constitution, U.S. laws, and treaties are the supreme law of the land.

Supreme Court: The highest court in the federal system and the only court which the U.S. Constitution mentions by name. Under current law, the Court has nine members, eight associate justices and a chief.

Susan B. Anthony Amendment: Another name for the Nineteenth Amendment, which granted women's suffrage. The name comes from one of the original and most consistent supporters of the amendment.

Suspect Classes: Groups, like racial minorities and aliens, to whom the Court has extended extra judicial scrutiny because of past use of such classifications in a discriminatory fashion.

Symbolic Speech: Communications other than through written or verbal words. The Court has extended protections to such speech through the First and Fourteenth Amendments.

Takings Clause: The provision found in the Fifth Amendment that forbids government from taking private property without providing just compensation.

Three-Fifths Clause: The provision in Article I, Section 2 of the U.S. Constitution specifying that slaves would count as three-fifths of a person for purposes of taxation and representation.

Titles of Nobility: Honors bestowed by foreign governments. Article I, Section 9 prohibits Americans from accepting such titles except with congressional permission.

Total Incorporation: The view that the Fourteenth Amendment intended to apply all the provisions in the Bill of Rights to the states. Prominent advocates of this view have included Justice John Marshall Harlan I and Justice Hugo Black.

Total Incorporation Plus: The view that the Fourteenth Amendment intended to apply all the provisions of the Bill of Rights to the states but that it was not limited to this objective.

Treason: Defined by Article III, Section 3 of the Constitution as "levying War" or "adhering to their [the nation's] Enemies, giving them Aid and Comfort," this is one of three stated grounds for which Congress may impeach and remove public officers.

Treaties: Formal agreements with foreign nations negotiated by the president and requiring two-thirds majority approval by the Senate.

Undue Burden: The U.S. Supreme Court has decided that laws limiting abortion may not impose an "undue burden" on individuals seeking abortions.

Unenumerated Rights: Rights that the Constitution does not specially list but that may nonetheless deserve protection. The Ninth Amendment to the Constitution recognizes the existence of such rights.

Unicameralism: A system, like that under the Articles of Confederation, that provides for a single house of the legislative branch.

Unitary Government: A governmental system in which primary powers rest with the central government, which acts directly on individual citizens.

Unreasonable Searches and Seizures: Searches and seizures that officials initiate without just cause or proper warrant procedures as specified in the Fourth Amendment.

Unwritten Constitution: A system of customs and usages like those of Great Britain that set the pattern for governmental operations but that are not collected together in a single written document. Under many such constitutions, the legislature is, at least in theory, sovereign.

Veto: A negative. Under the U.S. Constitution, if the president vetoes a bill, it does not become law unless a two-thirds majority of both houses of Congress subsequently readopts it.

Viability: The point at which a fetus can survive outside a mother's womb. In *Roe v. Wade* (1973), the Supreme Court used this point—then thought to be at the end of the second trimester of pregnancy—as the point at which a state could prohibit abortions, except when necessary to save the life or health of the mother.

Virginia and Kentucky Resolutions: Resolutions, which Thomas Jefferson and James Madison authored and which these two state legislatures adopted in 1799 in opposition to the Alien and Sedition Acts of the previous year.

Virginia Plan: The first and most important plan that delegates introduced at the Constitutional Convention of 1787. The origin of such ideas as the separation of powers and bicameralism, the plan favored the larger states and called for a new national government much stronger than that under the Articles of Confederation.

Virtual Representation: The position, which the British advocated in the dispute with the American colonies in which the British argued that, since members of Parliament represented all Englishmen, the colonists were virtually represented there and Parliament thus had authority over them.

Voir Dire: The name of the process by which a judge, and/or opposing counsel, ask questions of potential jurors in order to decide who will sit in on a trial and render a verdict.

Vote of No-Confidence: A mechanism that parliamentary governments employ by which the Parliament can bring down the elected government and trigger new elections by voting against a major initiative of the majority party or coalition.

War Powers Resolution of 1973: A law, which Congress adopted over President Nixon's veto, that provided for consultation between the president and Congress, notification of new troops deployments, and the termination of such new deployments after ninety days absent congressional approval.

Washington, George: The leader of American revolutionary forces in the war against England and subsequent first president of the new republic.

Washington's decision to attend the Constitutional Convention of 1787, and his service as President, contributed to the success of its deliberations.

Writ of Certiorari: Petitions by which cases are appealed to the U.S. Supreme Court. The Court has broad discretion over which of these petitions it will accept.

Writ of Habeas Corpus: A privilege upheld in Article I, Section 9 of the Constitution whereby governments have to inform defendants of the charges against them.

Writ of Mandamus: A judicial order requiring the performance of a ministerial act. An appeal for such a writ was at issue in *Marbury v. Madison* (1803).

Writs of Assistance: General warrants used by the British in colonial America and prohibited by the Fourth Amendment.

Written Constitution: A document, like that which the Constitutional Convention of 1787 formulated, that outlines the distribution of governmental powers and limits and that Congress cannot change through ordinary legislative means.

Highlights of Constitutional History

1215   King John I signs the Magna Carta.

1619   Virginia establishes its House of Burgesses.

1620   Passengers on the *Mayflower* sign a "Compact" before debarking from their ship.

1641   Massachusetts adopts its "Body of Liberties."

1688   Britain deposes James II and installs King William and Queen Mary.

1689   The British Parliament establishes a Bill of Rights outlining fundamental liberties.

1692   Nineteen persons are hanged and one is pressed to death as a result of the Salem Witch Trials.

1735   A colonial jury acquits Peter Zenger of seditious libel.

1754   The French and Indian War.
–1763

1754   The Albany Congress calls for a continental plan of union.

1765   British Parliament adopts the Stamp Act. Nine colonies respond in the Stamp Act Congress.

1770   The Boston Massacre reflects rising tensions between Britain and the colonies.

1773   The Boston Tea Party protests British taxes on tea.

1774   Britain adopts the Coercive Acts.

1775   The colonists convene the First Continental Congress in response to Britain's Coercive Acts.

1775   Armed conflict breaks out between the colonists and the British at Lexington and Concord, Massachusetts.

       The Second Continental Congress convenes in Philadelphia.

1776   Virginia adopts its Declaration of Rights.

       Thomas Paine publishes *Common Sense*.

       The Second Continental Congress adopts the Declaration of Independence.

       States begin replacing colonial charters with new constitutions.

1777   The Second Continental Congress proposes the Articles of Confederation.

1781   George Washington defeats British forces at Yorktown.

       The last state ratifies the Articles of Confederation.

1783   The Treaty of Paris establishes peace between the United States and Britain.

       Washington resigns as commander of the military and returns home.

1785   Delegates from Virginia and Maryland meet at Mount Vernon to discuss navigation on mutual waterways.

1786   Five states send representatives to the Annapolis Convention.

       Virginia adopts its pathbreaking Bill for Establishing Religious Freedom.

       Shay's Rebellion in Massachusetts signals weaknesses under the Articles of Confederation.

1787   The Confederal Congress adopts the Northwest Ordinance.

       Delegates from twelve states meet in Philadelphia and draw up a new constitution.

       Hamilton, Madison, and Jay begin writing the *Federalist Papers*.

1788   The required number of states ratify the new Constitution.

1789   The new Constitution goes into effect, and George Washington is inaugurated as president.

       Congress proposes the Bill of Rights.

       Congress adopts the Judiciary Act outlining the federal court system.

1791   The states ratify the Bill of Rights.

1795   States ratify the Eleventh Amendment, clarifying judicial jurisdiction.

1798   Congress adopts the Alien and Sedition Acts.

       James Madison and Thomas Jefferson author the Kentucky and Virginia Resolutions.

1800   U.S. capital moved to the District of Columbia.

1801   Thomas Jefferson and his Democratic-Republican Party win the national election and replace the Federalist Party, but the House of Representatives has to resolve a tie between Jefferson and putative running mate, Aaron Burr.

       John Adams appoints John Marshall as Chief Justice of the U.S. Supreme Court.

1803   The Supreme Court establishes its power of judicial review over federal legislation in *Marbury v. Madison*.

       The United States purchases the Louisiana Territory.

1804   The states ratify the Twelfth Amendment to clear up a problem in the electoral college.

1805   The Senate fails to convict Supreme Court Justice Samuel Chase on impeachment charges.

1807   The national government fails to convict Aaron Burr of treason.

1811   The charter of the first U.S. bank lapses.

1812   The United States and Britain go to war.

1814   Representatives from New England states discuss the possibility of secession at the Hartford Convention.

       The United States and Britain sign the Treaty of Ghent officially ending the War of 1812.

1815   U.S. forces, unaware that war in over, win a decisive battle over the British at New Orleans.

1816   Congress reestablishes a national bank.

1819   Chief Justice Marshall upholds the constitutionality of the national
        bank using the doctrine of implied powers in *McCulloch v. Mary-
        land.*

        Dartmouth College v. Woodward prohibits New Hampshire from
        impairing a contract that had been issued by the English Crown.

1820   Congress adopts the Missouri Compromise limiting slavery in the
        northern territories.

        James Monroe runs unopposed for president, and wins all but one
        electoral vote.

1823   President James Monroe announces the Monroe Doctrine, designed
        to keep European powers out of the Western Hemisphere.

1824   The U.S. House of Representatives resolves a disputed presidential
        election and decides on John Quincy Adams over Andrew Jackson
        and Henry Clay.

        The U.S. Supreme Court affirms the supremacy of federal over state
        commerce regulations in *Gibbons v. Ogden.*

        Both Thomas Jefferson and John Adams die on July 4, the fiftieth
        anniversary of the adoption of the Declaration of Independence.

1828   Andrew Jackson is elected president.

        Congress adopts a tariff that Southerners label the Tariff of
        Abominations.

1833   *Barron v. Baltimore* decides that the Bill of Rights applies only to
        the national government.

1835   President Andrew Jackson appoints Roger Taney as Chief Justice of
        the U.S. Supreme Court.

1837   In *Charles River Bridge Co. v. Warren River Bridge Co.*, the Su-
        preme Court announces that it will interpret ambiguities in contracts
        on behalf of the state.

1841   John Tyler becomes the first vice president to succeed a president in
        office upon the death of William Henry Harrison.

1848   Congress declares war on Mexico.

        Delegates meet at Seneca Falls, New York, to advocate women's
        rights.

1850   Congress adopts the Compromise of 1850 in an unsuccessful attempt to solve the problem of slavery.

1854   The Kansas-Nebraska Act renews conflict over slavery in the territories.

1857   The U.S. Supreme Court rules in the *Dred Scott Decision* that blacks are not, and cannot become, U.S. citizens. The court exercised judicial review by invalidating the Missouri Compromise of 1820.

1858   Abraham Lincoln and Stephen A. Douglas participate in a series of debates in running for a Senate seat from Illinois.

1859   John Brown and his supporters launch an unsuccessful revolution in (West) Virginia.

1860   Abraham Lincoln is elected as the nation's first Republican president.

1861   U.S. Civil War.
–1865

1863   Lincoln issues the Emancipation Proclamation.

       Lincoln delivers his Gettysburg Address.

1865   Abraham Lincoln is assassinated.

       The states ratify the Thirteenth Amendment, abolishing slavery.

1868   The states ratify the Fourteenth Amendment guaranteeing basic rights of citizens to all persons born or naturalized in the United States.

       The Senate falls a single vote short of convicting President Andrew Johnson of impeachment charges.

1870   States ratify the Fifteenth Amendment prohibiting denial of the right to vote on the basis of race.

1873   The *Slaughterhouse Cases* restrictively interpret the privileges and immunities clause of the Fourteenth Amendment.

       Bradwell v. Illinois upholds a state law banning women from the practice of law.

1875   Civil Rights Act bans racial discrimination in places of public accommodation.

1876   The presidential election has to be resolved by a special commission.

The United States celebrates the centennial of the Declaration of Independence.

1877   The United States withdraws its troops from the former Confederacy, thus ending the period of Reconstruction that began in 1865.

1883   The *Civil Rights Cases* invalidate the Civil Rights Act of 1875 and provide a restrictive interpretation of the Fourteenth Amendment.

1886   In *Santa Clara County v. Southern Pacific Railroad Co.*, the U.S. Supreme Court recognizes corporations as "persons" protected by the Fourteenth Amendment.

1887   The United States celebrates the centennial of the U.S. Constitution.

1895   *Pollock v. Farmers' Loan & Trust Co.* outlaws the national income tax.

1896   *Plessy v. Ferguson* legitimizes the doctrine of "separate but equal" to uphold Jim Crow segregation laws.

1898   A war with Spain leads to the American acquisition of foreign territories.

1905   The U.S. Supreme Court invalidates a New York law regulating the hours of bakers in *Lochner v. New York*.

1913   States ratify the Sixteenth Amendment, legalizing the national income tax.

States ratify the Seventeenth Amendment, providing for direct election of U.S. Senators.

1914   *Weeks v. United States* applies the exclusionary rule to the national government.

1917   The United States enters World War I.

A revolution installs communists in power in Russia.

Congress adopts Espionage Act.

1918   U.S. Supreme Court decision in *Hammer v. Dagenhart* invalidates federal regulation of child labor.

Congress adopts a Sedition Act.

1919   States ratify the Eighteenth Amendment, providing for the prohibition of alcohol.

Justice Oliver Wendell Holmes, Jr. articulates the "clear and present danger" test in *Schenck v. United States*.

1919 U.S. Senate rejects the Treaty of Versailles and U.S. participation in
–1920 the League of Nations.

Nation deports aliens during the "Red Scare," stimulated by the Russian Revolution and domestic anarchist bombings.

1920 States ratify the Nineteenth Amendment, prohibiting states from denying the right to vote on the basis of sex.

1924 Congress extends citizenship to Native American Indians.

1925 The U.S. Supreme Court applies the free speech provision of the First Amendment to the states in *Gitlow v. New York*.

The Scopes trial in Tennessee examines the issue of evolution in the public schools.

1926 *U.S. v. Myers* establishes broad power for the president to dismiss individuals he has appointed to nonjudicial positions.

1929 The stock market crash initiates the Great Depression and leads to increased pressures for governmental regulations of the economy.

1932 Franklin D. Roosevelt is elected president.

1933 States ratify the Twentieth Amendment, designed to reduce the problem of "lame ducks."

States ratify the Twenty-first Amendment, repealing prohibition.

President Franklin D. Roosevelt becomes president and inaugurates his New Deal programs.

1935 The U.S. Supreme Court moves into its own building.

1936 President Franklin D. Roosevelt proposes his "court-packing" plan.

1937 The U.S. Supreme Court makes its "switch-in-time-that-saved-nine."

In *Palko v. Connecticut*, Justice Cardozo articulates the doctrine of "selective incorporation."

1938 Justice Harlan Fiske Stone writes footnote four in the *Carolene Products Case*.

1941 The Japanese attack on Pearl Harbor leads to United States participation in World War II.

1943 *West Virginia State Board of Education v. Barnette* overturns *Minersville School District v. Gobitis* (1940) and rules that public schools cannot force Jehovah's Witnesses to salute the flag.

1944   The U.S. Supreme Court validates the exclusion of Japanese Americans from the West Coast in *Korematsu v. United States*.

1945   The use of two atomic bombs against Japan brings World War II to an end. The United Nations is formed.

1946   The United States and the Soviet Union begin a long cold war.

1950   President Truman responds to North Korean attack on South Korea without specifically asking Congress to declare war.

1951   States ratify the Twenty-second Amendment limiting presidents to two full terms.

1952   In the *Steel Seizure Case*, the U.S. Supreme Court overturns President Truman's seizure of U.S. steel mills.

1953   President Eisenhower appoints Earl Warren as Chief Justice of the U.S. Supreme Court.

1954   The U.S. Supreme Court overturns *de jure* segregation in *Brown v. Board of Education*.

1955   The U.S. Supreme Court declares in *Brown v. Board of Education II* that racial desegregation shall take place "with all deliberate speed."

        Rosa Parks's refusal to move to the back of a bus launches the Montgomery Bus Boycott.

1960   John F. Kennedy becomes the first Roman Catholic ever to be elected U.S. president.

1961   States ratify the Twenty-third Amendment, granting electoral college representation to the District of Columbia.

1962   The U.S. Supreme Court outlaws public prayer in public schools in *Engel v. Vitale*.

        The U.S. Supreme Court decides in *Baker v. Carr* that it will not longer regard the issue of legislative apportionment as a "political question."

        Mapp v. Ohio extends the exclusionary rule to the states.

        The Cuban Missile Crisis highlights the dangers of the Cold War.

1963   *Gideon v. Wainwright* extends the right to counsel to indigents accused of felonies.

        Dr. Martin Luther King, Jr. leads the March on Washington.

President John F. Kennedy's assassination points to potential for presidential disability.

1964   States ratify the Twenty-fourth Amendment, eliminating poll taxes in national elections.

New York Times v. Sullivan establishes that public figures must establish "actual malice" before they can win libel suits.

1964   Congress adopts a comprehensive Civil Rights Bill that outlaws racial discrimination in places of public accommodation.

Congress adopts the Gulf of Tonkin Resolution, which President Lyndon Johnson uses to widen U.S. participation in Vietnam.

1965   Dr. Martin Luther King leads a March on Washington to push for civil rights.

Congress adopts the Voting Rights Act of 1965.

The U.S. Supreme Court recognizes a right to privacy in *Griswold v. Connecticut*.

1966   The U.S. Supreme Court establishes the Miranda Rules.

1967   States ratify the Twenty-fifth Amendment to provide for cases of presidential disability.

Thurgood Marshall becomes the first African American to be appointed to the U.S. Supreme Court.

1968   Martin Luther King and Robert Kennedy are assassinated.

1969   President Nixon appoints Warren Burger as Chief Justice of the U.S. Supreme Court.

Brandenburg v. Ohio limits restrictions of speech that does not pose the threat of imminent lawless action.

1971   The Twenty-sixth Amendment lowers the voting age to eighteen.

New York Times Co. v. United States allows for publication of the Pentagon Papers.

Reed v. Reed uses the equal protection clause to overturn a law that prefers males to females in the administration of estates.

The U.S. Supreme Court formulates the Lemon Test for cases involving the establishment clause.

1972   Congress proposed the Equal Rights Amendment, but the necessary number of states fail to ratify.

U.S. Supreme Court invalidates existing death penalty laws in *Furman v. Georgia.*

Presidential operatives are arrested trying to break in to the Democratic National Headquarters in the Watergate Complex in Washington, D.C.

1973   The U.S. Supreme Court allows for most abortions in *Roe v. Wade.*

The United States creates the Miller Test for ascertaining whether works are pornographic.

Congress adopts the War Powers Resolution.

Gerald Ford begins first individual selected as vice president under the terms of the Twenty-fifth Amendment.

1974   In *U.S. v. Nixon*, the U.S. Supreme Court rejects Nixon's expansive claims of executive privilege.

President Richard Nixon resigns under threat of impeachment and Gerald Ford becomes president.

President Gerald Ford pardons Nixon for all offenses he might have committed while in office.

1976   The United States celebrates bicentennial of the Declaration of Independence.

Gregg v. Georgia validates the constitutionally of capital punishment laws that provide for bifurcated trials and for consideration of mitigating and aggravating factors.

1978   The Supreme Court strikes down racial quotas but permits use of race to achieve academic diversity in *Regents of the University of California v. Bakke.*

1981   Sandra Day O'Connor becomes the first woman to be appointed to the U.S. Supreme Court.

1983   The Supreme Court invalidates the legislative veto in *Immigration and Naturalization Service v. Chadha.*

1986   President Reagan appoints William Rehnquist as Chief Justice of the U.S. Supreme Court.

1987   The United States celebrates bicentennial of the U.S. Constitution.

1989   *U.S. v. Johnson* affirms the First Amendment rights of protestors to burn the American flag.

1989   The fall of the Iron Curtain leads to hopes of reduced world tensions.

1991   The United States drives Iraqi troops out of Kuwait.

1992   States ratify the Twenty-seventh Amendment, relative to Congressional salaries.

1995   *U.S. Term Limits v. Thornton* declares that states do not have the power to limit the terms of their members in Congress.

1998   *Clinton v. City of New York* declares a presidential item veto to be unconstitutional.

1999   The Senate acquits President William J. Clinton of impeachment charges.

2000   George W. Bush narrowly wins the electoral college while failing to secure as many popular votes as his rival Al Gore. The Supreme Court decision in *Bush v. Gore* ends official vote counts.

       In response to a state court decision, Vermont makes provision for legalizing civil unions between gay couples.

2001   Terrorist attacks on the United States raise questions about U.S. security and prompt adoption of the U.S. Patriot Act.

2003   In *Lawrence v. Texas*, the U.S. Supreme Court overturns a Texas law prohibiting private acts of sodomy.

       The United States launches a second invasion of Iraq and deposes Saddam Hussein.

       Virginia v. Black affirms the right of states to ban cross-burnings that are carried out for the purpose of intimidation.

       Gratz v. Bollinger rejects the undergraduate system of admissions at the University of Michigan while *Grutter v. Bollinger* accepts the system at the law school against charges that it violates the equal protection clause.

2004   In *Elk Grove Unified School District v. Newdow*, the Supreme Court declared that an individual challenging the words "under God" in the pledge of allegiance to the flag did not have proper standing.

       Massachusetts recognizes same-sex marriages.

2005   The U.S. Senate accepts a compromise that averts a threatened vote
       that might have ended Senate filibusters of federal judicial nomi-
       nees.

       The identity of "Deep Throat," a key source for reporters during the
       Watergate investigation, is revealed to be W. Mark Felt, deputy
       director of the F.B.I.

       The U.S. Supreme Court votes in *Gonzales v. Raich* to strike down
       California's law allowing for the medicinal use of marijuana.

       Chief Justice William Renquist dies; John G. Roberts is confirmed
       to take his place.

FOR FURTHER READING

Alpheus Thomas Mason and Donald Grier Stephenson, Jr., *American Constitutional Law: Introductory Essays and Selected Cases*, 13th ed. (Upper Saddle River,
NJ: Prentice-Hall, 2002).

David Schultz and John R. Vile, eds., *The Encyclopedia of Civil Liberties in
America*, 2 vols. (Armonk, NY: M.E. Sharpe, 2005).

John R. Vile, *Encyclopedia of Constitutional Amendments, Proposed Amendments, and Amending Issues, 1789–2002*, 2nd ed. (Santa Barbara, CA: ABC-CLIO,
2003).

U.S. Supreme Court Justices

Some scholars have likened the U.S. Supreme Court to a continuous constitutional convention. Like other federal judges, Supreme Court justices are nominated by the president and confirmed by the U.S. Senate. Because the line between interpreting and writing a constitution is so fine, Supreme Court justices must often define the contours of the document.

This chart lists the justices who have served on the U.S. Supreme Court, the presidents who appointed them, and their years of service. As first among equals, chief justices not only preside over deliberations but also set the tone of a court; the chart accordingly designates the names and years of their service in bold type. The chart lists the terms of justices who have served as both associates and as chief justices separately (an asterisk designates chiefs who have been elevated from the bench).

John Jay	George Washington	**1789–1795**
John Rutledge	George Washington	1789–1791
William Cushing	George Washington	1789–1810
James Wilson	George Washington	1789–1798
John Blair, Jr.	George Washington	1789–1795
James Iredell	George Washington	1790–1799
Thomas Johnson	George Washington	1791–1793
William Paterson	George Washington	1793–1806
John Rutledge	George Washington	**1795**
Oliver Ellsworth	George Washington	**1796–1800**
Bushrod Washington	John Adams	1798–1829

Alfred Moore	John Adams	1800–1804
John Marshall	John Adams	**1801–1835**
William Johnson	Thomas Jefferson	1804–1834
Henry Brokholst Livingston	Thomas Jefferson	1806–1823
Thomas Todd	Thomas Jefferson	1807–1826
Gabriel Duvall	James Madison	1811–1835
Joseph Story	James Madison	1811–1845
Smith Thomas	James Monroe	1823–1843
Robert Trimble	John Quincy Adams	1826–1828
John McLean	Andrew Jackson	1829–1861
Henry Baldwin	Andrew Jackson	1830–1844
James Moore Wayne	Andrew Jackson	1835–1867
Roger Brooke Taney	Andrew Jackson	**1836–1864**
Philip Pendleton Barbour	Andrew Jackson	1836–1841
John Catron	Andrew Jackson	1836–1841
John McKinley	Martin Van Buren	1837–1852
Peter Vivian Daniel	Martin Van Buren	1841–1860
Samuel Nelson	John Tyler	1845–1872
Levi Woodbury	James K. Polk	1846–1851
Robert Cooper Grier	James K. Polk	1846–1870
Benjamin Robbins Curtis	Millard Fillmore	1851–1857
John Archibald Campbell	Franklin Pierce	1853–1861
Nathan Clifford	James Buchanan	1858–1881
Noah Haynes Swayne	Abraham Lincoln	1862–1881
Samuel Freeman Miller	Abraham Lincoln	1862–1890
David Davis	Abraham Lincoln	1862–1877
Stephan Johnson Field	Abraham Lincoln	1863–1897
Salmon Portland Chase	Abraham Lincoln	**1864–1873**
William Strong	Ulysses S. Grant	1870–1880
Joseph B. Bradley	Ulysses S. Grant	1870–1892
Ward Hunt	Ulysses S. Grant	1872–1882
Morrison Remick Waite	Ulysses S. Grant	**1874–1888**
John Marshall Harlan	Rutherford B. Hayes	1877–1911
William Burnham Woods	Rutherford B. Hayes	1880–1887
Stanley Matthews	James G. Garfield	1881–1889
Horace Gray	Chester A. Arthur	1881–1902
Samuel Blatchford	Chester A. Arthur	1882–1893
Lucius Quintus Cincinnatus Lamar	Grover Cleveland	1888–1893
Melville Weston Fuller	Grover Cleveland	**1888–1910**
David Josiah Brewer	Benjamin Harrison	1889–1910
Henry Billings Brown	Benjamin Harrison	1890–1906

George Shiras, Jr.	Benjamin Harrison	1892–1903
Howell Edmunds Jackson	Benjamin Harrison	1893–1895
Edward Douglass White	Grover Cleveland	1894–1910
Rufus Wheeler Peckham	Grover Cleveland	1895–1909
Joseph McKenna	William McKinley	1898–1925
Oliver Wendell Holmes, Jr.	Theodore Roosevelt	1902–1932
William Rufus Day	Theodore Roosevelt	1903–1922
William Henry Moody	Theodore Roosevelt	1906–1910
Horace Harmon Lurton	William Howard Taft	1909–1914
Charles Evans Hughes	William Howard Taft	1910–1916
Edward D. White*	William Howard Taft	**1910–1921**
Willis Van Devanter	William Howard Taft	1910–1937
Joseph Rucker Lamar	William Howard Taft	1910–1916
Mahlon Pitney	William Howard Taft	1912–1922
James Clark McReynolds	Woodrow Wilson	1914–1941
Louis Dembitz Brandeis	Woodrow Wilson	1916–1939
John Hessin Clarke	Woodrow Wilson	1916–1922
William Howard Taft	Warren G. Harding	**1921–1930**
George Sutherland	Warren G. Harding	1922–1938
Pierce Butler	Warren G. Harding	1922–1939
Edward Terry Sanford	Warren G. Harding	1923–1930
Harlan Fiske Stone	Calvin Coolidge	1925–1941
Charles Evans Hughes	Herbert Hoover	**1930–1941**
Owen Josephus Roberts	Herbert Hoover	1930–1945
Benjamin Nathan Cardozo	Herbert Hoover	1932–1938
Hugo Lafayette Black	Franklin D. Roosevelt	1937–1971
Stanley Forman Reed	Franklin D. Roosevelt	1938–1957
Felix Frankfurter	Franklin D. Roosevelt	1939–1962
William Orville Douglas	Franklin D. Roosevelt	1939–1975
William Francis (Frank) Murphy	Franklin D. Roosevelt	1940–1949
Harlan Fiske Stone*	Franklin D. Roosevelt	**1941–1946**
James Francis Byrnes	Franklin D. Roosevelt	1941–1942
Robert Houghwout Jackson	Franklin D. Roosevelt	1941–1954
Wiley Blount Rutledge	Franklin D. Roosevelt	1943–1949
Harold Hitz Burton	Harry S. Truman	1945–1958
Frederick Moore Vinson	Harry S. Truman	**1946–1953**
Tom Campbell Clark	Harry S. Truman	1949–1967
Sherman Minton	Harry S. Truman	1949–1956
Earl Warren	Dwight D. Eisenhower	**1953–1969**
John Marshall Harlan	Dwight D. Eisenhower	1955–1971
William Joseph Brennan, Jr.	Dwight D. Eisenhower	1956–1990

Charles Evans Whittaker	Dwight D. Eisenhower	1957–1962
Potter Stewart	Dwight D. Eisenhower	1958–1981
Byron Raymond White	John F. Kennedy	1962–1993
Arthur Joseph Goldberg	John F. Kennedy	1962–1965
Abe Fortas	Lyndon B. Johnson	1965–1969
Thurgood Marshall	Lyndon B. Johnson	1967–1991
Warren Earl Burger	Richard M. Nixon	**1969–1986**
Harry Andrew Blackmun	Richard M. Nixon	1970–1994
Lewis Franklin Powell, Jr.	Richard M. Nixon	1971–1987
William Hubbs Rehnquist	Richard M. Nixon	1971–1986
John Paul Stevens	Gerald R. Ford	1975–
Sandra Day O'Connor	Ronald Reagan	1981–2005
William Rehnquist*	Ronald Reagan	**1986–2005**
Antonin Scalia	Ronald Reagan	1986–
Anthony McLeod Kennedy	Ronald Reagan	1988–
David H. Souter	George H. W. Bush	1990–
Clarence Thomas	George H. W. Bush	1991–
Ruth Bader Ginsburg	William Jefferson Clinton	1993–
Stephen G. Breyer	William Jefferson Clinton	1994–
John G. Roberts	George W. Bush	**2005–**
Samuel A. Alito	George W. Bush	2006–

For Further information see: Kermit L. Hall, ed., *The Oxford Companion to the Supreme Court of the United States* (New York: Oxford, 1992) and David Schultz, *Encyclopedia of American Law* (New York: Facts on File, 2002).

Appendix

The Constitution of the United States

We the People of the United States, in Order to form a more perfect Union, establish Justice, insure domestic Tranquility, provide for the common defence, promote the general Welfare, and secure the Blessings of Liberty to ourselves and our Posterity, do ordain and establish this Constitution for the United States of America.

Article. I.

Section. 1. All legislative Powers herein granted shall be vested in a Congress of the United States, which shall consist of a Senate and House of Representatives.

Section. 2. The House of Representatives shall be composed of Members chosen every second Year by the People of the several States, and the Electors in each State shall have the Qualifications requisite for Electors of the most numerous Branch of the State Legislature.

No Person shall be a Representative who shall not have attained to the Age of twenty five Years, and been seven Years a Citizen of the United States, and who shall not, when elected, be an Inhabitant of that State in which he shall be chosen.

[*Representatives and direct Taxes shall be apportioned among the several States which may be included within this Union, according to their respective Numbers, which shall be determined by adding to the whole Number of free Persons, including those bound to Service for a Term of Years, and excluding Indians not taxed, three fifths of all other Persons.*]* The actual Enumeration shall be made

*Changed by Section 2 of the Fourteenth Amendment.

within three Years after the first Meeting of the Congress of the United States, and within every subsequent Term of ten Years, in such Manner as they shall by Law direct. The Number of Representatives shall not exceed one for every thirty Thousand, but each State shall have at Least one Representative; and until such enumeration shall be made, the State of New Hampshire shall be entitled to chuse three. Massachusetts eight, Rhode-Island and Providence Plantations one, Connecticut five, New-York six, New Jersey four, Pennsylvania eight, Delaware one, Maryland six, Virginia ten, North Carolina five, South Carolina five, and Georgia three.

When vacancies happen in the Representation from any State, the Executive Authority thereof shall issue Writs of Election to fill such Vacancies.

The House of Representatives shall chuse their Speaker and other Officers; and shall have the sole Power of Impeachment.

Section. 3. The Senate of the United States shall be composed of two Senators from each State, [*chosen by the Legislature thereof,*]* for six Years, and each Senator shall have one Vote.

Immediately after they shall be assembled in Consequence of the first Election, they shall be divided as equally as may be into three Classes. The Seats of the Senators of the first Class shall be vacated at the Expiration of the second Year, of the second Class at the Expiration of the fourth Year, and of the third Class at the Expiration of the sixth Year, so that one third may be chosen every second Year; [*and if Vacancies happen by Resignation, or otherwise, during the Recess of the Legislature of any State, the Executive thereof may make temporary Appointments until the next Meeting of the Legislature, which shall then fill such Vacancies.*]**

No Person shall be a Senator who shall not have attained to the Age of thirty Years, and been nine Years a Citizen of the United States, and who shall not, when elected, be an Inhabitant of that State for which he shall be chosen.

The Vice President of the United States shall be President of the Senate, but shall have no Vote, unless they be equally divided.

The Senate shall chuse their other Officers, and also a President pro tempore, in the Absence of the Vice President, or when he shall exercise the Office of President of the United States.

The Senate shall have the sole Power to try all Impeachments. When sitting for that Purpose, they shall be on Oath or Affirmation. When the President of the United States is tried, the Chief Justice shall preside: And no Person shall be convicted without the Concurrence of two thirds of the Members present.

---

*Changed by the Seventeenth Amendment.

**Changed by the Seventeenth Amendment.

Judgment in Cases of Impeachment shall not extend further than to removal from Office, and disqualification to hold and enjoy any Office of honor, Trust or Profit under the United States: but the Party convicted shall nevertheless be liable and subject to Indictment, Trial, Judgment and Punishment, according to Law.

Section. 4. The Times, Places and Manner of holding Elections for Senators and Representatives, shall be prescribed in each State by the Legislature thereof; but the Congress may at any time by Law make or alter such Regulations, except as to the Places of chusing Senators.

The Congress shall assemble at least once in every Year, and such Meeting shall be [*on the first Monday in December,*]* unless they shall by Law appoint a different Day.

Section. 5. Each House shall be the Judge of the Elections, Returns and Qualifications of its own Members, and a Majority of each shall constitute a Quorum to do Business; but a smaller Number may adjourn from day to day, and may be authorized to compel the Attendance of absent Members, in such Manner, and under such Penalties as each House may provide.

Each House may determine the Rules of its Proceedings, punish its Members for disorderly Behaviour, and, with the Concurrence of two thirds, expel a Member.

*Changed by Section 2 of the Twentieth Amendment.

Each House shall keep a Journal of its Proceedings, and from time to time publish the same, excepting such Parts as may in their Judgment require Secrecy; and the Yeas and Nays of the Members of either House on any question shall, at the Desire of one fifth of those Present, be entered on the Journal.

Neither House, during the Session of Congress, shall, without the Consent of the other, adjourn for more than three days, nor to any other Place than that in which the two Houses shall be sitting.

Section. 6. The Senators and Representatives shall receive a Compensation for their Services, to be ascertained by Law, and paid out of the Treasury of the United States. They shall in all Cases, except Treason, Felony and Breach of the Peace, be privileged from Arrest during their Attendance at the Session of their respective Houses, and in going to and returning from the same; and for any Speech or Debate in either House, they shall not be questioned in any other Place.

No Senator or Representative shall, during the Time for which he was elected, be appointed to any civil Office under the Authority of the United States, which shall have been created, or the Emoluments whereof shall have been encreased during such time; and no Person holding any Office under the United States, shall be a Member of either House during his Continuance in Office.

Section. 7. All Bills for raising Revenue shall originate in the House of Representatives; but the Senate may propose or concur with Amendments as on other Bills.

Every Bill which shall have passed the House of Representatives and the Senate, shall, before it becomes a Law, be presented to the President of the United States; If he approve he shall sign it, but if not he shall return it, with his Objections to that House in which it shall have originated, who shall enter the Objections at large on their Journal, and proceed to reconsider it. If after such Reconsideration two thirds of that House shall agree to pass the Bill, it shall be sent, together with the Objections, to the other House, by which it shall likewise be reconsidered, and if approved by two thirds of that House, it shall become a Law. But in all such Cases the Votes of both Houses shall be determined by yeas and Nays, and the Names of the Persons voting for and against the Bill shall be entered on the Journal of each House respectively. If any Bill shall not be returned by the President within ten Days (Sundays excepted) after it shall have been presented to him, the Same shall be a Law, in like Manner as if he had signed it, unless the Congress by their Adjournment prevent its Return, in which Case it shall not be a Law.

Every Order, Resolution, or Vote to which the Concurrence of the Senate and House of The Constitution of the United States Representatives may be necessary (except on a question of Adjournment) shall be presented to the President of the United States; and before the Same shall take Effect, shall be approved by him, or being disapproved by him, shall be repassed by two thirds of the Senate and House of Representatives, according to the Rules and Limitations prescribed in the Case of a Bill.

Section. 8. The Congress shall have Power To lay and collect Taxes, Duties, Imposts and Excises, to pay the Debts and provide for the common Defence and general Welfare of the United States; but all Duties, Imposts and Excises shall be uniform throughout the United States;

To borrow Money on the credit of the United States;

To regulate Commerce with foreign Nations, and among the several States, and with the Indian Tribes;

To establish an uniform Rule of Naturalization, and uniform Laws on the subject of Bankruptcies throughout the United States;

To coin Money, regulate the Value thereof, and of foreign Coin, and fix the Standard of Weights and Measures;

To provide for the Punishment of counterfeiting the Securities and current Coin of the United States;

To establish Post Offices and post Roads;

To promote the Progress of Science and useful Arts, by securing for limited Times to Authors and

Inventors the exclusive Right to their respective Writings and Discoveries;

To constitute Tribunals inferior to the supreme Court;

To define and punish Piracies and Felonies committed on the high Seas, and Offenses against the Law of Nations;

To declare War, grant Letters of Marque and Reprisal, and make Rules concerning Captures on Land and Water;

To raise and support Armies, but no Appropriation of Money to that Use shall be for a longer Term than two Years;

To provide and maintain a Navy;

To make Rules for the Government and Regulation of the land and naval Forces;

To provide for calling forth the Militia to execute the Laws of the Union, suppress Insurrections and repel Invasions;

To provide for organizing, arming, and disciplining, the Militia, and for governing such Part of them as may be employed in the Service of the United States, reserving to the States respectively, the Appointment of the Officers, and the Authority of training the Militia according to the discipline prescribed by Congress;

To exercise exclusive Legislation in all Cases whatsoever, over such District (not exceeding ten Miles square) as may, by Cession of particular States, and the Acceptance of Congress, become the Seat of the Government of the United States,

and to exercise like Authority over all Places purchased by the Consent of the Legislature of the State in which the Same shall be, for the Erection of Forts, Magazines, Arsenals, dock-Yards and other needful Buildings;—And

To make all Laws which shall be necessary and proper for carrying into Execution the foregoing Powers, and all other Powers vested by this Constitution in the Government of the United States, or in any Department or Officer thereof.

Section. 9. The Migration or Importation of such Persons as any of the States now existing shall think proper to admit, shall not be prohibited by the Congress prior to the Year one thousand eight hundred and eight, but a Tax or duty may be imposed on such Importation, not exceeding ten dollars for each Person.

The Privilege of the Writ of Habeas Corpus shall not be suspended, unless when in Cases of Rebellion or Invasion the public Safety may require it.

No Bill of Attainder or ex post facto Law shall be passed.

[*No Capitation, or other direct, Tax shall be laid, unless in Proportion to the Census or Enumeration herein before directed to be taken.*]*

No Tax or Duty shall be laid on Articles exported from any State.

No Preference shall be given by any Regulation of Commerce or

*Changed by the Sixteenth Amendment.

Revenue to the Ports of one State over those of another: nor shall Vessels bound to, or from, one State, be obliged to enter, clear, or pay Duties in another.

No Money shall be drawn from the Treasury, but in Consequence of Appropriations made by Law; and a regular Statement and Account of the Receipts and Expenditures of all public Money shall be published from time to time.

No Title of Nobility shall be granted by the United States: And no Person holding any Office of Profit or Trust under them, shall, without the Consent of the Congress, accept of any present, Emolument, Office, or Title, of any kind whatever, from any King, Prince, or foreign State.

Section. 10. No State shall enter into any Treaty, Alliance, or Confederation; grant Letters of Marque and Reprisal; coin Money; emit Bills of Credit; make any Thing but gold and silver Coin a Tender in Payment of Debts; pass any Bill of Attainder, ex post facto Law, or Law impairing the Obligation of Contracts, or grant any Title of Nobility.

No State shall, without the Consent of the Congress, lay any Imposts or Duties on Imports or Exports, except what may be absolutely necessary for executing it's inspection Laws: and the net Produce of all Duties and Imposts, laid by any State on Imports or Exports, shall be for the Use of the Treasury of the United States; and all such Laws shall be subject to the Revision and Controul of the Congress.

No State shall, without the Consent of Congress, lay any Duty of Tonnage, keep Troops, or Ships of War in time of Peace, enter into any Agreement or Compact with another State, or with a foreign Power, or engage in War, unless actually invaded, or in such imminent Danger as will not admit of delay.

Article. II.

Section. 1. The executive Power shall be vested in a President of the United States of America. He shall hold his Office during the Term of four Years, and, together with the Vice President, chosen for the same Term, be elected, as follows: Each State shall appoint, in such Manner as the Legislature thereof may direct, a Number of Electors, equal to the whole Number of Senators and Representatives to which the State may be entitled in the Congress: but no Senator or Representative, or Person holding an Office of Trust or Profit under the United States, shall be appointed an Elector.

[*The Electors shall meet in their respective States, and vote by Ballot for two Persons, of whom one at least shall not be an Inhabitant of the same State with themselves. And they shall make a List of all the Persons voted for, and of the Number of Votes for each; which List they shall sign and certify, and* *transmit sealed to the Seat of the Government of the United States, directed to the President of the Senate. The President of the Senate shall, in the Presence of the Senate and House of Representatives, open all the Certificates, and the Votes shall then be counted. The Person having the greatest Number of Votes shall be the President, if such Number be a Majority of the whole Number of Electors appointed, and if there be more than one who have such Majority, and have an equal Number of Votes, then the House of Representatives shall immediately chuse by Ballot one of them for President, and if no Person have a Majority, then from the five highest on the List the said House shall in like Manner chuse the President. But in chusing the President, the Votes shall be taken by States, the Representation from each state having one Vote; A quorum for this Purpose shall consist of a Member or Members from two thirds of the States, and a Majority of all the States shall be necessary to a Choice. In every Case, after the Choice of the President, the Person having the greatest Number of Votes of the Electors shall be the Vice President. But if there should remain two or more who have equal Votes, the Senate shall chuse from them by Ballot the Vice President.]**

The Congress may determine the Time of chusing the Electors, and the Day on which they shall give their Votes; which Day shall be the same throughout the United States.

No Person except a natural born Citizen, or a Citizen of the United States, at the time of the Adoption of this Constitution, shall be eligible to the Office of the President; neither shall any person be eligible to that Office who shall not have attained to the Age of thirty five Years, and been fourteen Years a Resident within the United States.

[In Case of the Removal of the President from Office, or of his Death, Resignation, or Inability to discharge the Powers and Duties of the said Office, the Same shall devolve on the Vice President, and the Congress may by Law provide for the Case of Removal, Death, Resignation or Inability, both of the President and Vice President, declaring what Officer shall then act as President, and such Officer shall act accordingly, until the Disability be removed, or a President shall be elected.]**

The President shall, at stated Times, receive for his Services, a Compensation, which shall neither be increased nor diminished during the Period for which he shall have been elected, and he shall not receive within that Period any other Emolument from the United States, or any of them.

Before he enter on the Execution of his Office, he shall take the following Oath or Affirmation:—"I do solemnly swear (or affirm) that I will

---

*Changed by the Twelfth Amendment.

**Changed by the Twenty-fifth Amendment.

faithfully execute the Office of President of the United States, and will to the best of my Ability, preserve, protect and defend the Constitution of the United States."

Section. 2. The President shall be Commander in Chief of the Army and Navy of the United States, and of the Militia of the several States, when called into the actual Service of the United States; he may require the Opinion, in writing, of the principal Officer in each of the executive Departments, upon any Subject relating to the Duties of their respective Offices, and he shall have Power to grant Reprieves and Pardons for Offenses against the United States, except in Cases of Impeachment.

He shall have Power, by and with the Advice and Consent of the Senate, to make Treaties, provided two thirds of the Senators present concur; and he shall nominate, and by and with the Advice and Consent of the Senate, shall appoint Ambassadors, other public Ministers and Consuls, Judges of the supreme Court, and all other Officers of the United States, whose Appointments are not herein otherwise provided for, and which shall be established by Law: but the Congress may by Law vest the Appointment of such inferior Officers, as they think proper, in the President alone, in the Courts of Law, or in the Heads of Departments.

The President shall have Power to fill up all Vacancies that may happen during the Recess of the Senate, by granting Commissions which shall expire at the End of their next Session.

Section. 3. He shall from time to time give to the Congress Information of the State of the Union, and recommend to their Consideration such Measures as he shall judge necessary and expedient; he may, on extraordinary Occasions, convene both Houses, or either of them, and in Case of Disagreement between them, with Respect to the Time of Adjournment, he may adjourn them to such Time as he shall think proper; he shall receive Ambassadors and other public Ministers; he shall take Care that the Laws be faithfully executed, and shall Commission all the Officers of the United States.

Section. 4. The President, Vice President and all civil Officers of the United States, shall be removed from Office on Impeachment for, and Conviction of, Treason, Bribery, or other high Crimes and Misdemeanors.

Article. III.

Section. 1. The judicial Power of the United States, shall be vested in one supreme Court, and in such inferior Courts as the Congress may from time to time ordain and establish. The Judges, both of the supreme and inferior Courts, shall hold their Offices during good Behaviour, and shall, at stated Times, receive for their Services, a Compensation, which shall not be diminished during their Continuance in Office.

Section. 2. The judicial Power shall extend to all Cases, in Law and Equity, arising under this Constitution, the Laws of the United States, and Treaties made, or which shall be made, under their Authority;—to all Cases affecting Ambassadors, other public Ministers and Consuls;—to all Cases of admiralty and maritime Jurisdiction;—to Controversies to which the United States shall be a Party,—to Controversies between two or more states; [*between a State and Citizens of another State;—*]* between Citizens of different States—between Citizens of the same State claiming Lands under Grants of different States, [*and between a State, or the Citizens thereof, and foreign States, Citizens or Subjects.*]*

In all Cases affecting Ambassadors, other public Ministers and Consuls, and those in which a State shall be Party, the supreme Court shall have original Jurisdiction. In all the other Cases before mentioned, the supreme Court shall have appellate Jurisdiction, both as to Law and Fact, with such Exceptions, and under such Regulations as the Congress shall make.

The Trial of all Crimes, except in Cases of Impeachment, shall be by Jury; and such Trial shall be held in the State where the said Crimes shall have been committed, but

*Changed by the Eleventh Amendment.

when not committed within any State, the Trial shall be at such Place or Places as the Congress may by Law have directed.

Section. 3. Treason against the United States, shall consist only in levying War against them, or in adhering to their Enemies, giving them Aid and Comfort. No Person shall be convicted of Treason unless on the Testimony of two Witnesses to the same overt Act, or on Confession in open Court.

The Congress shall have Power to declare the Punishment of Treason, but no Attainder of Treason shall work Corruption of Blood, or Forfeiture except during the Life of the Person attainted.

Article. IV.

Section. 1. Full Faith and Credit shall be given in each State to the public Acts, Records, and judicial Proceedings of every other State; And the Congress may by general Laws prescribe the Manner in which such Acts, Records and Proceedings shall be proved, and the Effect thereof.

Section. 2. The Citizens of each State shall be entitled to all Privileges and Immunities of Citizens in the several States.

A Person charged in any State with Treason, Felony, or other Crime, who shall flee from Justice, and be found in another State, shall on Demand of the executive Authority of the State from which he fled, be delivered up, to be removed to the State having Jurisdiction of the Crime.

[*No Person held to Service or Labour in one State, under the Laws thereof, escaping into another, shall, in Consequence of any Law or Regulation therein, be discharged from such Service or Labour, but shall be delivered up on Claim of the Party to whom such Service or Labour may be due.*]*

Section. 3. New States may be admitted by the Congress into this Union; but no new State shall be formed or erected within the Jurisdiction of any other State; nor any State be formed by the Junction of two or more States, or Parts of States, without the Consent of the Legislatures of the States concerned as well as of the Congress.

The Congress shall have Power to dispose of and make all needful Rules and Regulations respecting the Territory or other Property belonging to the United States; and nothing in this Constitution shall be so construed as to Prejudice any Claims of the United States, or of any particular State.

Section. 4. The United States shall guarantee to every State in this Union a Republican Form of Government, and shall protect each of them against Invasion; and on Application of the Legislature, or of the Executive (when the Legislature cannot be convened) against domestic Violence.

*Changed by the Thirteenth Amendment.

Article. V.

The Congress, whenever two thirds of both Houses shall deem it necessary, shall propose Amendments to this Constitution, or, on the Application of the Legislatures of two thirds of the several States, shall call a Convention for proposing Amendments, which, in either Case, shall be valid to all Intents and Purposes. as Part of this Constitution, when ratified by the Legislatures of three fourths of the several States, or by Conventions in three fourths thereof, as the one or the other Mode of Ratification may he proposed by the Congress; Provided that no Amendment which may he made prior to the Year One thousand eight hundred and eight shall in any Manner affect the first and fourth Clauses in the Ninth Section of the first Article; and that no State, without its Consent, shall be deprived of its equal Suffrage in the Senate.

Article. VI.

All Debts contracted and Engagements entered into, before the Adoption of this Constitution, shall be as valid against the United States under this Constitution, as under the Confederation.

This Constitution, and the Laws of the United States which shall he made in Pursuance thereof; and all Treaties made, or which shall be made, under the Authority of the

United States, shall be the supreme Law of the Land; and the Judges in every State shall he bound thereby, any Thing in the Constitution or Laws of any State to the Contrary notwithstanding.

The Senators and Representatives before mentioned, and the Members of the several State legislatures, and all executive and judicial Officers, both of the United States and of the several States, shall be bound by Oath or Affirmation, to support this Constitution; but no religious Test shall ever be required as a Qualification to any Office or public Trust under the United States.

Article. VII.

The Ratification of the Conventions of nine States, shall be sufficient for the Establishment of this Constitution between the States so ratifying the Same.

[D]one in Convention by the Unanimous Consent of the States present the Seventeenth Day of September in the Year of our Lord one thousand seven hundred and Eighty seven and of the Independence of the United States of America the Twelfth In Witness whereof We have here unto subscribed our Names,

G. Washington—Presid: and deputy
from Virginia

New Hampshire	John Langdon
	Nicholas Gilman
Massachusetts	Nathaniel Gorham
	Rufus King
Connecticut	Wm. Saml. Johnson
	Roger Sherman
New York	Alexander Hamilton
New Jersey	Wil: Livingston
	David Brearley
	Wm. Paterson
	Jona Dayton
Pennsylvania	B. Franklin
	Thomas Mifflin
	Robt. Morris
	Geo. Clymer
	Thos. FitzSimons
	Jan d Ingersoll
	James Wilson
	Gouv Morris
Delaware	Geo: Read
	Gunning Bedford jun
	John Dickinson
	Richard Bassett
	Jaco: Broom
Maryland	James McHenry
	Dan of St Thos. Jenifer
	Danl Carroll
Virginia	John Blair—
	James Madison Jr.
North Carolina	Wm. Blount
	Richd. Dobbs Spaight
	Hu Williamson
South Carolina	I Rutledge
	Charles Cotesworth Pinckney
	Charles Pinckney
	Pierce Butler
Georgia	William Few
	Abr Baldwin

Attest William Jackson Secretary

In Convention Monday September 17th 1787.

Present The States of

New Hampshire, Massachusetts, Connecticut, Mr Hamilton from New York, New Jersey, Pennsylvania, Delaware, Maryland, Virginia, North Carolina, South Carolina and Georgia

Resolved,

That the preceeding Constitution be laid before the United States in Congress assembled, and that it is the Opinion of this Convention, that it should afterwards be submitted to a Convention of Delegates chosen in each State by the People thereof, under the Recommendation of its Legislature for their Assent and Ratification, and that each Convention assenting to, and ratifying the Same, should give Notice thereof to the United States in Congress assembled. Resolved, That it is the Opinion of this Convention, that as soon as the Conventions of nine States shall have ratified this Constitution, the United States in Congress assembled should fix a Day on which Electors should be appointed by the States which shall have ratified the same, and a day on which the Electors should assemble to vote for the President, and the Time and Place for commencing Proceedings under this Constitution.

That after such Publication the Electors should be appointed, and the Senators and Representatives elected: That the Electors should meet on the Day fixed for the Election of the President, and should transmit their Votes certified, signed, sealed and directed, as the Constitution requires, to the Secretary of the United States in Congress assembled, that the Senators and Representatives should convene at the Time and Place assigned; that the Senators should appoint a President of the Senate, for the sole Purpose of receiving, opening and counting the Votes for President; and, that after he shall be chosen, the Congress, together with the President, should, without Delay, proceed to execute this Constitution.

By the unanimous Order of the Convention
G. WASHINGTON—Presid:
W. JACKSON Secretary.

AMENDMENTS TO THE CONSTITUTION OF THE UNITED STATES OF AMERICA

ARTICLES IN ADDITION TO, AND AMENDMENT OF, THE CONSTITUTION OF THE UNITED STATES OF AMERICA, PROPOSED BY CONGRESS, AND RATIFIED BY THE SEVERAL STATES, PURSUANT TO THE FIFTH ARTICLE OF THE ORIGINAL CONSTITUTION.

Amendment I.*

Congress shall make no law respecting an establishment of religion, or prohibiting the free exercise thereof; or abridging the freedom of speech, or of the press, or the right of the people peaceably to assemble, and to petition the Government for a redress of grievances.

*The first ten Amendments (Bill of Rights) were ratified effective December 15, 1791.

Amendment II.

A well regulated Militia, being necessary to the security of a free State, the right of the people to keep and bear Arms, shall not be infringed.

Amendment III.

No Soldier shall, in time of peace be quartered in any house, without the consent of the Owner, nor in time of war, but in a manner to be prescribed by law.

Amendment IV.

The right of the people to be secure in their persons, houses, papers, and effects, against unreasonable searches and seizures, shall not be violated, and no Warrants shall issue, but upon probable cause, supported by Oath or affirmation, and particularly describing the place to be searched, and the persons or things to be seized.

Amendment V.

No person shall be held to answer for a capital, or otherwise infamous crime, unless on a presentment or indictment of a Grand Jury, except in cases arising in the land or naval forces, or in the Militia, when in actual service in time of War or public danger; nor shall any person be subject for the same offence to be twice put in jeopardy of life or limb; nor shall be compelled in any criminal case to be a witness against himself, nor be deprived of life, liberty, or property, without due process of law; nor shall private property be taken for public use, without just compensation.

Amendment VI.

In all criminal prosecutions, the accused shall enjoy the right to a speedy and public trial, by an impartial jury of the State and district wherein the crime shall have been committed; which district shall have been previously ascertained by law, and to be informed of the nature and cause of the accusation; to be confronted with the witnesses against him; to have compulsory process for obtaining witnesses in his favor, and to have the Assistance of Counsel for his defence.

Amendment VII.

In Suits at common law, where the value in controversy shall exceed twenty dollars, the right of trial by jury shall be preserved, and no fact tried by a jury shall be otherwise re-examined in any Court of the United States, than according to the rules of the common law.

Amendment VIII.

Excessive bail shall not be required, nor excessive fines imposed, nor cruel and unusual punishments inflicted.

Amendment IX.

The enumeration in the Constitution of certain rights shall not be construed to deny or disparage others retained by the people.

Amendment X.

The powers not delegated to the United States by the Constitution, nor prohibited by it to the States, are reserved to the States respectively, or to the people.

Amendment XI.*

The Judicial power of the United States shall not be construed to extend to any suit in law or equity, commenced or prosecuted against one of the United States by Citizens of another State, or by Citizens or Subjects of any Foreign State.

Amendment XII.**

The Electors shall meet in their respective states, and vote by ballot for President and Vice-President, one of whom, at least, shall not be an inhabitant of the same state with themselves; they shall name in their ballots the person voted for as President, and in distinct ballots the person voted for as Vice-President, and they shall make distinct lists of all persons voted for as President, and of all persons voted for as Vice-

*The Eleventh Amendment was ratified February 7, 1795.
**The Twelfth Amendment was ratified June 15, 1804.

President, and of the number of votes for each, which lists they shall sign and certify, and transmit sealed to the seat of the government of the United States, directed to the President of the Senate;—The President of the Senate shall, in the presence of the Senate and House of Representatives, open all the certificates and the votes shall then be counted;— The person having the greatest number of votes for President, shall be the President, if such number be a majority of the whole number of Electors appointed; and if no person have such majority, then from the persons having the highest numbers not exceeding three on the list of those voted for as President, the House of Representatives shall choose immediately, by ballot, the President. But in choosing the President, the votes shall he taken by states, the representation from each state having one vote; a quorum for this purpose shall consist of a member or members from two-thirds of the states, and a majority of all the states shall be necessary to a choice. [*And if the House of Representatives shall not choose a President whenever the right of choice shall devolve upon them, before the fourth day of March next following, then the Vice-President shall act as President, as in the case of the death or other constitutional disability of the President—*]* The person having the greatest number of votes as Vice-President, shall be the Vice-President, if such number be a majority of the whole number of Electors appointed, and if no person have a majority, then from the two highest numbers on the list, the Senate shall choose the Vice-President; a quorum for the purpose shall consist of two-thirds of the whole number of Senators, and a majority of the whole number shall be necessary to a choice. But no person constitutionally ineligible to the office of President shall be eligible to that of Vice-President of the United States.

Amendment XIII.*

Section. 1. Neither slavery nor involuntary servitude, except as a punishment for crime whereof the party shall have been duly convicted, shall exist within the United States, or any place subject to their jurisdiction.

Section. 2. Congress shall have power to enforce this article by appropriate legislation.

Amendment XIV.**

Section. 1. All persons born or naturalized in the United States and subject to the jurisdiction thereof, are citizens of the United States and of the State wherein they reside. No State shall make or enforce any law

---

*Superseded by section 3 of the Twentieth Amendment.

*The Thirteenth Amendment was ratified December 6, 1865.
**The Fourteenth Amendment was ratified July 9, 1868.

which shall abridge the privileges or immunities of citizens of the United States; nor shall any State deprive any person of life, liberty, or property, without due process of law; nor deny to any person within its jurisdiction the equal protection of the laws.

Section. 2. Representatives shall be apportioned among the several States according to their respective numbers, counting the whole number of persons in each State, excluding Indians not taxed. But when the right to vote at any election for the choice of electors for President and Vice President of the United States, Representatives in Congress, the Executive and Judicial officers of a State, or the members of the Legislature thereof, is denied to any of the male inhabitants of such State, being twenty-one years of age, and citizens of the United States, or in any way abridged, except for participation in rebellion, or other crime, the basis of representation therein shall be reduced in the proportion which the number of such male citizens shall bear to the whole number of male citizens twenty-one years of age in such State.

Section. 3. No person shall be a Senator or Representative in Congress, or elector of President and Vice President, or hold any office, civil or military, under the United States, or under any State, who, having previously taken an oath, as a member of Congress, or as an officer of the United States, or as a member of any State legislature, or as an executive or judicial officer of any State, to support the Constitution of the United States, shall have engaged in insurrection or rebellion against the same, or given aid or comfort to the enemies thereof. But Congress may by a vote of two-thirds of each House, remove such disability.

Section. 4. The validity of the public debt of the United States, authorized by law, including debts incurred for payment of pensions and bounties for services in suppressing insurrection or rebellion, shall not be questioned. But neither the United States nor any State shall assume or pay any debt or obligation incurred in aid of insurrection or rebellion against the United States, or any claim for the loss or emancipation of any slave; but all such debts, obligations and claims shall be held illegal and void.

Section. 5. The Congress shall have power to enforce, by appropriate legislation, the provisions of this article.

Amendment XV.*

Section. 1. The right of citizens of the United States to vote shall not be denied or abridged by the United States or by any State on account of race, color, or previous condition of servitude.

*The Fifteenth Amendment was ratified February 3, 1870.

Section. 2. The Congress shall have power to enforce this article by appropriate legislation.

Amendment XVI.*

The Congress shall have power to lay and collect taxes on incomes, from whatever source derived, without apportionment among the several States, and without regard to any census or enumeration.

Amendment XVII.**

The Senate of the United States shall be composed of two Senators from each State, elected by the people thereof, for six years; and each Senator shall have one vote. The electors in each State shall have the qualifications requisite for electors of the most numerous branch of the State legislatures.

When vacancies happen in the representation of any State in the Senate, the executive authority of such State shall issue writs of election to fill such vacancies: Provided, That the legislature of any State may empower the executive thereof to make temporary appointments until the people fill the vacancies by election as the legislature may direct.

This amendment shall not be so construed as to affect the election or term of any Senator chosen before

it becomes valid as part of the Constitution.

Amendment XVIII.*

Section. 1. [*After one year from the ratification of this article the manufacture, sale, or transportation of intoxicating liquors within, the importation thereof into, or the exportation thereof from the United States and all territory subject to the jurisdiction thereof for beverage purposes is hereby prohibited.*

Section. 2. *The Congress and the several States shall have concurrent power to enforce this article by appropriate legislation.*

Section. 3. *This article shall be inoperative unless it shall have been ratified as an amendment to the Constitution by the legislatures of the several States, as provided in the Constitution, within seven years from the date of the submission hereof to the States by the Congress.*]

Amendment XIX.**

The right of citizens of the United States to vote shall not be denied or abridged by the United States or by any State on account of sex.

Congress shall have power to enforce this article by appropriate legislation.

*The Sixteenth Amendment was ratified February 3, 1913.
**The Seventeenth Amendment was ratified April 8, 1913.

*The Eighteenth Amendment was ratified January 16, 1919. It was repealed by the Twenty-First Amendment, December 5, 1933.
**The Nineteenth Amendment was ratified August 18, 1920.

Amendment XX.*

Section. 1. The terms of the President and Vice President shall end at noon on the 20th day of January, and the terms of Senators and Representatives at noon on the 3d day of January, of the years in which such terms would have ended if this article had not been ratified; and the terms of their successors shall then begin.

Section. 2. The Congress shall assemble at least once in every year, and such meeting shall begin at noon on the 3d day of January, unless they shall by law appoint a different day.

Section. 3. If, at the time fixed for the beginning of the term of the President, the President elect shall have died, the Vice President elect shall become President. If a President shall not have been chosen before the time fixed for the beginning of his term, or if the President elect shall have failed to qualify, then the Vice President elect shall act as President until a President shall have qualified; and the Congress may by law provide for the case wherein neither a President elect nor a Vice President elect shall have qualified, declaring who shall then act as President, or the manner in which one who is to act shall be selected, and such person shall act accordingly until a President or Vice President shall have qualified.

Section. 4. The Congress may by law provide for the case of the death of any of the persons from whom the House of Representatives may choose a President whenever the right of choice shall have devolved upon them, and for the case of the death of any of the persons from whom the Senate may choose a Vice President whenever the right of choice shall have devolved upon them.

Section. 5. Sections 1 and 2 shall take effect on the 15th day of October following the ratification of this article.

Section. 6. This article shall be inoperative unless it shall have been ratified as an amendment to the Constitution by the legislatures of three-fourths of the several States within seven years from the date of its submission.

Amendment XXI.**

Section. 1. The eighteenth article of amendment to the Constitution of the United States is hereby repealed.

Section. 2. The transportation or importation into any State, Territory, or possession of the United States for delivery or use therein of intoxicating liquors, in violation of the laws thereof, is hereby prohibited.

---

*The Twentieth Amendment was ratified January 23, 1933.

**The Twenty-First Amendment was ratified December 5, 1933.

Section. 3. This article shall be inoperative unless it shall have been ratified as an amendment to the Constitution by conventions in the several States, as provided in the Constitution, within seven years from the date of the submission hereof to the States by the Congress.

Amendment XXII.*

Section. 1. No person shall be elected to the office of the President more than twice, and no person who has held the office of President, or acted as President, for more than two years of a term to which some other person was elected President shall be elected to the office of the President more than once. But this Article shall not apply to any person holding the office of President when this Article was proposed by the Congress, and shall not prevent any person who may be holding the office of President, or acting as President, during the term within which this Article becomes operative from holding the office of President or acting as President during the remainder of such term.

Section. 2. This article shall be inoperative unless it shall have been ratified as an amendment to the Constitution by the legislatures of three-fourths of the several States within seven years from the date of its submission to the States by the Congress.

Amendment XXIII.*

Section. 1. The District constituting the seat of Government of the United States shall appoint in such manner as the Congress may direct:

A number of electors of President and Vice President equal to the whole number of Senators and Representatives in Congress to which the District would be entitled if it were a State, but in no event more than the least populous State; they shall be in addition to those appointed by the States, but they shall be considered, for the purposes of the election of President and Vice President, to be electors appointed by a State, and they shall meet in the District and perform such duties as provided by the twelfth article of amendment.

Section. 2. The Congress shall have power to enforce this article by appropriate legislation.

Amendment XXIV.**

Section. 1. The right of citizens of the United States to vote in any primary or other election for President or Vice President, for electors for President or Vice President, or for Senator or Representative in Congress, shall not be denied or abridged by the United States or any State by reason of failure to pay any poll tax or other tax.

---

*The Twenty-Second Amendment was ratified February 27, 1951.

*The Twenty-Third Amendment was ratified March 29, 1961.
**The Twenty-Fourth Amendment was ratified January 23, 1964.

Section. 2. The Congress shall have power to enforce this article by appropriate legislation.

Amendment XXV.*

Section. 1. In case of the removal of the President from office or of his death or resignation, the Vice President shall become President.

Section. 2. Whenever there is a vacancy in the office of the Vice President, the President shall nominate a Vice President who shall take office upon confirmation by a majority vote of both Houses of Congress.

Section. 3. Whenever the President transmits to the President pro tempore of the Senate and the Speaker of the House of Representatives his written declaration that he is unable to discharge the powers and duties of his office, and until he transmits to them a written declaration to the contrary, such powers and duties shall be discharged by the Vice President as Acting President.

Section. 4. Whenever the Vice President and a majority of either the principal officers of the executive departments or of such other body as Congress may by law provide, transmit to the President pro tempore of the Senate and the Speaker of the House of Repre-

sentatives their written declaration that the President is unable to discharge the powers and duties of his office, the Vice President shall immediately assume the powers and duties of the office as Acting President.

Thereafter, when the President transmits to the President pro tempore of the Senate and the Speaker of the House of Representatives his written declaration that no inability exists, he shall resume the powers and duties of his office unless the Vice President and a majority of either the principal officers of the executive department or of such other body as Congress may by law provide, transmit within four days to the President pro tempore of the Senate and the Speaker of the House of Representatives their written declaration that the President is unable to discharge the powers and duties of his office. Thereupon Congress shall decide the issue, assembling within forty-eight hours for that purpose if not in session. If the Congress, within twenty-one days after receipt of the latter written declaration, or, if Congress is not in session, within twenty-one days after Congress is required to assemble, determines by two-thirds vote of both Houses that the President is unable to discharge the powers and duties of his office, the Vice President shall continue to discharge the same as Acting President; otherwise, the President shall resume the powers and duties of his office.

*The Twenty-Fifth Amendment was ratified February 10, 1967.

Amendment XXVI.*

Section. 1. The right of citizens of the United States, who are eighteen years of age or older, to vote shall not be denied or abridged by the United States or by any State on account of age.

Section. 2. The Congress shall have power to enforce this article by appropriate legislation.

Amendment XXVII.**

No law, varying the compensation for the services of the Senators and Representatives, shall take effect, until an election of Representatives shall have intervened.

---

*The Twenty-sixth Amendment was ratified July 1, 1971.

**The Twenty-seventh Amendment was ratified May 8, 1992.

Appendix

The Declaration of Independence*

In Congress, July 4, 1776, The unanimous Declaration of the United States of America,

When in the Course of human events, it becomes necessary for one people to dissolve the political bands which have connected them with another, and to assume among the Powers of the earth, the separate and equal station to which the Laws of Nature and of Nature's God entitle them, a decent respect to the opinions of mankind requires that they should declare the causes which impel them to the separation.

We hold these truths to be self-evident, that all men are created equal, that they are endowed by their Creator with certain unalienable Rights, that among these are Life, Liberty, and the pursuit of Happiness. That to secure these rights, Governments are instituted among Men, deriving their just powers from the consent of the governed, That whenever any Form of Government becomes destructive of these ends, it is the Right of the People to alter or to abolish it, and to institute new Government, laying its foundation on such principles and organizing its powers in such form, as to them shall seem most likely to effect their Safety and Happiness. Prudence, indeed, will dictate that Governments long established should not be changed for light and transient causes; and accordingly all experience hath shown, that mankind are more disposed to suffer, while evils are sufferable, than to

*From *Documents of American History*, ed. by Henry Steele Commager (New York: Appleton-Century-Crofts, 8th edition. 1968).

right themselves by abolishing the forms to which they are accustomed. But when a long train of abuses and usurpations, pursuing invariably the same Object evinces a design to reduce them under absolute Despotism, it is their right, it is their duty, to throw off such Government, and to provide new Guards for their future security.—Such has been the patient sufferance of these Colonies; and such is now the necessity which constrains them to alter their former Systems of Government. The history of the present King of Great Britain is a history of repeated injuries and usurpations, all having in direct object the establishment of an absolute Tyranny over these States. To prove this, let Facts be submitted to a candid world.

He has refused his Assent to Laws, the most wholesome and necessary for the public good.

He has forbidden his Governors to pass Laws of immediate and pressing importance, unless suspended in their operation till his Assent should be obtained; and, when so suspended, he has utterly neglected to attend to them.

He has refused to pass other Laws for the accommodation of large districts of people, unless those people would relinquish the right of Representation in the Legislature, a right inestimable to them and formidable to tyrants only.

He has called together legislative bodies at places unusual, uncomfortable, and distant from the depository of their Public Records, for the sole purpose of fatiguing them into compliance with his measures.

He has dissolved Representative Houses repeatedly, for opposing with manly firmness his invasions on the rights of the people. He has refused for a long time, after such dissolutions, to cause others to be elected; whereby the Legislative Powers, incapable of Annihilation, have returned to the People at large for their exercise; the State remaining in the mean time exposed to all the dangers of invasion from without, and convulsions within.

He has endeavoured to prevent the population of these States; for that purpose obstructing the Laws of Naturalization of Foreigners; refusing to pass others to encourage their migrations hither, and raising the conditions of new Appropriations of Lands.

He has obstructed the Administration of Justice, by refusing his Assent to Laws for establishing Judiciary Powers.

He has made Judges dependent on his Will alone, for the tenure of their offices, and the amount and payment of their salaries.

He has erected a multitude of New Offices, and sent hither swarms of Officers to harass our People, and eat out their substance.

He has kept among us, in times of peace, Standing Armies without the Consent of our legislature.

He has affected to render the Military independent of and superior to the Civil Power.

He has combined with others to subject us to a jurisdiction foreign to our constitution, and unacknowledged by our laws; giving his Assent to their Acts of pretended legislation:

For quartering large bodies of armed troops among us:

For protecting them, by a mock Trial, from Punishment for any Murders which they should commit on the Inhabitants of these States:

For cutting off our Trade with all parts of the world:

For imposing taxes on us without our Consent:

For depriving us in many cases, of the benefits of Trial by Jury:

For transporting us beyond Seas to be tried for pretended offences:

For abolishing the free System of English Laws in a neighbouring Province, establishing therein an Arbitrary government, and enlarging its Boundaries so as to render it at once an example and fit instrument for introducing the same absolute rule into these Colonies:

For taking away our Charters, abolishing our most valuable Laws, and altering fundamentally the Forms of our Governments:

For suspending our own Legislature, and declaring themselves invested with Power to legislate for us in all cases whatsocver.

He has abdicated Government here, by declaring us out of his Protection and waging War against us.

He has plundered our seas, ravaged our Coasts, burnt our towns, and destroyed the lives of our people.

He is at this time transporting large armies of foreign mercenaries to compleat the works of death, desolation and tyranny, already begun with circumstances of Cruelty & perfidy scarcely paralleled in the most barbarous ages, and totally unworthy the Head of a civilized nation.

He has constrained our fellow Citizens taken Captive on the high Seas to bear Arms against their Country, to become the executioners of their friends and Brethren, or to fall themselves by their Hands.

He has excited domestic insurrections amongst us, and has endeavoured to bring on the inhabitants of our frontiers, the merciless Indian Savages, whose known rule of warfare, is an undistinguished destruction of all ages, sexes, and conditions.

In every stage of these Oppressions We have Petitioned for Redress in the most humble terms: Our repeated Petitions have been answered only by repeated injury. A Prince, whose character is thus marked by every act which may define a Tyrant, is unfit to be the ruler of a free People.

Nor have We been wanting in attention to our Brittish brethren. We have warned them from time to time of attempts by their legislature to extend an unwarrantable jurisdiction over us. We have reminded them of the circumstances of our emigration and settlement here. We have appealed to their native justice and magnanimity, and we have conjured them by the ties of our common kindred to disavow these usurpations, which, would inevitably interrupt our connections and correspondence. They too have been deaf to the voice of justice and of consanguinity. We must, therefore, acquiesce in the necessity, which denounces our Separation, and hold them, as we hold the rest of mankind, Enemies in War, in Peace Friends.

We, therefore, the Representatives of the united States of America, in General Congress, Assembled, appealing to the Supreme Judge of the world for the rectitude of our intentions, do, in the Name, and by Authority of the good People of these Colonies, solemnly publish and declare, That these United Colonies are, and of Right ought to be Free and Independent States; that they are Absolved from all Allegiance to the British Crown, and that all political connection between them and the State of Great Britain, is and ought to be totally dissolved; and that as Free and Independent States, they have full Power to levy War, conclude Peace, contract Alliances, establish Commerce, and to do all other Acts and Things which Independent States may of right do. And for the support of this Declaration, with a firm reliance on the Protection of Divine Providence, we mutually pledge to each other our Lives, our Fortunes and our sacred Honor.

JOHN HANCOCK.

New Hampshire
JOSIAH BARTLETT,
WM. WHIPPLE,
MATTHEW THORNTON.

Massachusetts Bay
SAML. ADAMS,
JOHN ADAMS,
ROBT. TREAT PAINE,
ELBRIDGE GERRY.

Rhode Island
STEP. HOPKINS,
WILLIAM ELLERY.

Connecticut
ROGER SHERMAN,
SAM'EL HUNTINGTON,
WM. WILLIAMS,
OLIVER WOLCOTT.

New York
WM. FLOYD,
PHIL. LIVINGSTON,
FRANS. LEWIS,
LEWIS MORRIS.

Pennsylvania
ROBT. MORRIS,
BENJAMIN RUSH,
BENJA. FRANKLIN,
JOHN MORTON,
GEO. CLYMER,
JAS. SMITH,
GEO. TAYLOR,
JAMES WILSON,
GEO. ROSS.

Delaware
CAESAR RODNEY,
GEO. READ,
THO. M KEAN.

Georgia
BUTTON GWINNETT,
LYMAN HALL,
GEO. WALTON.

Maryland
SAMUEL CHASE,
WM. PACA,
THOS. STONE,
CHARLES CARROLL OF
CARROLLTON.

Virginia
GEORGE WYTHE,
RICHARD HENRY LFE,
TH. JEFFERSON,
BENJA. HARRISON,
THS. NELSON, JR.
FRANCIS LIGHTFOOT LEE,
CARTER BRAXTON.

North Carolina
WM. HOOPER,
JOSEPH HEWES,
JOHN PENN.

South Carolina
EDWARD RUTLEDGE,
THOS. HEYWARD, JUNR.,
THOMAS LYNCH, JUNR.,
ARTHUR MIDDLETON.

New Jersey
RICHD. STOCKTON,
JNO. WITHERSPOON,
FRAS. HOPKINSON,
JOHN HART,
ABRA. CLARK.

Appendix

The Articles of Confederation*

To all to whom these Presents shall come, we the undersigned Delegates of the States affixed to our names send greeting.

Whereas the Delegates of the United States of America in Congress assembled did on the fifteenth day of November in the Year of our Lord One Thousand Seven Hundred and Seventy seven, and in the Second Year of the Independence of America agree to certain articles of Confederation and perpetual Union between the States of Newhampshire, Massachusetts-bay, Rhodeisland and Providence Plantations, Connecticut, New-York, New-Jersey, Pennsylvania, Delaware, Maryland, Virginia, North-Carolina, South-Carolina and Georgia in the Words following, viz.

"Articles of Confederation and perpetual Union between the states of Newhampshire, Massachusetts-bay, Rhodeisland and Providence Plantations, Connecticut, New-York, New-Jersey, Pennsylvania, Delaware, Maryland, Virginia, North-Carolina, South-Carolina and Georgia.

Article I. The Stile of this confederacy shall be "The United States of America."

Article II. Each state retains its sovereignty, freedom and independence, and every Power, Jurisdiction and right, which is not by this confederation expressly delegated to the United States, in Congress assembled.

Article III. The said states hereby severally enter into a firm league of friendship with each other, for their common defence, the security of their

---

*Source: Thorpe, ed., 1 *Federal and State Constitutions* 9 (1909).

Liberties, and their mutual and general welfare, binding themselves to assist each other, against all force offered to, or attacks made upon them, or any of them, on account of religion, sovereignty, trade, or any other presence whatever.

Article IV. The better to secure and perpetuate mutual friendship and intercourse among the people of the different states in this union, the free inhabitants of each of these states, paupers, vagabonds and fugitives from Justice excepted, shall be entitled to all privileges and immunities of free citizens in the several states; and the people of each state shall have free ingress and regress to and from any other state, and shall enjoy therein all the privileges of trade and commerce, subject to the same duties, impositions and restrictions as the inhabitants thereof respectively, provided that such restriction shall not extend so far as to prevent the removal of property imported into any state, to any other state of which the Owner is an inhabitant; provided also that no imposition, duties or restriction shall be laid by any state, on the property of the united states, or either of them.

If any Person guilty of, or charged with treason, felony, or other high misdemeanor in any state, shall flee from Justice, and be found in any of the united states, he shall upon demand of the Governor or executive power, of the state from which he fled, be delivered up and removed to the state having jurisdiction of his offence.

Full faith and credit shall be given in each of these states to the records, acts and judicial proceedings of the courts and magistrates of every other state.

Article V. For the more convenient management of the general interests of the united states, delegates shall be annually appointed in such manner as the legislature of each state shall direct, to meet in Congress on the first Monday in November, in every year, with a power reserved to each state, to recal its delegates, or any of them, at any time within the year, and to send others in their stead, for the remainder of the Year.

No state shall be represented in Congress by less than two, nor by more than seven Members; and no person shall be capable of being a delegate for more than three years in any term of six years; nor shall any person, being a delegate, be capable of holding any office under the united states, for which he, or another for his benefit receives any salary, fees or emolument of any kind.

Each state shall maintain its own delegates in a meeting of the states, and while they act as members of the committee of the states.

In determining questions in the united states, in Congress assembled, each state shall have one vote.

Freedom of speech and debate in Congress shall not be impeached or questioned in any Court, or place out of Congress, and the members of congress shall be protected in their persons from arrests and imprisonments, during the time of their going to and from, and attendance on congress, except for treason, felony, or breach of the peace.

Article VI. No state without the Consent of the united states in congress assembled, shall send any embassy to, or receive any embassy from, or enter into any conference, agreement, or alliance or treaty with any King, prince or state; nor shall any person holding any office of profit or trust under the united states, or any of them, accept of any present, emolument, office or title of any kind whatever from any king, prince or foreign state; nor shall the united states in congress assembled, or any of them, grant any title of nobility.

No two or more states shall enter into any treaty, confederation or alliance whatever between them, without the consent of the united states in congress assembled, specifying accurately the purposes for which the same is to be entered into, and how long it shall continue.

No state shall lay any imposts or duties, which may interfere with any stipulations in treaties, entered into by the united states in congress assembled, with any king, prince or state, in pursuance of any treaties already proposed by congress, to the courts of France and Spain.

No vessels of war shall be kept up in time of peace by any state, except such number only, as shall be deemed necessary by the united states in congress assembled, for the defence of such state, or its trade; nor shall any body of forces be kept up by any state, in time of peace, except such number only, as in the judgment of the united states, in congress assembled, shall be deemed requisite to garrison the forts necessary for the defence of such state; but every state shall always keep up a well regulated and disciplined militia, sufficiently armed and accoutred, and shall provide and constantly have ready for use, in public stores, a due number of field pieces and tents, and a proper quantity of arms, ammunition and camp equipage.

No state shall engage in any war without the consent of the united states in congress assembled, unless such state be actually invaded by enemies, or shall have received certain advice of a resolution being formed by some nation of Indians to invade such state, and the danger is so imminent as not to admit of a delay, till the united states in congress assembled can be consulted: nor shall any state grant commissions to any ships or vessels of war, nor letters of marque or reprisal, except it be after a declaration of war by the united states in congress assembled, and then only against the kingdom or state and the subjects thereof, against which war has been so declared, and under such regulations as shall be established by the united states in congress assembled, unless such state be infested by pirates. in which case vessels of war may be fitted out for that occasion, and kept so long as the danger shall continue, or until the united states in congress assembled shall determine otherwise.

Article VII. When land-forces are raised by any state for the common defence, all officers of or under the rank of colonel, shall be appointed by the legislature of each state respectively by whom such forces shall be raised, or in such manner as such state shall direct, and all vacancies shall be filled up by the state which first made the appointment.

Article VIII. All charges of war, and all other expences that shall be incurred for the common defence or general welfare, and allowed by the united states in congress assembled, shall be defrayed out of a common treasury, which shall be supplied by the several states, in proportion to the value of all land within each state, granted to or surveyed for any Person, as such land and the buildings and improvements thereon shall be estimated according to such mode as the united states in congress assembled, shall from time to time direct and appoint. The taxes for paying that proportion shall be laid and levied by the authority and direction of the legislatures of the several states within the time agreed upon by the united states in congress assembled.

Article IX. The united states in congress assembled shall have the sole and exclusive right and power of determining on peace and war, except in the cases mentioned in the sixth article—of sending and receiving ambassadors— entering into treaties and alliances, provided that no treaty of commerce shall be made whereby the legislative power of the respective states shall be restrained from imposing such imposts and duties on foreigners, as their own people are subjected to, or from prohibiting the exportation or importation of any species of goods or commodities whatsoever—of establishing rules for deciding in all cases, what captures on land or water shall be legal, and in what manner prizes taken by land or naval forces in the service of the united states shall be divided or appropriated—of granting letters of marque and reprisal in times of peace—appointing courts for the trial of piracies and felonies committed on the high seas and establishing courts for receiving and determining finally appeals in all cases of captures, provided that no member of congress shall be appointed a judge of any of the said courts.

The united states in congress assembled shall also be the last resort on appeal in all disputes and differences now subsisting or that hereafter may arise between two or more states concerning boundary, jurisdiction or any other cause whatever; which authority shall always be exercised in the manner following. Whenever the legislative or executive authority or lawful agent of any state in controversy with another shall present a petition to congress, stating the matter in question and praying for a hearing, notice thereof shall be given by order of congress to the legislative or executive authority of the other state in controversy, and a day assigned for the appearance of the parties by their lawful agents, who shall then be directed to appoint by joint consent, commissioners or judges to constitute a court for hearing and determining the matter in question: but if they cannot agree, congress shall name three persons out of each of the united states, and from the list of such persons each party shall alternately strike out one, the petitioners beginning, until the number shall be reduced to thirteen; and from that number nor less than seven, nor more than nine names as congress shall direct, shall in the presence of congress be drawn out by lot, and the persons whose names shall be so drawn or any five of them, shall be commissioners or judges, to hear and finally determine the controversy, so always as a major part of the judges who shall hear the cause shall agree in the determination: and if either party shall neglect to attend at the day appointed, without strewing reasons, which congress shall judge sufficient, or being present shall refuse to strike, the congress shall proceed to nominate three persons out of each state, and the secretary of congress shall strike in behalf of such party absent or refusing; and the judgment and sentence of the court to be appointed, in the manner before prescribed, shall be final and conclusive; and if any of the parties shall refuse to submit to the authority of such court, or to appear or defend their claim or cause, the court shall nevertheless proceed to pronounce sentence, or judgment, which shall in like manner be final and decisive, the judgment or sentence and other proceedings being in either case transmitted to congress, and lodged among the acts of congress for the security of the parties concerned: provided that every commissioner, before he sits in judgment, shall take an oath to be administered by one of the judges of the supreme or superior court of the state, where the cause shall be tried, "well and truly to hear and determine the matter in question, according to the best of his judgment, without favour, affection or hope of reward:" provided also that no state shall be deprived of territory for the benefit of the united states.

All controversies concerning the private right of soil claimed under different grants of two or more states, whose jurisdictions as they may respect such lands, and the states which passed such grants are adjusted, the said grants or either of them being at the same time claimed to have originated antecedent to such settlement of jurisdiction, shall on the petition of either party to the congress of the united states, be finally determined as near as may be in the same manner as is before prescribed for deciding disputes respecting territorial jurisdiction between different states.

The united states in congress assembled shall also have the sole and exclusive right and power of regulating the alloy and value of coin struck by their own authority, or by that of the respective states—fixing the standard of weights and measures throughout the united states.—regulating the trade and managing all affairs with the Indians, not members of any of the states, provided that the legislative right of any state within its own limits be not infringed or violated—establishing and regulating post-offices from one state to another, throughout all the united states, and exacting such postage on the papers passing thro' the same as may be requisite to defray the expences of the said office—appointing all officers of the land forces, in the service of the united states, excepting regimental officers.—appointing all the officers of the naval forces, and commissioning all officers whatever in the service of the united states—making rules for the government and regulation of the said land and naval forces, and directing their operations.

The united states in congress assembled shall have authority to appoint a committee, to sit in the recess of congress, to be denominated "a Committee of the States," and to consist of one delegate from each state; and to appoint such other committees and civil officers as may be necessary for managing the general affairs of the united states under their direction—to appoint one of their number to preside, provided that no person be allowed to serve in the office of president more than one year in any term of three years; to ascertain the necessary sums of Money to be raised for the service of the united states, and to appropriate and apply the same for defraying the public expences—to borrow money, or emit bills on the credit of the united states, transmitting every half year to the respective states an account of the sums of money so borrowed or emitted,—to build and equip a navy—to agree upon the number of land forces, and to make requisitions from each State for its quota, in proportion to the number of white inhabitants in such state; which requisition shall be binding, and thereupon the legislature of each state shall appoint the regimental officers, raise the men and cloath, arm and equip them in a soldier like manner, at the expence of the united states, and the officers and men so cloathed, armed and equipped shall march to the place appointed, and within the time agreed on by the united states in congress assembled: But if the united states in congress assembled shall, on consideration of circumstances judge proper that any state should not raise men, or should raise a smaller number than its quota, and that any other state should raise a greater number of men than the quota thereof, such extra number shall be raised, officered, cloathed, armed and equipped in the same manner as the quota of such state, unless the legislature of such state shall judge that such extra number cannot be safely spared out of the same, in which case they shall raise officer, cloath, arm and equip as many of such extra number as they judge can be safely spared. And the officers and men so cloathed, armed and equipped, shall march to the place appointed, and within the time agreed on by the united states in congress assembled.

The united states in congress assembled shall never engage in a war, nor grant letters of marque and reprisal in time of peace, nor enter into any treaties or alliances, nor coin money, nor regulate the value thereof, nor ascertain the sums and expenses necessary for the defence and welfare of the united states, or any of them, nor emit bills, nor borrow money on the credit of the united states, nor appropriate money, nor agree upon the number of vessels of war, to be built or purchased, or the number of land or sea forces to be raised, nor appoint a commander in chief of the army or navy, unless nine states assent to the same: nor shall a question on any other point, except for adjourning from day to day be determined, unless by the votes of a majority of the united states in congress assembled.

The congress of the united states shall have power to adjourn to any time within the year, and to any place within the united states, so that no period of adjournment be for a longer duration than the space of six Months, and shall publish the Journal of their proceedings monthly, except such parts thereof relating to treaties, alliances or military operations as in their judgment require secrecy; and the yeas and nays of the delegates of each state on any question shall be entered on the Journal, when it is desired by any delegate; and the delegates of a state, or any of them, at his or their request shall be furnished with a transcript of the said Journal, except such parts as are above excepted, to lay before the legislatures of the several states.

Article X. The committee of the states, or any nine of them, shall be authorised to execute, in the recess of congress, such of the powers of congress as the united states in congress assembled, by the consent of nine states, shall from time to time think expedient to vest them with; provided that no power be delegated to the said committee, for the exercise of which, by the articles of confederation, the voice of nine states in the congress of the united states assembled is requisite.

Article XI. Canada acceding to this confederation, and joining in the measures of the united states, shall be admitted into, and entitled to all the advantages of this union: but no other colony shall be admitted into the same, unless such admission be agreed to by nine states.

Article XII. All bills of credit emitted, monies borrowed and debts contracted by, or under the authority of congress, before the assembling of the united states, in pursuance of the present confederation, shall be deemed and considered as a charge against the united states, for payment and satisfaction whereof the said united states, and the public faith are hereby solemnly pledged.

Article XIII. Every state shall abide by the determinations of the united states in congress assembled, on all questions which by this confederation are submitted to them. And the Articles of this confederation shall be inviolably observed by every state, and the union shall be perpetual; nor shall any alteration at any time hereafter be made in any of them; unless such alteration be agreed to in a congress of the united states, and be afterwards confirmed by the legislatures of every state.

And Whereas it hath pleased the Great Governor of the World to incline the hearts of the legislatures we respectively represent in congress, to approve of, and to authorize us to ratify the said articles of confederation and perpetual union. Know Ye that we the undersigned delegates, by virtue of the power and authority to us given for that purpose, do by these presents, in the name and in behalf of our respective constituents, full and entirely ratify and confirm each and every of the said articles of confederation and perpetual union, and all and singular the matters and things therein contained: And we do further solemnly plight and engage the faith of our respective constituents, that they shall abide by the determinations of the united states in congress assembled, on all questions, which by the said confederation are submitted to them. And that the articles thereof shall be inviolably observed by the states we respectively represent, and that the union shall be perpetual. In Witness whereof we have hereunto set our hands in Congress. Done at Philadelphia in the state of Pennsylvania the ninth Day of July in the Year of our Lord one Thousand seven Hundred and Seventy-eight, and in the third year of the independence of America.

On the part & behalf of the State of New Hampshire
JOSIAH BARTLETT
JOHN WENTWORTH JUN[r]
August 8th 1778

On the part and behalf of The State of Massachusetts Bay
JOHN HANCOCK
SAMUEL ADAMS
ELBRIDGE GERRY
FRANCIS DANA
JAMES LOVELL
SAMUEL MOLTEN

*On the part and behalf of the State of Rhode-Island
and Providence Plantations*
WILLIAM ELLERY
HENRY MARCHANT
JOHN COLLINS

On the part and behalf of the State of Connecticut
ROGER SHERMAN
SAMUEL HUNTINGTON
OLIVER WOLCOTT
TITUS HOSMER
ANDREW ADAMS

On the Part and Behalf of the State of New York
JA[s] DUANE
FRA[s] LEWIS
W[M] DUER
GOUV MORRIS

*On the Part and in Behalf of the State of New Jersey
Nov[r] 26, 1778.—*
JNO WITHERSPOON
NATH[L] SCUDDER

On the part and behalf of the State of Pennsylvania
ROB^T MORRIS
DANIEL ROBERDEAU
JON^A BAYARD SMITH.
WILLIAM CLINGAN
JOSEPH REED 22d July 1778

On the part & behalf of the State of Delaware
THO M:KEAN Feby 12 1779
JOHN DICKINSON
May 5th 1779
NICHOLAS VAN DYKE,

On the part and behalf of the State of Maryland
JOHN HANSON LEE
March 1 1781
DANIEL CARROLL d^o

On the Part and Behalf of the State of Virginia
RICHARD HENRY LEE
JOHN BANISTER
THOMAS ADAMS
JN^o HARVIE
FRANCIS LIGHTFOOT LEE

On the part and Behalf of the State of No Carolina
JOHN PENN July 21st 1778
CORN^S HARNETT
JN^o WILLIAMS

On the part & behalf of the State of South-Carolina
HENRY LAURENS
WILLIAM HENRY DRAYTON
JN^o MATHEWS
RICH^D HUTSON
THO^S HEYWARD JUN^r

On the part & behalf of the State of Georgia
JN^o WALTON 24th July 1778
EDW^D TELFAIR
EDW^D LANGWORTHY

Index

About the Author

JOHN R. VILE is Professor and Chair of the Political Science Department at Middle Tennessee State University.